The Politics of
Problem Definition

STUDIES IN GOVERNMENT AND PUBLIC POLICY

The Politics of Problem Definition
Shaping the Policy Agenda

Edited by David A. Rochefort
and Roger W. Cobb

University Press of Kansas

© 1994 by the University Press of Kansas

Published by the University Press of Kansas (Lawrence, Kansas 66049), which was organized by the Kansas Board of Regents and is operated and funded by Emporia State University, Fort Hays State University, Kansas State University, Pittsburg State University, the University of Kansas, and Wichita State University

Library of Congress Cataloging-in-Publication Data

The Politics of problem definition : shaping the policy agenda /
    edited by David A. Rochefort, Roger W. Cobb.
        p.   cm. — (Studies in government and public policy)
    Includes bibliographical references and index.
    ISBN 0-7006-0646-7. — ISBN 0-7006-0647-5 (pbk.)
    1. Policy sciences—Case studies.   I. Rochefort, David A.
II. Cobb, Roger W.   III. Series.
H97.P6677   1995
320'.6—dc20   94-11031

British Library Cataloguing in Publication Data is available.

Printed in the United States of America

10 9 8 7 6 5 4 3 2 1

The paper used in this publication meets the minimum requirements of the American National Standard for Permanence of Paper for Printed Library Materials Z39.48-1984.

Contents

Preface

"Problem definition" has to do with what we choose to identify as public issues and how we think and talk about these concerns. In recent years, problem definition has acquired increasing importance in the study of public policymaking along two often separate tracks. First, researchers interested in the appearance of new issues have investigated how the description of a given social problem can affect its rise or decline before government. Second, public policy specialists working in diverse fields have linked such descriptions to the solutions that government devises.

As editors of this volume, we brought to the task different backgrounds reflecting this larger division of scholarship. David Rochefort, a specialist in social welfare and health policy development, had earlier examined the "social images" of problems and their impact on policy design. Roger Cobb, a student of agenda building and symbolic politics, had explored the public rhetoric of issue descriptions and their political significance. Problem definition, then, became the academic common ground that enabled us to pursue what we saw as a needed integration within the policy analysis literature. Joining us was a talented group of authors with varying substantive interests but a shared enthusiasm about the intellectual direction of our project.

The book is intended to serve both students and fellow policy researchers. In our view, appreciating the dynamics of problem definition is essential to even the most rudimentary understanding of public policymaking; accordingly, this volume presents the key insights from past research on problem definition as well as a set of lively contemporary case studies, all written to be suitable for an undergraduate course on public policy. Scholars, approaching the work on a different level, will find a vocabulary and method of analysis that can be adapted to the study of problem definition in any policy context and a guide to future research needs.

The plan of the book is as follows. In Chapter 1, we introduce the concept of problem definition in public policy analysis, trace its multidisciplinary origins, and set out central propositions concerning the relationship between specific definitional forms and agenda access and policy formulation. The next several chapters illustrate these general observations via detailed policymaking histories encompassing a broad array of issues.

In Chapter 2, John Portz looks at competing definitions of plant closings and their part in shaping the local community response. In Chapter 3, Frank Baumgartner and Bryan Jones consider how problem definitions may change over time with special reference to air transportation. In Chapter 4, Ellen Frankel Paul traces the emergence of sexual harassment as a major political issue in the 1990s and the related debate over its proper definition. In Chapter 5, Elaine Sharp turns to recurring national episodes of antidrug policymaking, which feature elements of continuity as well as change in interpretations of the drug use problem. In Chapter 6, Gary Mucciaroni provides a comparative analysis of two policy areas, tax policy and agriculture, using a problem definition framework to explain the divergent courses of action within each. In Chapter 7, Joseph Coughlin highlights the cultural conflict that underlies discussion of transportation policy, and he shows how different sides attempt to manipulate definitional issues to strengthen their positions. In Chapter 8, we conclude the series of case studies with a focus on instrumental versus expressive approaches to AIDS policymaking.

Finally, in Chapter 9, Christopher Bosso weighs the special contribution to political and policy analysis that is offered by a problem definition perspective. Additionally, he relates the tenets of this perspective to other factors important in the workings of government.

We wish to acknowledge the able assistance of the editorial group at the University Press of Kansas, including especially Fred Woodward, director, and Susan McRory, senior production editor. We also express our appreciation for the support of the Groupe de recherche sur les aspects sociaux de la prévention (GRASP), University of Montreal, where David spent the fall of 1993 as a visiting researcher while finishing his work on this book. Jeffrey Henig, of the University of Maryland, and Rita Mae Kelly, of Arizona State University, reviewed our manuscript for the publisher and offered many insightful suggestions. We also thank Paul Pezza, of Providence College, for his comments on our AIDS chapter. A preliminary version of some of the ideas in Chapter 1 first appeared in David A. Rochefort and Roger W. Cobb, "Problem Definition, Agenda Access, and Policy Choice," *Policy Studies Journal* 21, 1: (1993): 56–71. Paula Woolley prepared the index with skillful attention to detail.

David A. Rochefort
Northeastern University

Roger W. Cobb
Brown University

1

Problem Definition:
An Emerging Perspective

David A. Rochefort and Roger W. Cobb

In his classic work of political analysis, *The Semi-Sovereign People*, E. E. Schattschneider (1960) opened by describing a riot in New York City during the Second World War. In August 1943, a fight in a Harlem hotel lobby between a black soldier and a white policeman quickly escalated. Rumors about the conflict spread throughout the community and angry crowds gathered at the police station, in front of the hotel, and elsewhere. Violence soon erupted and hundreds subsequently were hurt. For Schattschneider, this incident illustrated how a conflict can quickly expand beyond those immediately involved and how the original contestants maintain little control over such a struggle once it develops.

Another riot nearly fifty years later, this one in Los Angeles, California, again illustrates the contagion of social conflict, as well as other political dynamics. On March 3, 1991, a black man, Rodney King, was stopped by city police after a high-speed chase. He did not respond to police commands to acquiesce and was beaten severely by four officers for "resisting arrest." Part of the incident was videotaped by a spectator, who gave a copy to a local television station. The tape was played repeatedly throughout the nation. On that basis, charges were brought against the four officers who beat King. A trial was set to be held in Simi Valley, a white community north of Los Angeles.

When the trial took place in the spring of 1992, it attained national visibility. The widespread presumption was that the videotape sealed the officers' guilt. However, on April 29, 1992, the jury returned with a verdict of not guilty. Shortly after the verdict was announced, violence broke out in the South-Central section of the city, a predominantly black area. By the time the National Guard was called in to quell the unrest some days later, the statistics were grim: 44 dead, 2,000 hurt, and property damage in excess of $1 billion (Mathews et al. 1992: 30).

1

Soon after the violence started, charges and countercharges began to fly. First, the primary figures in the conflict were blamed. For example, the attention of some commentators focused on the nonblack jury, who did not live near blacks, did not interact with them, and seemed to feel that blacks were violence prone. As one Los Angeles politician stated, this verdict was "a modern-day lynching" (Mathews et al. 1992: 33). King's lawyer said: "It may be that 12 white jurors aren't going to convict four white cops for beating a black man—it may be as simple as that" (Mathews et al. 1992: 34). Others focused on Police Chief Daryl Gates and the Los Angeles Police Department. The department's slow reaction to the riots was surprising to many, since Gates had long been criticized for overreacting to other incidents in minority areas. But the day the riot began, the police chief had attended a political fund-raiser and did not return to his office until the events in South-Central Los Angeles were well under way. Neither did lower-level police officials act to send force into the area. The *New York Times* called it a "new embarrassment for the department" (Mydans 1992: A25). Finally, some blamed the mayor, Tom Bradley. Following the verdict, Bradley had spoken out and called it "senseless"; he said that the police defendants "were not fit to wear a uniform" (Mathews et al. 1992: 33–34). These struck some as reckless and inflammatory remarks that encouraged people to engage in unlawful acts.

A second set of charges was made along ethnic lines. The blacks in the South-Central community were blamed for taking "justice into their own hands." Others criticized the Mexican-American community. Pat Buchanan, a presidential aspirant, attributed the outbreak to Mexicans "coming into this country illegally and helping to burn down one of the greatest cities in America" (Apple 1992: A20).

A third set of charges focused on law and order. A fine line distinguishes between people reacting to injustice and people behaving irresponsibly. As one noted sociologist commented: "If the violence in Los Angeles had been minimal, I think there would have been general sympathy for the rioters . . . . But as the rioting goes on and the looters come out of stores, people shift their anger toward the rioters" (Wilson 1992: 51). So it was that a U.S. Senate candidate from California blamed the riot on the "rotten" looters and arsonists (Apple 1992: A20). President Bush also pointed his finger at criminal elements in the area, stating that "federal assistance offers no reward for rioting. To the criminals who subjected this city to three days of rioting and hate, the message has got to be unequivocal. Lawlessness cannot be explained away" (*Providence Journal-Bulletin* 1992: A4).

A fourth set of accusations were partisan in orientation. Prior to the riot, President Bush had claimed that the failed programs of Lyndon Johnson's Great Society made social problems worse rather than better. In this vein, one week after the riot started, Marlin Fitzwater, White House press spokesperson, said, "We believe that many of the root problems that have resulted in inner-city difficulties were started in the 60's and 70's [Democratic programs] and that they [these programs] have failed." Further, he asserted that liberal Democrats in Congress were responsible for frustrating President Bush's efforts to enact policies that would have averted such rioting (Wines 1992: A26). The Democratic presidential candidate, Bill Clinton, sparred with the White House over the question of culpability. He linked the riots to Reagan and Bush's neglect of race relations, urban programs, and domestic social policy in general (Pear 1992: A24).

Still a fifth set of causes was proposed by Vice-President Dan Quayle. He argued that the "lawless social anarchy" occurring in Los Angeles had resulted from a more general "poverty of values."The riots were "directly related to the breakdown of family structure, personal responsibility and social order in too many areas of society." He maintained, further, that television had also contributed to the moral decay by making a heroine out of a women who gave birth out of wedlock. "It doesn't help matters when prime-time TV has Murphy Brown . . . mocking the importance of fathers by bearing a child alone" (Jehl 1992: A1, A6).

The Los Angeles riots rank among the most disturbing outbreaks of social violence in recent U.S. history. Accordingly, the debate they sparked was well publicized. Only now, nearly two years later, is the controversy abating. However, this kind of disagreement over who or what is responsible for a problem in society is not at all uncommon with public issues. At the nexus of politics and policy development lies persistent conflict over where problems come from and, based on the answer to this question, what kinds of solutions should be attempted. In Los Angeles, for example, directing attention to racial and economic inequalities as underlying causes of the riots presumed a certain kind of response, one built around social justice measures, including expanded economic and educational opportunities for the disadvantaged. By contrast, a focus on the police's inability to control the disorder pointed toward improving police management, training, and hiring. In this way, every retrospective analysis in problem definition is also a look ahead and an implicit argument about what government should be doing next.

But problem definition is about much more than just finding someone or something to blame. Further disputes can surround a situation's perceived social significance, meaning, implications, and urgency. By dramatizing or downplaying the problem and by declaring what is at stake, these descriptions help to push an issue onto the front burners of policymaking or result in officials' stubborn inaction and neglect.

The name policy researchers have given to this process of characterizing problems in the political arena is "problem definition." In part, government action is a result of institutional structure and formal and informal procedure. The partisan balance of power will also direct decisionmaking. But, according to the problem definition perspective, public policymaking must also be understood as a function of the perceived nature of the problems being dealt with, and the qualities that define this nature are never incontestable (even though they may sometimes be taken for granted).

The defining process occurs in a variety of ways, but always it has major import for an issue's political standing and for the design of public solutions. Cultural values, interest group advocacy, scientific information, and professional advice all help to shape the content of problem definition. Once crystallized, some definitions will remain long-term fixtures of the policymaking landscape; other definitions may undergo constant revision or be replaced altogether by competing formulations (for a case study of this in the legal realm, see Polisar and Wildavsky 1989).

This book examines this most central topic of public policy analysis. It seeks to document the importance of the problem definition phenomenon from both political and policymaking perspectives, to map out the rhetoric most frequently employed by problem definers, and to analyze the scenarios by which definitions are built or crumble. The contributors to this volume supply a rich collection of case studies for comparative analysis. Through this approach it will become plain that the process described is always pivotal to government problem-solving in general, although its specific expressions are multiform.

In the remainder of this chapter, we will present the concept of problem definition at greater length, first by bringing together the several major streams of literature from which it has emerged. We will discuss the "mechanics" of cognition and argument by which problems are defined with tremendous flexibility, as well as the role played by political stakeholders. Finally, we will profile the dimensions of definition that are most frequently invoked when social problems are put up for governmental consideration.

CONVERGING PERSPECTIVES ON PROBLEM DEFINITION

Contemporary policy analysis is multidisciplinary in its techniques and orientation, and perhaps nowhere more so than in the burgeoning study of problem definition. Thus, it is possible to locate within political science, sociology, and even literary theory a number of points of origin for the critical concepts relating to this subject. From such diverse intellectual sources, too often discussed without relation to each other, come insights that help to make sense of the fluidity of social problem selection and interpretation by public policymakers.

Social Conflict and Politics

Schattschneider (1960) was one of the very first scholars to underscore the importance of social conflict for political life. In his words, "At the nub of politics are, first, the way in which the public participates in the spread of conflict and, second, the processes by which the unstable relation of the public to the conflict is controlled" (p. 3). For Schattschneider, a conflict's outcome depended directly on the number of people who come to be involved in it. And it is always in the interest of the weaker side to seek to expand involvement by recruiting new participants to its support. Whoever can control this expansion, whether by accelerating or limiting it, gains the political upper hand.

Definition of issues or problems is crucial in the development of a conflict because, as Schattschneider pointed out, the outside audience does not enter the fray randomly or in equal proportion for the competing sides. Rather, the uninterested become engaged in response to the way participants portray their struggle. In short, "the definition of the alternatives is the supreme instrument of power" (Schattschneider 1960: 68). Applying these ideas, Baumgartner (1989: 75) identifies three levels of political conflict, which can be about (1) whether a problem exists, (2) what the best solution is, and (3) what the best means of implementation are.

In political conflict, then, issue definition and redefinition can serve as tools used by opposing sides to gain advantage. To restrict participation, issues may be defined in procedural or narrow technical terms (Nelkin 1975). To heighten participation, issues may be connected to sweeping social themes, such as justice, democracy, and liberty. Conflict is inherently spontaneous and confusing, but activists and organized interests attempt to direct its course by strategic maneuvers based on problem definition. This framework of analysis is applicable to political developments within a host of contexts, from national electoral campaigns to backroom legislative lobbying.

The Social Construction of Reality

Northcott (1992: 1-2; see also Berger and Luckmann 1967) concisely summarizes the sociological perspective that focuses on the "social construction of reality":

> individuals, groups and societies tend to place interpretations upon reality—interpretations which may or may not be true in an absolute sense. These definitions, explanations and assertions are constructed to help us make sense of those things and events that we experience and to help us decide how to respond to those experiences. In the face of uncertainty and ambiguity, these social constructions themselves are fre-

quently based on "fashionable" and therefore changeable assumptions and value judgments.

When applied to the study of social issues, this perspective emphasizes the distinction between "objective conditions" and the definition of some conditions as "problems." According to Seidman and Rappaport (1986: 1), "the definition of a social problem is time, place, and context bound." Spector and Kitsuse (1977), who helped establish the constructionist approach to social problem analysis, redirected attention away from the "putative" problems, probing instead the activities by which such problems are brought to light and presented as needing solution. They described the groups and individuals involved in this problem-naming process as "claims-makers" sustained by "interests or values, or a combination of them" (p. 88).

Claims-makers do more than just identify social problems. In Best's (1989: xx) phrase, they also "typify" them by characterizing the problem's nature. This can be done by advancing a particular orientation (moral, criminal, political, and so forth), or by seizing on so-called representative examples of the problem that accentuate certain features over others. For example, a major interest in the recent sociological literature has been the means by which problems in modern society become "medicalized," bringing to bear concepts of disease, treatment, and professional authority (see, for example, Conrad and Schneider 1980).

The social-constructionist approach has been employed in a large body of studies of different social problem areas. One collection (Best 1989) contains chapters on child abuse, missing children, AIDS, elder abuse, learning disabilities, infertility, the crack epidemic, popular music, smoking, drunk driving, wife abuse, urine testing, and Mexican immigration. Other recent book-length analyses concern population aging (Northcott 1992) and systems of psychiatric diagnosis (Kirk and Kutchins 1992). The direct relevance of this model to public policymaking lies both in the explanation offered for which issues come to be the subject of public discussion, and in the connection between the socially dominant understanding of a problem and the sorts of programmatic interventions deemed to be appropriate and reasonable. As Best (1989: xx) writes, "an orientation locates the problem's cause and recommends a solution."

Among analysts who portray problems and other cultural phenomena as socially constructed, there is some ambiguity as to the precise agency of meaning investment. Gamson (1990: 263–264) outlines two models often found in the literature. A "reflection theory" describes the construction as a direct representation of beliefs, values, and sentiments that are prevalent in the social 'psyche.' " A "hypodermic theory" locates responsibility with particular powerful political and cultural leaders who impose their stance on others, thereby achieving an ideological hegemony. Gamson also proposes another alternative, in which a complex open contest takes place involving a wide range of players who are constrained by shifts in the site of decision-making as well as accidents of history.

Practitioners readily describe the social constructionist understanding of social problems as a work-in-progress (see, for example, Miller and Holstein 1993). Widely utilized, it has nonetheless drawn numerous criticisms, the most telling of which from a political vantage point may be an insufficient concern with the impact of institutional forces in the problem-naming process.

Postmodernism

Postmodernism may be described most generally as an intellectual style concerned with examining the unquestioned value assumptions embodied in culture and society. The primary method of analysis associated with postmodernism is "deconstruction," a way of revealing hidden differences and contradictions within a seemingly unified whole. The most extensive applications of postmodern thinking have occurred in the fields of literature and philosophy. Yet the school is now "sweeping the social sciences," too, including several areas relevant to government, such as public administration, planning and management, and organizational theory (Rosenau 1993: 1).

Postmodernism advances several themes that stress the importance of studying how problems or issues come to be defined in the policy arena. For example, postmodernism rejects the notion of impartial rationality, a popular linear model used in past descriptions of public policymaking (Dye 1984). It disputes, further, that "policy is or can be objective or ideologically neutral" (Rosenau 1993: 3). Policy becomes, instead, a series of conclusions, choices, and rejections of alternatives that are assembled to compose a constructed totality. In politics as in literature, the use of rhetoric is key to the process by which these decisions are justified, promoted, and even placed beyond questioning. Especially relevant to government is "argument from authority," in which the speaker seeks to persuade by reference to a moral mandate (Hogan 1990: 41–47; see also Edelman 1988).

There are other, more sweeping historical and philosophical claims to postmodernism relating to "the cultural logic of capitalism" (Jameson 1991) and the utter indeterminacy of standards of truth. One need not, however, subscribe to such doctrines wholesale to recognize the connection between the theory's lesser claims and the notion of public policymaking as a representation of disputable definitions over the existence and character of social conditions. In this sense, students of problem definition and postmodernism are one in a belief that "policy proposals cry out to be deconstructed, torn apart from within" (Rosenau 1993: 2).

A "Political" Policy Analysis

There are two, quite different, senses in which problem definition has come to be important in the literature of policy analysis. The first usage, which is technical, comes out of the tradition of policy analysis as an applied profession. Under this approach, policy analysis consists of a set of logical steps for diagnosing problems and devising cost-effective solutions, typically in the service of some policymaking authority (Dery 1984: 14–15). Here, problem definition refers to formulating "an 'actionable' statement of issue dynamics from which expenditures can be made, personnel deployed, and procedures developed that will reduce or eliminate the undesirable state of affairs without undue harmful consequences to related activities" (Guess and Farnham 1989: 7).

Yet, as so many policy researchers have pointed out, problem definition can never be purely a technical exercise (see, for example, Dery 1984; Wildavsky 1979; Hogwood and Gunn 1984). Stakeholders have their own assumptions and interests that lead to particular favored definitions, not all of which are compatible (Guess and Farnham 1989: 18–20). And policy choices are always statements of values, even if some value positions are so dominant that their influence goes unexamined or so unrepresented that their neglect goes unnoticed. An explicitly political analysis of public policy-making attempts to relate governmental process and result to this contest of different perspectives.

Scholars in the social constructionist school long ago identified the need to view social problems in terms of a career wherein a problem first emerges, next gains attention and legitimacy, and then receives official programmatic response (see, for example, Blumer 1971; Spector and Kitsuse 1977). With several transition points presenting contingencies capable of blocking advancement, completion of this pathway is never assured. It is these very concerns that contemporary students of agenda-setting have moved to the center of policy analysis. Cobb and Elder (1983), for example, emphasize the expansion of participation and the characteristics of issues as key interrelated factors determining which problems will gain access to the agendas of society and of government. Also, they point out how opponents can keep issues off the agenda by effective argumentation in relation to these same characteristics. A related area of inquiry in the social-constructionist literature has to do with "rhetorical idioms" and "counterrhetorical strategies" (Ibarra and Kitsuse 1993). However described, the result is a debate that must vie for attention against a backdrop of the limited processing capacities of government (see also Hilgartner and Bosk 1988).

The agenda-setting model does not cast problem definition as an abstract conflict of ideas separable from the operation of public institutions. Rather, as Petracca (1992: 1) puts it, "how an issue is defined or redefined, as the case may be, influences: (1) The type of politicking which will ensue around it; (2) Its chances of reaching the agenda of a particular political institution; and (3) The probability of a policy outcome favorable to advocates of the issue." More specifically, different public arenas—legislatures, courts, bureaucracies, the media—have different "selection principles" that are satisfied more or less well by different problem definitions (Hilgartner and Bosk 1988). Baumgartner and Jones (1993) explain how a change in an issue's tone from positive to negative—for example, from images of progress to images of danger in nuclear power—can lead to destruction of a policy monopoly by a few groups or institutional structures that control decisionmaking, and its replacement by an unstable disequilibrium involving many policymaking jurisdictions. But the connection between problem definition and institutional process in this framework is interactive: "Where the rhetoric begins to change, venue changes become more likely. Where venue changes occur, rhetorical changes are facilitated" (Baumgartner and Jones 1993: 37).

The uses of language are crucial to the political analysis of public policymaking and problem definition. Language is essential to understanding, argument, and individual and group expression, which all figure into the definition of social problems for public attention. Language can be the vehicle for employing symbols that lend legitimacy to one definition and undermine the legitimacy of another—as when professional groups try to gain control over the way a problem is perceived by introducing symbols of their expertise and authority (Elder and Cobb 1983). Stone (1988) points out four prominent forms of language and symbolic representation in political discourse: (1) stories, which provide explanations; (2) synecdoches, in which parts of things are said to depict the whole; (3) metaphors, which claim likenesses between things; and (4) ambiguity, in which multiple meanings are evoked simultaneously.

If policymaking is a struggle over alternative realities, then language is the medium that reflects, advances, and interprets these alternatives (Edelman, 1988; Ibarra and Kitsuse 1993). Inside the realm of political institutions, language can also offer a powerful tool for structuring decisionmaking so as to favor one result and diminish the likelihood of another (Riker 1986). Always the question to ask is, who is speaking and to what end? A student of Canadian politics (Lee 1989: 12) describes the growing use of "camouflanguage" to present self-serving versions of events:

As we approached the dying decade of the second millenium . . . a thing contained by a name was often less significant than the name itself. The trend was so ubiquitous it was seldom noticed. Civic leaders borrowed military terms when they wished to convey a sense of action; a committee became a task force, even though it was still a committee.

The military borrowed medical terms to lend a sense of healing to an act of destruction; a bombing became a surgical strike, even though it was still a bombing. Medicine borrowed the language of accountants to apply a sense of fiscal prudence to acts of political revolt; extra billing became balanced billing, even though it was still a violation of medicare [Canada's national health insurance program].

MULTIPLICATION OF MEANINGS— DIVISION OF SUPPORT

Cognitive psychologists distinguish between general and phenomenal realities. The former refers to the actual bases of existence. The latter refers to "the constellation of thoughts, perceptions, and feelings" that makes up each person's "constructed reality" (Wegner and Vallacher 1977: 4). The physical environment, other people's behavior, even one's own qualities as an individual all enter into this construction and are taken as true. Applying this same insight politically, Hogwood and Gunn (1984: 109) state, "we each create our own 'reality,' and this is nowhere more true than in the way we identify problems or issues, and interpret and relate them to our mental map of some larger situation." To understand the process of problem definition in public policymaking, it is necessary to take into account both the specific component elements of political discussion and the methods by which these elements may be assembled.

The Complexity of Social Reality

A basic social science perspective on causality illuminates the intricate nature of social reality and how it may be cast in different lights. Figure 1.1 outlines three alternative models of directional action. The first model, multiple and simultaneous influence, represents a situation at a single point in time where several independent variables exercise shared impact on a given dependent variable. Model 2, sequential influence, depicts a longitudinal chain in which several independent variables working forward in time determine the dependent variable. In Model 3, component influence, two or more independent variables are nested in their relationship to the dependent variable. Still more complex causal pictures are possible through an infinite variety of combinations of these models.

The point is not that one or another of these depictions offers a preferable outline of experience, but that the world works in all of these ways all the time. No observer is able to capture the full picture. Combs (1981: 55) explains: "Reality is always more complex, inchoate, contradictory, and inexplicable than our images and metaphors of it." No two observers are likely

Model 1 - Multiple and Simultaneous Causation

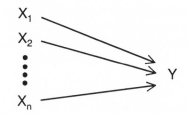

Model 2 - Sequential Causation

Model 3 - Component Causation

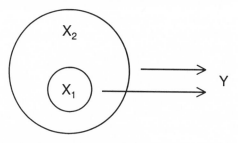

Figure 1.1. Three Social Science Causal Models
Source: Based on Watson and McGaw (1980), chapter 15.

even to see the partial picture in exactly the same way. This divergence is what underpins the political struggle over problem definition, with causal understandings inevitably predisposing certain kinds of policy solutions, foreclosing others, and directing the allocation of authority and resources to cope with a problem (Stone 1988: 160–165).

Emphasis. The choice of which cause to emphasize is a main determinant of differences in problem definition. In a picture of many possible influences, selecting certain factors to the exclusion of others is an act of explanation that aggressively promotes a particular version of reality. For example, mental illness is a longstanding social problem with clearly complex sources.

Researchers have identified numerous categories of causal factors, among them social stress, family interactions, genetics, and biology. Such influences often operate in conjunction and are difficult to disentangle. Yet mental health policymakers and advocates in different historical periods have tended to be selective in their focus, resulting in recurring shifts in the theory and practice of mental health care and the uses of public funding for this policy area (Rochefort 1988).

In the following passage, economist Ellwood (1989: 8) illustrates concretely the impossibility of reaching consensus on the *one* real cause of poverty in the case of a two-parent family:

> Suppose we find that a two-parent family with three children is poor even though the father is working full time. What is the cause of the family's poverty? One could say that the father's wages are too low, that the mother is not willing to work, that the family cannot find affordable day care, that the couple was irresponsible to have children when they could not support them, or that the father did not get enough education or has not worked hard enough to get a "good" job. Even if we talked to the family, it is possible that we would not be able to agree on just one "true" reason.

Level of Analysis. Often, selecting which independent variables to emphasize in a complicated, explanation-rich situation hinges on the observer's level of analysis. In terms of the model of component influence outlined in Figure 1.1, this might mean seeing the interior of the causal picture to the neglect of an enclosing structure. Where, on the continuum from microindividual behavior to macrosocial forces, does the problem-definer focus attention? The Los Angeles riot offers a perfect example of a complicated social event involving individual and group behavior within a context of specific short-term stimuli and more general long-term social and racial inequalities. At what level should we focus in understanding this situation? As we have seen, this question can be answered very differently, prompting a debate that is as much about social philosophy as the facts of the riot itself.

Similarly, child neglect can be approached on different levels—individual, social system, and the plane of fundamental beliefs and cultural agreements (Lally 1984). A narrow clinical view that tends to focus on family behavior alone gives limited preventive possibilities. This same behavior, however, can also be embedded as a component of larger processes that point to interventions aimed at business and technology, economics, and other social forces.

Measurement. Measurement is a process that always involves discretion and inconsistency. No two analysts will approach the task of gauging a social problem's magnitude, rate of change, or distribution in quite the same way. Whether a problem exists, how bad it is, who or what is responsible, and what future trends will occur are all perceptions that can depend on the measuring approach applied. The use of "optimistic" versus "pessimistic" assumptions is one well-known tactic in attacking or defending a government program (Light 1985: 55). And deciding how to categorize the objects or events to be counted and why is another common point of contention in political life, especially between the parties and between incumbents and office seekers. Far from strict mathematics, political measurement is an activity of such flexibility that Stone (1988: 127) likens it to poetry rather than science. Consider the following examples of numerical controversies:

Were the 1980s a period of growing social inequality in American society? The statistical evidence varies depending on baseline year selected; mean versus median family income; which forms of taxation are included in the analysis; and which public programs are classified as "social spending" (DeParle 1991; Gosselin 1992).

How many times did George Bush as President, and Bill Clinton as Governor of Arkansas, raise taxes? The question surfaced forcefully in the 1992 campaign. At one point, the Bush camp claimed that its candidate had raised taxes but once, while his opponent was guilty of 128 counts. Yet the Clinton team's reexamination of the Bush record yielded a much higher total of 178 increases in taxes, fees, and related "revenue enhancements" (Kantor 1992).

What is the U.S. poverty rate? The official counting method originally was devised in the early 1960s. Today, there is debate about the price of nonfood costs, about how to factor in the value of in-kind benefits (such as food stamps and medical insurance), and about the types of taxes to be subtracted from income, among other issues (Ruggles 1990). The 1992 *Statistical Abstract of the United States* (U.S. Bureau of the Census 1992) reports the poverty level using 15 different definitions!

What was the ratio of tax increases to spending cuts in the first Clinton budget? Republican opponents pushed the answer in one direction (inflating the tax increases); Democratic backers pulled the other way (exaggerating the spending cuts). Aiding these partisan foes and friends of the document was the intrinsic ambiguity of many governmental actions. One example: an increase in taxation of Social Security benefits by which the Treasury would recapture a portion of spending under the program (Greenhouse 1993).

Interconnections. Reactions to an issue can depend on its perceived relationship to other issues of importance to the observer. The standard political ideologies like liberalism and conservatism provide one form of possible linkage across issues. Each of us also has his or her own internal attitudinal fields in which more idiosyncratic principles of association may be at work (Milburn 1991). In addition, media coverage can juxtapose contemporaneous subjects so that one thing tends to remind us of another.

An analysis of voter reaction to the free trade issue in Canada during the 1988 election shows the complexity and importance of such interconnections for problem definition (Lee 1989: 13–14). A longitudinal opinion survey assessed public response to the "Mulroney trade deal" and to the "Canada–U.S. trade agreement," using these different denotations with randomly selected portions of the sample group. Not only did support levels vary according to the designation used, but changing attitudes over time for the "Mulroney trade deal" hinged on shifts in the general popularity of the prime minister, while support for the "Canada–U.S. trade agreement" was unaffected by such shifts. Supposedly, all of those being polled were reacting to the same policy issue. Yet how the issue was named and what associations this name carried in the minds of the voters made a world of difference.

The Struggle for Problem Ownership

A basic concept for the study of problem definition is "problem ownership" (Gusfield 1981). One aspect of problem ownership is domination of the way that a social concern is thought of and acted upon in the public arena, that is, by serving as the recognized authority on essential questions of causes, consequences, and solutions. From an institutional angle, problem ownership can also refer to jurisdictional control over policy decisions and appropriations for a problem area.

For many types of social problems, one can identify a well-delineated, specialized "community of operatives" (Hilgartner and Bosk 1988) that advances the theories and data on which policies are based. When the paradigm of explanation shaping policy development goes without serious challenge, or when challengers are effectively kept on the sidelines in the decisionmaking process—these are signs of ownership in public policymaking. Such political property rights may be sought by professional, disciplinary, religious, economic, or ideological groups, depending on the issue. And the motivations for seeking ownership are equally varied (and potentially intertwined), from territorial protection and expansion, to the search for truth, to moral expression.

A policy area today that features an obvious unresolved struggle for problem ownership is homelessness (Rochefort and Cobb 1992). At least three different major points of view have surfaced—of homelessness as housing shortage, as economic dislocation, and as product of mental hospital deinstitutionalization. For each explanation, there are well-organized advocates and providers, armed with study findings, who desire expanded public financing for services within their domain, be it affordable housing, economic development and job training, or expanded community mental health programs. Hard-pressed to decide which of these aspects of homelessness will receive their primary attention, policymakers have often adopted a holistic approach that spreads resources thinly among all the leading claimant groups, an inclusive but ultimately unfocused strategy that is yet to be demonstrated as effective.

THE RHETORIC OF PROBLEM DEFINITION AND ITS POLICYMAKING CONSEQUENCES

As political discourse, the function of problem definition is at once to explain, to describe, to recommend, and, above all, to persuade. It is a distinctive form of public rhetoric made up of a habitual vocabulary. Building on what has been demonstrated so far in this chapter about the malleability of social issues, we now proceed to set out several recurrent categories of problem definition claims, noting their relationship to agenda access and to program design (see, for example, Hogwood and Gunn 1984: 115–127; Peters 1993: 48–53; and Anderson 1990: 78–82 for related discussions).

Causality

The way a problem is defined invariably entails some statement about its origins. As already suggested, the question of culpability is the most prominent of all aspects of problem definition. One important distinction is whether attribution is made to individual versus impersonal causes. Much of the traditional debate between liberalism and conservatism can in fact be explained by the stress given these two competing perspectives. Consider, for example, the poverty problem. Those on the left highlight failures of the economic and cultural system, while those on the right commonly cite the lack of individual or group effort (Patterson 1981).

In the realm of technology, much attention has been given to the role of human versus equipment error in accounting for complex system failures, such as in nuclear power plants or airline disasters. The latter association is more likely to result in stronger standards and regulation because responsibility is not linked to idiosyncratic human performance and capability. Stone (1988; see also Stone 1989) proposes a framework for classifying causal statements in politics based on different types of actions (unguided versus purposeful) and their consequences (intended versus unintended). Within her approach, the clearest contrast in problem definition is found between causes considered to be intentional and accidental. Intentional causes refer to some purposive human action undertaken to bring about a particular result. If the action is perceived to be in the public interest and effective, it is labeled a rational success; if the outcome is harmful, an investigation into the action often ensues, often in terms of "victims" and "conspiracies." Accidental causes have to do with "the realm of accident and fate," such as a natural disaster, and there is no one on whom to place responsibility.

Blaming is one of the great pastimes of politics. Generating blame, however, is a "strategic choice that has both potential benefits and costs" (Weaver 1988: 2). It may be a way to create momentum for a particular policy thrust or to rule out seeming alternatives; but those being blamed are bound to do all they can to deflect incrimination. Fault-finding lay at the heart of a flap involving former Secretary of Education Lauro Cavazos, the nation's first Hispanic-American cabinet member. It was Cavazos himself who started the controversy by blaming Hispanic parents for undervaluing education and calling on them for a greater "commitment." A firestorm of angry protests erupted as several Hispanic leaders pointed to other sources of the dropout problem. "Hispanic parents know that education is the only way out of poverty for their children," one activist contradicted Cavazos. "He is wrong to say that the families are at fault when society is at fault for not supporting families that are overwhelmed by economic problems" (Suro 1990a: B8). San Antonio Mayor Henry Cisneros added his voice to the expression of resentment, similarly redirecting the locus of responsibility for this issue: "First of all, what he said is not true. And second, it hurts parents who are struggling and want the best for their families but who confront the reality of unequally financed school systems, the reality of low paying jobs, and language barriers" (Suro 1990b: 13).

A decision about problem causality can be the linchpin to a whole set of interdependent propositions that construct an edifice of understanding about a particular issue. Reuter (1992; see also Sharp in this volume), for example, characterizes the drug policy debate in terms of "hawks," "doves," and "owls," who respectively view drug usage as a problem of criminality, ill-conceived prohibitive legislation, and disease. Each position carries its own assumptions about why people use drugs, what the core of drug policy should be, and the consequences of policy failure. The alternatives before government that emerge from this conflict of perspectives are as different as tougher police enforcement, legalization of psychoactive substances, and more prevention and treatment services.

Certain problems are defined very simply, specifying single causal agents; others include a variety of influences. Problem definitions of these two types may predispose the political system to different outcomes. Generally, narrowing the focus to just one or two causal factors is a signal that the problem definer is ready for action. More complex formulations, on the other hand, may represent a strategy to head off prompt response (Stone 1988: chapter

8). Yet, depending on the circumstances, multicausal explanations and the multipronged solutions they engender can also be among the most sophisticated policy endeavors and also those that have the greatest chance of building support, as in tackling huge social program issues, such as the bail-out of Social Security (Light 1985) or reform of the health care system (White House Domestic Policy Council 1993).

Current research also underscores the impact of the media on the public's adoption of causal stances toward social problems (Iyengar 1991). Television, which is the primary source of most people's news, tends to frame issues either episodically (as particular incidents and acts) or thematically (within a political and economic context). The former style of broadcasting predominates and it renders viewers "less likely to hold public officials accountable for the existence of some problem and also less likely to hold them responsible for alleviating it" (Iyengar 1991: 2–3).

Severity

A social problem may be represented along many dimensions beyond that of causality. One of these facets is severity, that is, how serious a problem and its consequences are taken to be. Is this an issue meriting space on a crowded public policy agenda? How strongly the severity label gets applied is a contentious matter, since this element of problem definition is pivotal to capturing the attention of public officials and the media.

Global warming is an illustration of an issue whose severity is debated, with disputants vehemently disagreeing over the facts concerning its "extent, timing and impact" (Stevens 1991: B12; see also Samuelson 1992). Environmentalists warn that the situation is already grave, a looming disaster. Opponents of this view, however, including the former Bush administration and many industry groups, tend to characterize the problem as far from catastrophic, and they resist any corrective steps that could harm the economy.

Severity may also be communicated by a label that officially certifies that some germinating concern, having crossed a threshold, now qualifies as the definitive recurrence of a familiar public woe. Political disagreements in these circumstances revolve around when the label should be applied and by whom. Exactly this kind of discourse was seen with regard to using the "recession" label to describe this nation's worsening economic difficulties at the beginning of the decade. Excerpting from the reported statements of various public officials and economic onlookers during this period, Table 1.1 presents the semantic chronology by which this term ultimately gained acceptance as appropriate.

On the other hand, it is possible for a problem to grow steadily worse while onlookers adamantly resist labelling it as a new phenomenon. This, at least, is what Senator Daniel Moynihan (1993) maintains has been happen-

Table 1.1   A Semantic Chronology: Defining the Recession of 1990–91

August 23, 1990	In a *New York Times*/CBS News Poll, six in ten Americans surveyed said the nation was in a recession. The *New York Times* reported that the accepted academic definition of a recession, two consecutive quarters of declining national output, had not occurred, but many economists dispute this definition as unable "to capture fully the varieties of hard times."
September 25, 1990	At a meeting in Washington, D.C., the Group of Seven industrial nations (the United States, West Germany, Japan, France, Britain, Canada, and Italy) released a communiqué this week criticizing talk of recession as too pessimistic. The previous week, in testimony before the Joint Economic Committee of Congress, Federal Reserve Chairman Alan Greenspan proposed revising the traditional definition of recession in favor of a more stringent one representing a "cumulative unwinding of economic activity."
November 11, 1990	Expressing his observation that economic troubles were hitting the investment community much harder than middle America, a Prudential Bache analyst stated, "To a large extent, this is a yuppie recession."
November 11, 1990	In a feature in the *New York Times*, economist Leonard Silk described as premature the popular anxiety "that the American economy might be headed not just for another brief recession . . . but for a real depression."
November 12, 1990	Based on rising unemployment claims, *Newsweek* magazine concluded that "a recession betwen 'mild' and 'average' is developing" and speculated on the chances that it might turn into a national economic "collapse."
November 28, 1990	In testimony before the House Banking Committee, Alan Greenspan described the economy as undergoing "a meaningful downturn." He objected to one Democratic representative's remark that this "was a nice way of saying we've entered a recession."
November 29, 1990	In a speech President Bush summarized his view of economic conditions in the country by saying, "We are in a period that concerns me of a sluggish economy. Some are saying 'recession,' and some are saying 'slowdown' and some are going 'downturn.' But the one positive thing is that most if not all people are suggesting that whatever it is, it won't be long-lasting."
November 30, 1990	The Commerce Department released the government's index of leading economic indicators for October. It showed a 1.2 percent drop, the fourth straight monthly drop in a row. An economist for the First Boston Corporation commented that "it reinforces the view that the economy has entered at least a mild recession."

Continued

Table 1.1   (*continued*)

December 5, 1990	A survey by the Federal Reserve showed a decline in business activity around the country. Without using the term "recession," the survey reported that "business conditions are somewhat mixed in different parts of the country but on balance display a weaker pattern."
December 16, 1990	In the midst of a slow Christmas shopping season and faced with other bad economic news, Treasury Secretary Nicholas Brady said on *Meet the Press* that "I don't think it's the end of the world even if we have a recession. We'll pull back out of it again. No big deal."
December 29, 1991	The Dating Committee of the National Bureau of Economic Research, a prestigious committee of economists that is charged with determining the official onset of recessions, announced that the country was in a recession that probably began in August. The committee's standard policy is to make a ruling only after observing six or more months of poor economic performance. For the first time in its history the committee broke with this schedule because, in one commitee member's words, "if we had waited a few months to say something, when most people are convinced that we are in a recession now, then we might have been laughed at." The *New York Times* said, "It was as if the umpire had called a strike before the pitch crossed the plate."
January 2, 1991	In a television interview with journalist David Frost that had been taped on December 16, President Bush admitted the country was in a recession but claimed it was not a deep one and would end "not too many months from now."
January 13, 1991	An economist for the Bridgewater Group, a money management firm, told a *New York Times* reporter that he felt the economy was in a depression. Referring to a recent statement by the chairman of the Federal Deposit Insurance Corporation that the banking industry was not in a situation comparable to that of the Great Depression, the reporter wrote, "Sometimes, more can be learned about what is going on from what officials choose to deny than from what they affirm."

Sources: Douglas 1990; Gosselin 1990; Hershey 1990a and 1990b; Norris 1990 and 1991; Oreskes 1990; *Providence Journal-Bulletin* 1991; Rosenbaum 1990a and 1990b; Silk 1990; Thomas 1990; Uchitelle 1990a and 1990b.

ing in the U.S. with regard to social deviancy. In a much commented-upon essay in the *American Scholar*, Moynihan invokes the sociological theory that the level of deviancy a society will recognize remains relatively constant, irrespective of the actual frequency of that behavior. Examining trends in such areas as the rate of illegitimacy and violent crime, he concludes that we are normalizing, or becoming accustomed to, hitherto unacceptable levels of harmful behavior without naming the trend as "social pathology" and following through with the attempts at remedial action this definition would imply.

Incidence

Moynihan's concern with tabulation brings us directly to "incidence" as a descriptive component in problem definition. According to survey researchers, perceptions of the frequency and prevalence of a hazardous or unjust situation are a potent trigger to it being considered a social problem (Stafford and Warr 1985). And notwithstanding the senator's analysis of social deviance, sometimes a key issue politically *is* a problem's change over time— is it declining, stable, or growing, and if it is growing, at what rate? Linear or even exponential projections are the most ominous, and when accepted as valid, tend to create the most pressure for quick public intervention.

Often, as we have already seen, the argument is simply over selecting the most accurate, nondistorting statistic to represent a problem. Take, for example, the number of Americans without health insurance (Steinmetz 1993). The figure most commonly cited is 37 million. Yet, health reform advocates tell us, this count is a mere snapshot in time that falls well below the total number of people who drift into and out of the uninsured pool over a period of time; the number also excludes the underinsured who have inadequate coverage. Those who feel that the 37 million statistic exaggerates the U.S. health care problem—defenders of the private health insurance industry, to name one group—call attention to the relatively brief time that many people remain uninsured.

Incidence patterns across society can also be portrayed in varying fashions. An issue's social-class dimension may be brought to light or downplayed. Nelson (1984: 15) showed that the disassociation of child abuse from class-based concerns "had long lasting effects on the shape of child abuse policy" by giving the issue a much more universal appeal. Alternatively, a social issue may be identified with a particular population cohort in order to elicit sympathy and support or target resources. For example, advocates have long endeavored to call attention to the persistent problems experienced by Americans who fought in Vietnam, a war whose divisiveness at home exacerbated the readjustment of returning veterans. (Interestingly, however, some recent research refutes stereotypes of the Vietnam-era vet as a troubled misfit, documenting that at least in terms of labor force status, these individuals generally have better jobs than their peers [Cohany 1987]). Current discussions of the AIDS issue that focus on the sharply rising rates of HIV infection among teenagers, and especially females among them, make use of age and gender as the critical defining measures of incidence (*Newsweek* 1992).

Novelty

When an issue is described as novel, unprecedented, or trailblazing, it can have a couple of effects. One, of course, is to win attention. Then as time passes and the novelty wanes, the public and media become bored with an issue and are distracted from it (Downs 1973; Bosso 1989). But issues that have not been seen before are difficult to conceptualize and they lack familiar solutions. Thus a tension arises as the issue is publicized and onlookers expect resolution, yet no consensus exists within the political system on how to tackle the problem. For example, difficulties of this kind often occur with medical breakthroughs such as those in genetics research. Each new discovery brings with it a thicket of ethical and practical concerns requiring analysis.

Proximity

To characterize an issue as having proximity is to argue that it hits close to home or directly impinges on a person's interest. If the case can be made successfully, members of the audience will become concerned and may express their concern politically. For this reason, issue proponents constantly seek to expand their base by claims of personal relevancy. Viewed in this light, it was no surprise to hear the National Commission on Children, on the occasion of release of its new report on child poverty in America, describe this problem not only in terms of "personal tragedies" but also as "a staggering national tragedy." To quote panel chairman John D. Rockefeller IV: "The health and vitality of our economy and our democracy are increasingly in danger." Harvard Professor T. Berry Brazelton added, "We know these kids are going to cost us billions in the future. They're going to be the terrorists of the future" (*New York Times* 1990: A22).

Crisis

"Crisis" is undoubtedly one of the most-used terms in the political lexicon. It denotes a special condition of severity where corrective action is long overdue and dire circumstances exist. The dividing line between a mere problem and a full-blown crisis is indeed a hazy one, which advocates are prone to cross in their language when they see momentum for their cause waning. Within the social-constructionist school, crisis has been identified as a prevalent motif of the "rhetoric of calamity," used by claims-makers to elevate a concern when facing an environment overloaded with competing claims.

Sometimes the argument is made that other problems under discussion are mere symptoms or effects of the subsuming crisis condition (Ibarra and Kitsuse 1993).

The national deficit is an example of an issue that has frequently been associated with the term crisis, although not all politicians or economists agree that the label is appropriate (Ortner 1990). In 1986, the death of two prominent athletes from a drug overdose coupled with the appearance of a new form of cocaine helped convert the drug problem into a concern of "crisis proportions." Yet, ironically, some evidence indicates that at the time drug usage was actually declining (Baumgartner 1989: 201–210).

No policy area has received more attention under President Clinton than health care reform. Moreover, a seemingly endless flow of special television news features and newspaper and magazine reports has done much to publicize the cost, access, and other health system worries. Yet just as the administration made ready in January 1994 to commence a major push behind its legislative package, the fundamental assumption that the United States suffers a health care crisis came under attack (Knox 1994). Reacting to recent improvement in the annual rate of medical inflation and seeking to undercut an issue on which they saw little partisan gain, Republicans argued that the Clinton team was guilty of overdramatizing the health care situation. Even a prominent Democrat, Senator Moynihan, stated publicly that he felt "we don't have a health care crisis in this country" (a comment he later recanted); Moynihan did, however, believe that we have a "welfare crisis," highlighting an issue long of special concern to him. President Clinton well recognized the rhetorical power of the "crisis" label and he was loathe to surrender it, making it a major point of his State of the Union speech to portray America's health care crisis indisputably as such and to ridicule the naysayers. In this as in other matters of problem definition, of course, perceptions count for all, and it greatly favored the president's position that 84 percent of the American public agreed there is "a crisis today in health care" (*American Health Line* 1994).

"Emergency" is a term often used synonymously with crisis. Discussing the homelessness problem, Lipsky and Smith (1989) have explained how defining the situation as an emergency has enabled quick responses but also tended to produce temporary band-aid solutions such as shelters instead of more comprehensive, long-term reforms.

Problem Populations

Not only are problems given descriptive definition, so too are the afflicted groups and individuals. This is especially true in social welfare policymaking, whose purpose is to transfer resources or deliver services to specified target populations. Political willingness to make these commitments is generally conditioned by societal perceptions of the people who are going to benefit. Further, the balance between assistance and coercion in policy design is struck by how positive or negative these perceptions are.

Several attitudinal axes structure aggregate impressions. Is the group worthy or unworthy (deserving or undeserving) of assistance? Underlying this question is the recurrent notion of culpability. Are members of the group seen as familiar or strange? Social deviants and other out-group members do not receive equivalent consideration to persons with whom the public readily identifies. Related to these issues is the distinction between sympathetic and threatening populations. Understandings of the nature of the difficulties presented by members of a problem population are also formative in policymaking. Is their problem conceived to be psychological or nonpsychological, permanent or reversible, self-limiting or all-encompassing in its effects on a person's social functioning? Rochefort (1986) utilized these attributions to account for varying forms of public intervention concerning groups like the elderly, working and welfare poor, and the mentally ill—including the use of institutions, rehabilitation programs, and financial entitlements—as well as shifts in these policy orientations over time. Examining public opinion data, Cook (1979) also demonstrated a link between the favorability of attitudes toward different groups and popular support for providing aid to them. She concludes simply that "all things being equal people we like and find attractive and pleasant seem to get more help" (p. 41).

Working along these same lines, Schneider and Ingram (1993: 335–336) specify four types of socially constructed target populations:

> Advantaged groups are perceived to be both powerful and positively constructed, such as the elderly and business. Contenders, such as unions and the rich, are powerful but negatively constructed, usually as undeserving. Dependents might include children or mothers and are considered to be politically weak, but they carry generally positive constructions. Deviants, such as criminals, are in the worst situation, since they are both weak and negatively constructed.

Which category a target population is perceived to fall into influences the level and nature of public interest in its plight, the tools government selects for intervening (subsidies, punishments, inducements, services, outreach), and the forms of rhetoric with which policy action is justified.

Instrumental versus Expressive Orientations

An interesting twist on the theme of problem definition concerns the ends-means orientation of those defining the problem. In some situations issue advocates premise their stance on an instrumental basis, which sets out a deliberate course of action carefully calculated to achieve a desired end. At other times, however, the means and not the ends of public action will be uppermost for issue definers. In effect, this amounts to viewing public policy in expressive terms and the very process of implementation as the embodiment or corruption of certain cherished values. Curious debates can ensue when issue opponents differ in their focus on ends and means, for the two sides lack a shared psychological orientation essential to meaningful argument.

A current example of such an instrumental/expressive conflict is the disagreement over the new birth control device Norplant. Norplant consists of a half dozen small capsules, implanted under the skin, that release small amounts of a contraceptive hormone for up to five years. A long-term continual method of preventing births, it has been recommended for use as part of several social policy initiatives, including welfare reform. In its simplest and most extreme form, the idea is to mandate the contraceptive for Aid to Families with Dependent Children recipients. Without doubting the potential efficacy of such an instrumental strategy, many opponents fault the method as unacceptable. As one bioethicist has stated: "There are all sorts of reasons why policies that might achieve a good goal—like the reduction of welfare costs and fewer poor babies—give too much authority to the government. I'm not saying the goal is bad, but the means to get there will come at a terrible price, a scary price" (Kantrowitz and Wingert 1993: 37).

Solutions

As indicated by the Norplant example, the definitional struggle in policy-making extends from aspects of the problem and those affected by and interested in it to include descriptive qualities of the solution. Until and unless general political agreement crystallizes on this matter, government remains without the wherewithal to act (see, for example, Kingdon 1984). Brewer and deLeon (1983: 18) term this the "estimation" stage of policy analysis, which "emphasizes empirical, scientific, and projective issues to help determine the likelihoods and consequences of candidate options . . . [and] assessments of the desirability of such outcomes."

Interestingly, some policy researchers, upsetting the notion of linear policy development, point out that sometimes it is solutions that determine problem definition. Wildavsky (1979), for example, has argued that public officials will not take a problem seriously unless there is a proposed course of action attached to it. In a sense, the solution begets the problem. Or, as he states, "A problem is linked to a solution; a problem is a problem only if something can be done about it" (p. 42). Wildavsky also predicted that if any proposed solution is carried out, it creates a whole set of new issues, ensuring that no public problem ever really dies. Too, in the process of implementation, previously accepted problem definitions may well come unraveled (Weiss 1989).

Solutions can also predispose the identification of causes, in the sense that political actors who favor particular policy strategies highlight those causal factors in social problems that can be targeted by their strategies. In effect, advocates are always searching for opportunities to argue the value of their programmatic ideas as new problems come into view. For this reason, political scientists sometimes go so far as to argue that "problems and solutions ought to be analyzed separately in order to understand governmental decision-making" (Baumgartner and Jones 1993: 5; see also Kingdon 1984; Peters 1993: 52–53).

Whatever the direction of influence in public policymaking among recognizing problems, finding causes, and choosing solutions—the pattern will depend on the issue and on the audience—an essential concern in problem definition is solution *availability*: Do key actors believe that means exist to accomplish what needs to be done? Or does it seem folly and a waste of resources to invest in a given course of action? For better or worse, the political realm is a magnet for nostrums that have neither been applied nor evaluated on a macrosocial scale. Therefore, it often becomes a guessing game for decisionmakers—an exercise in faith or skepticism—to choose between aggressive intervention or restraint.

Nuclear power plants to produce cheap and reliable electricity, health education programs to promote better living habits in the population at large, employment and training initiatives to counter chronic welfare dependency, recycling to resolve a growing trash disposal problem—each of these interventions matches a widely recognized social goal with a touted solution whose practical effectiveness is the subject of unabating controversy. Following the Los Angeles riots, myriad suggestions were aired for the kinds of aid necessary to prevent similar occurrences in Los Angeles and other American cities. Included were housing programs, employment training, free enterprise zones, and more. Experts were quite open, however, about how little really is known about solving the problem of America's urban underclass (Deparle 1992a,b). Similarly on the crime issue, one well-known writer (Silberman 1994: 1) has put it bluntly: "The problem of crime can be attacked, but it cannot be solved," this by way of criticizing official enthusiasm for quick fixes like the "three strikes and you're out" mandatory life sentencing proposal. Of course, to claim that no solution is available to deal with a problem can simply be a strategy of obstruction by political interests who perceive it is inaction that best suits their purposes.

A solution's *acceptability* does not refer to effectiveness of action but to whether that action conforms to standard codes of behavior. In many ways, this attribute offers another vantage point on the ends-means distinction already introduced. The heart of the matter is ethical: Are there established social principles that forbid a certain remedial approach even as the problem at hand worsens and could feasibly be contained? War in the Middle East has once again raised the issue of chemical warfare. Experience shows these weapons to be a lethal component of a country's military arsenal, one capable of inspiring great terror among the enemy. But does a civilized nation unleash this kind of destructive power, no matter what the circumstances? The question of acceptability also frequently attends the development of new technologies. A recent example is the implantation of fetal tissue into the brains of sufferers of Parkinson's disease (Kolata 1990). Although the technique apparently holds great promise for combating this nervous condition, widespread opposition has arisen based on fear the surgery will encourage abortions.

Supposing a proposed policy intervention is agreed upon, available, and acceptable, one more potential barrier still remains, that of affordability. The issue is straightforward. Do political actors perceive that adequate resources exist to pay for what needs to be done? Especially in these days of government deficits, decisionmakers are cautious in making financial commitments. Meanwhile, demands are ongoing for expanding existing programs and for adding new ones. For example, the nation's high infant mortality is accepted as a serious social problem, and much is understood about the complex of prenatal services that could help the situation (Tolchin 1990). It remains controversial, however, just how these services will be provided and financed. Simply deciding on a proposal's anticipated costs, which is fundamental to any discussion of affordability, can be hard enough. Thus, in President Clinton's health reform plan, there are uncertainties about both the cost of the standard package of benefits and the possibility of savings in existing programs. Proponents and opponents may choose from a spectrum of financing estimates spanning several billion dollars to make their differing arguments (Freudenheim 1993; Wessel and Wartzman 1993).

Affordability debates invoke various kinds of standards depending on the rhetorical objectives of participants. Dollar comparisons with other operating or proposed programs, references to overall budgetary constraints, and estimates of the cost of action measured against the probable economic (and social) costs of failing to act are all common.

CONCLUSION

We began this chapter with a review of varied scholarly literatures that, despite differences in nomenclature, disciplinary styles, and research objectives, share an underlying interest in how public issues are identified and conceptualized. By focusing on areas of overlap and connection in these literatures, rather than the discrepancies, we have pulled together the fundamentals of an emerging problem definition approach to policy analysis, laying the groundwork for more refined policy case studies. The following several chapters supply such studies. Surveying a wide gamut of programmatic activities, they convey further and in very concrete terms just how often and how profoundly the governmental process revolves around definitional concerns, irrespective of the nature of the issue, level of government, or institutional arena.

Actions speak louder than words, it is commonly said. However, in the world of politics and policymaking, this is not necessarily so, and in any case the two are inextricable; actions and words influence and even stand for each other as embodiments of the ideas, arguments, convictions, demands, and perceived realities that direct the public enterprise. The study of problem definition offers a systematic way to unveil these interrelationships and their significance.

REFERENCES

American Health Line. 1994. "CNN/USA Today/Gallup: 84% See Health Care Crisis." January 25, pp. 5–7, 11.

Anderson, J. E. 1990. *Public Policymaking: An Introduction*. Boston: Houghton Mifflin.

Apple, R. W. 1992. "Politicians Warily Gauge the Effects of Los Angeles's Rioting at the Polls." *New York Times*, May 17, p. A20.

Baumgartner, F. R. 1989. *Conflict and Rhetoric in French Policymaking*. Pittsburgh: University of Pittsburgh Press.

Baumgartner, F. R., and B. D. Jones. 1993. *Agendas and Instability in American Politics*. Chicago: University of Chicago Press.

Berger, P. L., and T. L. Luckmann. 1967. *The Social Construction of Reality*. Garden City, N.Y.: Doubleday.

Best, J., ed. 1989. *Images of Issues: Typifying Contemporary Social Problems*. New York: Aldine de Gruyter.

Blumer, H. 1971. "Social Problems as Collective Behavior." *Social Problems* 18: 298–306.

Bosso, C. 1989. "Setting the Agenda: Mass Media and the Discovery of Famine in Ethiopia." Pp. 153–174 in *Manipulating Public Opinion*, ed. M. Margolis and G. Mauser. Pacific Grove, Calif.: Brooks-Cole.

Brewer, G. D., and P. deLeon. 1983. *The Foundations of Policy Analysis*. Homewood, Ill.: Dorsey Press.

Cobb, R. W., and C. D. Elder. 1983. *Participation in American Politics: The Dynamics of Agenda-Building*. Baltimore: Johns Hopkins University Press.

Cohany, S. 1987. "Labor Force Status of Vietnam-era Veterans." *Monthly Labor Review*, February, pp. 11–17.

Combs, J. E. 1981. "A Process Approach." Pp. 39–62 in *Handbook of Political Communication*, ed. D. D. Nimmo and K. R. Sanders. Beverly Hills, Calif.: Sage.

Conrad, P., and J. W. Schneider. 1980. *Deviance and Medicalization: From Badness to Sickness*. St. Louis: C. V. Mosby.

Cook, F. 1979. *Who Should Be Helped? Public Support for Social Services*. Beverly Hills, Calif.: Sage.

DeParle, J. 1991. "Painted by Numbers, 1980's Are Rosy to G.O.P., While Democrats See Red." *New York Times*, September 26, p. B10.

———. 1992a. "The Civil Rights Battle Was Easy Next to the Problems of the Ghetto." *New York Times*, May 17, Week in Review sec., p. 1.

———. 1992b. "At Poverty Conference, Gloom and Dashed Hope." *New York Times*, June 1, p. A13.

Dery, D. 1984. *Problem Definition in Policy Analysis*. Lawrence: University Press of

"Who's Afraid of the Big, Bad Recession?" *New York Times*, in Review, Sec. 4, p. 7.

and Down with Ecology—The Issue Attention Cycle." *Public*

tanding Public Policy. Englewood Cliffs, N.J.: Prentice-Hall.

Constructing the Political Spectacle. Urbana: University of Illi-

. W. Cobb. 1983. *The Political Uses of Symbols*. New York:

oor Support. New York: Basic Books.

Freudenheim, M. 1993. "Health Insurance Data Called Faulty." *New York Times*, October 8, p. A26.

Gamson, J. 1990. "Rubber Wars: Struggles over the Condom in the United States." *Journal of the History of Sexuality* 1: 262–282.

Gosselin, P. 1990. Greenspan Admits to a 'Downturn.'" *Boston Globe*, November 29, p. 61.

———. 1992. "Back to the Future." *Boston Globe*, May 3, p. 77.

Greenhouse, S. 1993. "Seeing Figures, 2 Sides Calculate Clinton's Math." *New York Times*, February 22, p. A14.

Guess, G. M., and P. G. Farnham. 1989. *Cases in Public Policy Analysis*. New York: Longman.

Gusfield, J. 1981. *The Culture of Public Problems*. Chicago: University of Chicago Press.

Hershey, R. D. 1990a. "Leading Indicators in 4th Drop." *New York Times*, December 1, p. 33.

———. 1990b. "Fed Survey Says Slump Has Spread." *New York Times*, December 6, p. D1.

Hilgartner, S., and C. L. Bosk. 1988. "The Rise and Fall of Social Problems: A Public Arenas Model." *American Journal of Sociology* 94: 53–78.

Hogan, P. C. 1990. *The Politics of Interpretation: Ideology, Professionalism, and the Study of Literature*. New York: Oxford University Press.

Hogwood, B. W., and L. G. Gunn. 1984. *Policy Analysis for the Real World*. London: Oxford University Press.

Ibarra, P. R. and J. I. Kitsuse. 1993. "Vernacular Constituents of Moral Discourse: An Interactionist Proposal for the Study of Social Problems." Pp. 21–54 in *Constructionist Controversies: Issues in Social Problems Theory*, ed. G. Miller and J. A. Holstein. New York: Aldine de Gruyter.

Iyengar, S. 1991. *Is Anyone Responsible? How Television Frames Political Issues*. Chicago: University of Chicago Press.

Jameson, F. 1991. *Postmodernism, or, The Cultural Logic of Late Capitalism*. Durham: Duke University Press.

Jehl, D. 1992. "Quayle Sees Breakdown of Family at Root of Riots." *Providence Journal-Bulletin*, May 20, p. A1.

Kantor, M. 1992. "Tax. Blame. Regret. Elect." *New York Times*, September 29, p. A23.

Kantrowitz, B., and P. Wingert. 1993. "The Norplant Debate." *Newsweek*, February 15, pp. 37–41.

Kingdon, J. 1984. *Agendas, Alternatives and Public Policies*. Boston: Little, Brown.

Kirk, S. A., and H. Kutchins. 1992. *The Selling of DSM: The Rhetoric of Science in Psychiatry*. New York: Aldine de Gruyter.

Knox, R. A. 1994. "What Crisis?—GOP to Tackle Views on Health." *Boston Globe*, January 27, p. 1.

Kolata, G. 1990. "Fetal Tissue Seems to Aid Parkinson Patient." *New York Times*, February 3, p. A1.

Lally, R. J. 1984. "Three Views of Child Neglect: Expanding Visions of Preventive Intervention." *Child Abuse and Neglect* 8: 243–254.

Lee, R. M. 1989. *One Hundred Monkeys: The Triumph of Popular Wisdom in Canadian Politics*. Toronto: MacFarlane Walter & Ross.

Light, P. 1985. *Artful Work: The Politics of Social Security Reform*. New York: Random House.

Lipsky, M., and S. R. Smith. 1989. "When Social Problems Are Treated as Emergencies." *Social Service Review* 63: 5–25.

Mathews, T., et al. 1992. "The Siege of L.A." *Newsweek*, May 11, pp. 30–38.

Milburn, M. A. 1991. *Persuasion and Politics: The Social Psychology of Public Opinion*. Pacific Grove, Calif.: Brooks/Cole.

Miller, G. and J. A. Holstein, eds. 1993. *Constructionist Controversies: Issues in Social Problems Theory*. New York: Aldine de Gruyter.

Moynihan, D. P. 1993. "Defining Deviancy Down." *American Scholar* 62: 17–30.

Mydans, S. 1992. "For the Police, A New Embarrassment." *New York Times*, May 25, p. A25.

Nelkin, D. 1975. The Political Impact of Technical Expertise. *Social Studies of Science* 5: 35–54.

Nelson, B. 1984. *Making an Issue of Child Abuse*. Chicago: University of Chicago Press.

New York Times. 1990. "U.S. Panel Warns on Child Poverty," April 27, p. A22.

Newsweek. 1992. "Teenagers and AIDS," August 3, pp. 45–50.

Norris, F. 1990. "Joking Aside, Maybe It's Just a Yuppie Recession." *New York Times*, November 11, sec. 3, p. 1.

————. 1991. "Listening for a Scary Word: Depression." *New York Times*, January 13, sec. 3, p. 1.

Northcott, H. C. 1992. *Aging in Alberta: Rhetoric and Reality*. Calgary, Alberta: Detselig Enterprises Ltd.

Oreskes, M. 1990. "Nearly 6 in 10 Americans Say Nation Is in a Recession." *New York Times*, August 24, p. A14.

Ortner, R. 1990. *Voodoo Deficits*. New York: Dow Jones-Irwin.

Patterson, J. T. 1981. *America's Struggle against Poverty, 1900–1980*. Cambridge, Mass.: Harvard University Press.

Pear, R. 1992. "Clinton, in Attack on President, Ties Riots to Neglect." *New York Times*, May 6, p. A1.

Peters, B. G. 1993. *American Public Policy: Promise and Performance*. 3d ed. Chatham, N.J.: Chatham House Publishers.

Petracca, M. P. 1992. "Issue Definitions, Agenda-building, and Policymaking." *Policy Currents* 2: 1, 4.

Polisar, D., and A. Wildavsky. 1989. "From Individual to System Blame: A Cultural Analysis of Historical Change in the Law of Torts." *Journal of Policy History* 1: 129–155.

Providence Journal-Bulletin. 1991. "Bush Says Recession Will Be Mild." January 2, p. A2.

Providence Journal-Bulletin. 1992. "Bush, in Los Angeles, Talks Tough about Crime." May 30, p. A4.

Reuter, P. 1992. "Hawks Ascendant: The Punitive Trend of American Drug Policy." *Daedalus* 121: 15–52.

Riker, W. H. 1986. *The Art of Political Manipulation*. New Haven, Conn.: Yale University Press.

Rochefort, D. A. 1986. *American Social Welfare Policy: Dynamics of Formulation and Change*. Boulder: Westview.

_____. 1988. "Policymaking Cycles in Mental Health: Critical Examination of a Conceptual Model." *Journal of Health Politics, Policy and Law* 13: 129–152.

Rochefort, D. A., and R. W. Cobb. 1992. "Framing and Claiming the Homelessness Problem." *New England Journal of Public Policy* 8: 49–65.

Rosenau, P. V. 1993. "Anticipating a Post-Modern Policy Current?" *Policy Currents* 3: 1–4.

Rosenbaum, D. 1990a. "Greenspan Says Nation's Economy Is in a Downturn." *New York Times*, November 29, p. A1.

_____. 1990b. "Once Again Bush Says Economy Will Improve." *New York Times*, November 30, p. D2.

Ruggles, P. 1990. *Drawing the Line: Alternative Poverty Measures and Their Implications for Public Policy*. Washington, D.C.: Urban Institute Press.

Samuelson, R. J. 1992. "The End Is Not at Hand." *Newsweek*, June 1, p. 43.

Schattschneider, E. E. 1960. *The Semi-Sovereign People: A Realist's View of Democracy in America*. New York: Holt, Rinehart, and Winston.

Schneider, A., and H. Ingram. 1993. "Social Construction of Target Populations: Implications for Politics and Policy." *American Political Science Review* 87: 334–347.

Seidman, E., and J. Rappaport. 1986. *Redefining Social Problems*. New York: Plenum Press.

Silberman, C. E. 1994. "Why the Best Hope in a 'War' on Crime May Be a Stalemate." *New York Times*, January 30, sec. 4, p. 1.

Silk, L. 1990. "Why It's Too Soon to Predict Another Great Depression." *New York Times*, November 11, sec. 4, p. 1.

Spector, M., and J. I. Kitsuse. 1977. *Constructing Social Problems*. Menlo Park, Calif.: Cummings.

Stafford, M. C., and M. Warr. 1985. "Public Perceptions of Social Problems: Some Propositions and a Test." *Journal of Applied Behavioral Science* 21: 307–316.

Steinmetz, G. 1993. "Shaky Statistic: Number of Uninsured Stirs Much Confusion in Health-Care Debate." *Wall Street Journal*, June 9, p. 1.

Stevens, W. K. 1991. "Urgent Steps Urged on Warming Threat." *New York Times*, April 11, p. B12.

Stone, D. 1988. *Policy Paradox and Political Reason*. Glenview: Scott, Foresman.

_____. 1989. "Causal Stories and the Formation of Policy Agendas." *Political Science Quarterly* 104: 281–300.

Suro, R. 1990a. Education Secretary Criticizes the Values of Hispanic Parents. *New York Times*, April 11, p. B8.

Suro, R. 1990b. "Hispanic Criticism of Education Chief." *New York Times*, April 15, sec. 1, p. 13.

Thomas, R. 1990. "The Nightmare Scenarios." *Newsweek*, November 12, p. 57.

Tolchin, M. 1990. "Two-thirds of States Have Programs to Cut Costs of Teen Pregnancies." *New York Times*, June 17, sec. 1, p. 24.

Uchitelle, L. 1990a. "When Is It a Recession? Defining a Recession." *New York Times*, September 26, p. D1.

———. 1990b. "Umpires Give an Early Call: It's a Recession." *New York Times*, December 30, sec. 1, p. 1.

U.S. Bureau of the Census. 1992. *Statistical Abstract of the United States: 1992.* Washington, D.C.: U.S. Government Printing Office.

Watson, G., and D. McGaw. 1980. *Statistical Inquiry*. New York: Wiley.

Weaver, R. K. 1988. "Generating Blame for Fun and Profit." Paper given at the Annual Meeting of the American Political Science Association, Washington, D.C., September 1–4.

Wegner, D., and R. Vallacher. 1977. *Implicit Psychology*. New York: Oxford University Press.

Weiss, J. 1989. "The Powers of Problem Definition: The Case of Government Paperwork." *Policy Sciences* 22: 97–121.

Wessel, D., and R. Wartzman. 1993. "To Find Out Whether Clinton Numbers Add Up in Health Plan, Ask People Who Crunched Them." *Wall Street Journal*, October 1, p. A12.

White House Domestic Council. 1993. *The President's Health Security Plan*. New York: Times Books.

Wildavsky, A. 1979. *Speaking Truth to Power*. Boston: Little, Brown.

Wilson, W. J. 1992. "Race: Our Dilemma Still." *Newsweek*, May 11, p. 51.

Wines, M. 1992. "White House Links Riots to Welfare." *New York Times*, May 5, p. A1.

2

Plant Closings, Community Definitions, and the Local Response

John Portz

On February 24, 1992, General Motors made its announcement—manufacturing plants in twelve communities would close and 16,300 workers would lose their jobs (Levin 1992). For workers, thoughts turned to lost wages, new job searches, relocation options, and similar issues. For community and government leaders, attention turned to convincing GM to delay or rethink the decision and, failing success in that effort, to finding a new employer to fill the upcoming void in employment and tax revenues.

Announcements like the one made by GM are not unique. In 1990, there were 3,600 "mass layoff events" affecting approximately 580,000 workers in forty-five states.[1] Two-fifths of the events were in manufacturing, but other sectors also experienced layoffs and closings. Common to these events was a loss of jobs and income that posed important challenges for government officials, community leaders, and individual workers.

What is often distinctive about individual plant closings, however, is how they are defined as problems. Different plant closings can be defined in different ways and, indeed, the same closing can be defined differently by various parties. Each definition typically contains one or more of the following elements: a causal explanation of the problem, a description of the nature of the problem, and a solution or course of preferred action (Gusfield 1981). Each definition establishes terms of debate and provides a basis for action or acquiescence.

Although problem definitions of plant closing vary in their details, three general orientations are common. First, a definition might focus on the *company's survival*. The closing itself is not the problem; rather, the problem is the economic viability of the business firm. This definition, often adopted by business firms, typically emphasizes the competitive nature of a market economy and the importance of business flexibility to respond. The cause of the problem typically is found in the changing forces of supply and demand, and the solution is to increase revenues and/or identify ways to reduce costs, including closing the plant.

A second orientation, often adopted by workers and community leaders, is to focus on the *closing event* itself as the central problem. In particular, the emphasis is on ways to either avert the closing of or reopen the facility. Survival of the plant is the major goal; the closing typically poses major negative consequences for workers and the community. Causation is seen as specific to the individual plant and often raises such factors as poor management decisions, high labor costs, and inefficient physical facilities. The solution focuses on financial assistance as well as various labor and/or management changes to make the plant competitive.

In a third orientation the problem definition focuses on the *consequences* of the closing. From this perspective the closing event itself is generally accepted as unavoidable; it is often portrayed as a private business matter, not part of the public debate. Instead, the problem definition focuses on the needs of workers and the community. Emphasis is placed on a solution including reemployment and retraining for workers as well as community-wide economic development strategies.

In a single plant closing experience these orientations are likely to overlap and compete for support. Determining which definition guides the community response is often a contentious affair in which different parties attempt, as Joseph Gusfield says, to establish "ownership" of the problem definition. "The structure of public problems is an arena of conflict in which a set of groups and institutions, often including governmental agencies, compete and struggle over ownership and disownership, the acceptance of causal theories, and the fixation of responsibility" (Gusfield 1981: 15). In the case of plant closings, business corporations, labor unions, and political officials maneuver to establish their definition as the favored one to shape the policy process.

This struggle for "ownership" is well represented by the following case studies of plant closings in three communities—Louisville, Kentucky; Waterloo, Iowa; and Pittsburgh, Pennsylvania (Portz 1990). In Louisville, the closing of a tobacco products plant highlights a problem definition in which the initial focus is on business survival, then the focus turns to the consequences of the closing. The impending demise of a meatpacking plant in Waterloo offers a quite different example in which the dominant problem definition focuses on averting the actual closing through a comprehensive solution involving labor, management, and government. And finally, the closing of a steel mill near Pittsburgh demonstrates a sharp clash of definitions between a company that refuses to reconsider the closing decision and a labor-supported organization seeking to avert the closing through worker and community control over economic decisions.

BROWN & WILLIAMSON CORPORATION AND LOUISVILLE

For most of the 1960s and 1970s Brown & Williamson Corporation (B & W) was a leading producer of cigarettes. Behind such brands as KOOL, Viceroy, and Raleigh, B & W captured 17.6 percent of the 1973 domestic market (Overton 1981). Planning for future growth, B & W added a new production facility in Macon, Georgia, to its existing plants in Petersburg, Virginia, and Louisville (Brown & Williamson Tobacco Corporation n.d.).

Yet no increase in sales took place. Hard times hit the tobacco industry and B & W. Citing a decline in product sales, technological changes, and its current operating capacity, the company issued a memo in November 1978 to its Louisville employees reporting that all "alternatives" were being considered, including closing the Louisville plant, but no "conclusions have been reached" (Garr 1978: A16).

However, the "conclusions" were not long in coming. Within two months, on January 18, 1979, the decision was announced—the Louisville plant would close. Louisville would lose approximately 3,000 production jobs. Although the company's headquarters and its 2,000 employees would remain in Louisville, operations at the production facility would be phased-out over a three-year period. Shortly after the announcement the company and labor unions began negotiations over the lay-off process and closing benefits for workers.

In Louisville the initial problem definition focused on the company's survival, while a second definition focused on the consequences of the closing. Both definitions were framed by the company (Teague 1981; U.S. Congress 1980; U.S. Department of Labor 1985). In essence, Brown & Williamson "owned" the problem definitions. A problem definition structured around avoiding the B & W closing never developed.

In the first definition B & W clearly established the problem; at stake was the long-term viability of the company, not just the Louisville production facility. In this definition the cause of the problem was rooted in a market economy. In simplest terms, it was a case of supply exceeding demand. Based on its internal studies the company concluded that an adjustment was needed "to balance manufacturing capability with developing market requirements" (Crowdus 1979a: 1). In short, production capacity at B & W surpassed market demand, and the company must make the most efficient use of all its facilities, even if that meant closing one plant. As one company official noted, "long-term survival" is the bottom line; "that's the reality of a capitalistic system" (Moeller 1979: E1).

Causation was impersonal, relatively simple and, to a degree, accidental. B & W was simply responding to market forces. Construction of the Macon facility was an effort to take advantage of an expanding market, while closing the Louisville plant was also a response to market forces. Negative consequences were regrettable, but they were part of the system. The drop in sales was a serious problem for the company and a solution had to be found. Options were weighed and the decision to close the Louisville facility became the solution to the problem.

Within the community this problem definition was broadly accepted. As one staff person in the city's economic development office recalled, the closing was "essentially a business decision over which the community had little control."[2] Another local official described the closing as an "internal business management decision." Even among those who disagreed with the company, there was begrudging acceptance of this definition. As one labor leader commented, "I don't think Jesus Christ could have come down here and changed that company's mind."

With the first problem—survival of the company—solved by closing the plant, a second problem definition focused around the consequences of the closing. As a company spokesman noted shortly after the closing announcement, our "next major concern as a company was to do the best we could for our people" (Moeller 1979: E5). The focus of attention shifted to the impact the closing would have on workers and the community.

Here again, Brown & Williamson put forth a problem definition that was generally accepted in the community. The company recognized that unemployment was a serious matter for its workers and pledged to assist with relocation options, retraining support, and job search assistance. The company followed through with this pledge and within one week of the closing announcement negotiations began and continued until an agreement was reached in early April that provided a variety of financial benefits and job search assistance programs. The settlement agreement received near-unanimous support from the local union. As the local president commented, "I think the company went the last mile on it" (Crowdus 1979b: B7).

Both definitions put forth by Brown & Williamson set the stage for a community response with a very limited government role. The closing decision was an internal company decision, and the consequences of the closing were addressed through labor-management negotiations. As one academic observer commented, the entire closing process was largely a "non-issue" from the government's perspective. Government officials were not part of either definition, and they played little part in the community response. Although they expressed concern, policymakers generally viewed the closing as outside the bounds of public policy. One local official commented that "city government assistance was not sought or given." In short, the plant closing problem never made it to the governmental agenda (Cobb and Elder 1983).

Brown & Williamson's problem definition is important in understanding the Louisville experience, but it is not a complete explanation. Important characteristics of the institutional environment and local political economy played a major part in paving the way for the acceptance of B & W's perspective.

For example, the loss of manufacturing jobs at Brown & Williamson was balanced by expansion of white collar and other professional jobs in downtown Louisville. In fact, the total labor force increased during the late 1970s, despite plant closings at B & W and other manufacturers. Furthermore, B & W's announcement that it would keep its corporate headquarters in Louisville meant 2,000 jobs would continue to be part of the growing service and professional base of the downtown economy. As one former city official recalled, "a good deal of the B & W money stayed in Louisville."

Institutional weaknesses in local government were also important factors. At the time of the closing, Louisville suffered from fragmented city and county economic development efforts, a weak-mayor form of government, and a divisive political battle between the incumbent mayor and board of aldermen. On the side of labor, the settlement agreement offered various benefits that were popular among many workers, and the labor union, while losing members in Louisville, had already been accepted as the bargaining agent for workers in Macon. Also, the general absence in Louisville of a leftist presence to challenge established values and practices contributed to a muted local response.

All of these factors are important for an explanation of the Louisville experience, but the power of B & W's problem definition still looms large. This definition shaped the discourse and established boundaries for action. It is a critical piece in the overall explanation of this plant closing response.

RATH PACKING COMPANY AND WATERLOO, IOWA

The impending closure of Rath Packing Company in Waterloo, Iowa, offers a quite different example of problem definition. The problem definition in Louisville never focused on the plant itself and involved little controversy and a limited role for public officials. The Rath closing response, however, was premised by a definition that focused on the closing event and involved a consensus-building process among different parties as to the cause, nature, and solution to the problem. In this definition political leaders played a more prominent role.

Founded in Waterloo in 1891, Rath Packing Company enjoyed many good years as a major employer in the community. Starting in the 1960s, however, financial troubles mounted. By 1978 the company could look back on profits in only eight of the previous eighteen years and showed losses of approximately $18 million in the previous four years. In May 1978 a closing appeared likely. Management informed employees of the difficulties faced by the company and asked for wage and benefit concessions to keep the company afloat. Even with concessions, management confessed that the future of the company was uncertain (*Waterloo Courier* 1978).

At this point, a single problem definition did not exist. Although most people recognized that the Rath plant was old and inefficient, opinions diverged from there. To some in the community, and many in the Rath workforce, the true cause of the problem lay with management and a series of poor decisions in such areas as marketing, plant modernization, and personnel. From this perspective the solution required major changes in management structure and policies.

Management, however, was not the only focus for a problem definition. Some members of the community, along with management, pointed to expensive labor practices as a primary contributor to the company's financial woes. Work rules and other union-backed labor practices were cited as inefficient and expensive, diminishing the company's ability to change in a very competitive industry.

Many local political leaders tried to find a middle path in this debate. Recognizing that the physical plant, management, and labor all contributed to the problem, local officials saw the loss of jobs as the central problem. Avoiding that loss was the driving motivation for government officials. This motivation prompted local officials, including both the Black Hawk County Economic Development Committee, an arm of the County Board of Supervisors, and the city of Waterloo, to seek federal government support.

Consensus on a problem definition came in September 1978 when a feasibility study of the plant was completed. This study, supported by a $60,000 grant from the federal Economic Development Administration (EDA), was conducted by a group of engineers, economists, and management experts (Development Planning and Research Associates 1978). As one local official noted, the study became a "keystone" element in the community's response. As Brown & Williamson did in Louisville, the feasibility study established ownership of the problem and defined the terms of debate and the basic options for the community's plant closing response.

Problem causation was, in some respects, similar to the Louisville experience—a competitive and changing market. The meatpacking industry, like the tobacco industry, was highly competitive with a low operating margin, and Rath was failing to keep pace. As with Brown & Williamson, the company's current operating structure and physical plant were simply not competitive. However, while the market dynamic was presented as largely impersonal and immutable in Louisville, the feasibility study in Waterloo provided a critique of the market that was more personal in character and allocated blame to all parties at the company. Labor was criticized for maintaining expensive labor practices, management was blamed for poor decisions, and the inefficiencies of the old, multi-story plant also contributed to the problem.

The problem as identified in the feasibility study was quite severe and at a critical point. The study detailed numerous inefficiencies at the plant and the consequences for the company. Short-term options were presented to keep the company afloat for three years, but without fundamental changes, including a new plant, the company would not survive. As the study stated, "in the longer-term, the Rath-Waterloo plant cannot be renovated to produce meat at economically competitive levels" (Development Planning and Research Associates 1978: IV, 8).

The solution as presented by the feasibility study centered on financial assistance to Rath and reducing costs at the company. It clearly focused on avoiding the closure, and outlined both a short-term and a long-term strategy. In the short-term, over the next three years, the company needed not only an infusion of cash, but numerous changes in labor and management practices to increase operating efficiency. Cooperation from all parties was essential. Government could provide financial support, labor could reduce costs by deferring wage increases and changing work rules, and management could also reduce costs through numerous operating changes. In the long-term, the study outlined several options for construction of a new plant to replace the old facility.

The problem definition outlined in the feasibility study placed Rath squarely on the government's agenda and became the catalyst for action. The County Economic Development Committee, led by county supervisor Lynn Cutler, led the charge. In a matter of seventeen days the Committee met, legally incorporated, applied for and received a $3 million grant from the federal EDA, and awarded a $2.98 million short-term loan to Rath. The city also played a part. City officials applied for and received a $4.6 million grant from the federal Department of Housing and Urban Development. This grant, however, took considerably longer to negotiate and a loan to Rath was not awarded until October 1980, when an employee stock ownership plan was finally in place.

Taken together, the pieces of this problem definition maintained a clear focus on averting the closure of Rath. The feasibility study put forth both a causal explanation and solution that were broad-based and called for action by all parties to avoid the closing. The problem, as portrayed in the study, was so severe that a community response was essential.

However, as in Louisville, the problem definition presented by the feasibility study tells only part of the story, albeit a significant part. The study's compatibility with past experiences and current sentiments was important. An assistance package for Rath, for example, was not a new idea. In previous years Rath had turned to a federal EDA-guaranteed loan as well as worker wage and benefit concessions to keep operating. Also, community support for taking action was very high. As the *Waterloo Courier* declared even before the feasibility study was conducted, "survival [of Rath] is now at stake and the partnership approach to this crisis is crucial" (*Waterloo Cou-*

rier 1978: 1). To be certain, there were some in the community skeptical of Rath's viability and others who viewed government assistance as simply a bail-out, but the hope of saving Rath carried the day.

The importance of Rath to the local economy was also an important factor. Rath was the second largest employer in the county and the largest locally-based company. Thus, the consequences of a Rath closing would be quite significant. In fact, the Black Hawk County Economic Development Committee issued a brief report earlier in the summer that highlighted the potential losses to area businesses and local government if Rath closed. This report also emphasized the difficulties of finding new employment for the relatively old workforce at Rath. Thus, the consequences of a closing would be severe not only for the company, as emphasized in the feasibility study, but for workers and the community as well.

In addition, the fact that the company was trying to keep the plant open was an obvious point that shaped the community response. If Rath management had preferred to close the plant, as Brown & Williamson did in Louisville, the recommendations of the feasibility study would have received a much different reception, as is true in the next case study. Rath's support for keeping the plant open complemented the definition proposed by the feasibility study and thus adds an important element to our understanding of the community response.

Although the problem definition set the stage for the community response, other factors in the political economy would determine the final outcome. In fact, broader economic and institutional forces ultimately led to the closing of Rath. The economic recession of the early 1980s, the competitive nature of the meatpacking industry, and the inability to construct a new facility contributed to the company's decline. Despite government assistance as well as ongoing wage and benefit concessions, the red ink continued. By November 1983 Rath was in bankruptcy court, and in December 1984 the plant closed. Several employee and management groups tried to revive the plant, but none were able to secure adequate financing. Finally, in May 1985, the courts approved sale of the trademark and liquidation began. As the judge concluded, "there comes a time when the memories of a grand past and the tantalizing promises of a better future must be squared with the hard realities of the present. That time has arrived in this case" (U.S. Bankruptcy Court for the Northern District of Iowa 1985: 4).

U.S. STEEL AND THE MONONGAHELA RIVER VALLEY

This third case study involves a much more divisive experience in which different parties clashed over very different problem definitions. While one party, the Tri-State Conference on Steel (a labor-community coalition), presented a definition that focused on averting plant closings, U.S. Steel presented two definitions, not unlike Brown & Williamson, that focused primarily on the firm's survival and, secondarily, on the consequences of a plant closing. The ensuing battle, both in rhetoric and actions, was guided by these different problem definitions.

The setting, the Monongahela River Valley (Mon Valley) south of Pittsburgh, was once one of America's largest steel-making regions. U.S. Steel was the leader, with six major integrated facilities employing twenty-eight thousand workers in 1979. By 1984, however, company employment in these facilities had dropped to less than six thousand (Deitch 1984). Included in this decline was the closing of the blast furnace, known as Dorothy 6, at the Duquesne works. Announced in December 1983, this closing provided the rallying point for a regional effort to stop plant closings in the steel industry. The stage was set for a major battle among business, government, and labor over quite different problem definitions and prescriptions for addressing economic change.

U.S. Steel presented a problem definition that bore striking similarity to the definition established by Brown & Williamson in Louisville. In essence, the problem was the survival of the firm in a competitive industry. As with Brown & Williamson, problem causation was rooted in the impersonal workings of the market. Overseas producers and domestic mini-mills were making it increasingly difficult for U.S. Steel's larger and older integrated mills, such as the Duquesne Works, to compete. Steel-making was a highly competitive industry, and U.S. Steel had to protect its overall financial position. In essence, the closing was not the company's fault. Rather, it was an appropriate response by the company to reduce production in an industry plagued by overcapacity (United States Steel Corporation 1985a).

From the company's perspective the problem was severe and near crisis proportions. However, it was a problem that involved the company's entire steel-making operations, not simply the Duquesne Works or any one community. It was a systemic problem that required an equally broad response. The company's cost structure in steel operations would no longer support a continuation of "business as usual."

From U.S. Steel's perspective the solution was clear. It must close steel-making operations and diversify; the solution required a "nationwide rationalization program" designed to reduce steel-making capacity, diversify operations, and make the company more competitive. "The strategic plan called for diversification to ensure that the Company would no longer be as tied to the cyclical extremes of the steel industry" (USX 1986). Thus, steel-making operations were closed and the company diversified through various acquisitions, such as the purchase of Marathon Oil. Between 1978 and 1983, steel revenues dropped from 73 percent to 33 percent of total company revenues. The 1986 decision to rename the company USX put the finishing touches on corporate restructuring (United States Steel Corporation 1985b).

While the primary problem of company competitiveness was addressed through plant closings and diversification, U.S. Steel did recognize that the consequences of closing the Duquesne mill posed a significant problem for workers at the mill and the community. To address these problems, the company proposed to work with city officials and private developers to turn part of the Duquesne mill site into an industrial park. For workers the company established a job search assistance center in Duquesne. Both efforts addressed the consequences of the closing, a problem that was secondary from the company's perspective.

In contrast to the company's definition, a coalition of labor, community, and political leaders put forth a quite different conception of the problem. This coalition, known as the Tri-State Conference on Steel, had been organizing since 1979 in opposition to plant closings in the region. Unlike U.S. Steel, which defined the problem according to the company's balance sheet, Tri-State established a problem definition with an explicit aim to avert closings (Tri-State Conference on Steel 1984; Baron and Martoni 1985; Deitch and Erickson 1987; Hornack and Lynd 1986; Stout 1983 and 1986).

Tri-State presented a markedly different perspective on problem causation. While Tri-State agreed that the steel industry was changing and was quite competitive, thereby requiring innovative responses, it refused to accept plant closings as impersonal and blameless consequences of a dynamic economy. Rather, corporate decision-making played a critical role. In particular, U.S. Steel's diversification strategy was a diversion of funds from the modernization of steel mills to the self-interested protection of the company's bottom line. The problem was not accidental, nor was it blameless. Corporate decision-making, based on a company's goals and assessments for profitability, played the critical role in determining whether a plant such as the Duquesne mill would close.

From Tri-State's perspective the nature of the problem was particularly apparent in the consequences of plant closings. From this perspective the problem was indeed severe—a crisis. Plant closings in the steel industry and manufacturing in general were decimating the region. Unemployment was reaching depression levels in the Mon Valley, public infrastructure was deteriorating, and many mill towns in the valley were on the "brink of bankruptcy" (Tri-State Conference on Steel 1984: 9).

Furthermore, plant closings were not isolated events. Rather, they were part of a general disinvestment pattern with implications for the entire community. Tri-State drew links between steel mill closings in one community and closings of other mills in the region. For example, the closing of the Duquesne mill was preceded by closings in nearby Youngstown, Ohio, and would be followed by other mill closings. In contrast, in both of the previous case studies plant closings were defined more as isolated occurrences than as part of a general pattern of disinvestment.

From Tri-State's perspective both the cause and nature of the problem pointed to a collective response. The solution required a combined effort of labor, community, and government to keep plants open and ensure community survival. This solution would require considerable legal and financial resources, particularly in instances where the current owner of the plant was not interested in keeping the plant open. As one pamphlet stated, "since private industry will not rebuild our steel industry, the workers and communities of the Mon Valley must be allowed to do it" (Tri-State Conference on Steel 1984: 6).

As a major step in this solution, Tri-State supported the creation of a regional political authority with eminent domain powers, bonding authority, and legal standing to develop industrial projects. As one supporter noted, the problem called for an "intermunicipal body that would deal with plant closings not just on a plant-by-plant basis, as the crises arise, but hopefully in a more systematic fashion" (DaParma 1985: C1). This political authority would be able to avert a plant closing, through eminent domain if necessary, and work with individuals and organizations interested in preserving the plant. Meetings and actions to establish such an entity began in 1984 and continued until January 1986, when nine communities in the Mon Valley (but not Duquesne) received state approval to establish the Steel Valley Authority.

Unlike the plant closing experiences in Waterloo and Louisville, problem definition in the Mon Valley case never reached a general consensus. The two camps—U.S. Steel and the Tri-State Conference on Steel—remained divided. While to U.S. Steel the problem focused on the company's competitiveness and survival, to Tri-State the problem centered on preventing plant closings. There was very little common ground. Each camp proceeded to act in a manner consistent with its own problem definition.

For the Duquesne mill, however, it was U.S. Steel's definition that ultimately prevailed. By 1986, when the Steel Valley Authority was formed, the most recent feasibility study had concluded that the mill could not survive in the current market, and parts of the facility had already been dismantled (Lazard Freres and Company 1986). Few held any hope that the mill could be reopened.

As in Waterloo and Louisville, problem definitions played a critical role in shaping a community response, but other factors in the political economy were also important for understanding the course of events. In this case, the confluence of many economic and institutional factors provided support for U.S. Steel's definition and undermined Tri-State's effort to redefine closings. The growth of professional and white-collar jobs in Pittsburgh, for example, provided economic compensation for the loss of manufacturing jobs in the

Mon Valley. To many community and business leaders as well as government officials, particularly at the regional level, this transition was an inevitable part of a changing economy. U.S. Steel should be allowed to take those actions necessary to compete in this environment.

Perhaps most important, U.S. Steel maintained control over the site and was adamant in its opposition to keeping the mill open. The company was willing to assist the community and workers after the closing, but it had no interest in keeping the plant open. As David Roderick, chairman of the board at U.S. Steel remarked, it would take "five minutes on the back of an envelope to show that Dorothy 6 was not worth keeping" (Dvorchak 1985: 18). As in Louisville, the ownership rights of the company put it in a clear position of power.

Tri-State and the Steel Valley Authority posed a problem definition that appealed to many in the Mon Valley, principally because it was consistent with the economic experiences of the smaller mill towns. Mon Valley unemployment rates ranged from 15 to 20 percent and were accompanied by family break-ups, mental stress, and demand for numerous social services (Cunningham and Martz 1986). In addition, closings created major fiscal strain for local government budgets. For example, 50–60 percent of revenues for the city of Duquesne were derived from wage taxes, parking meter revenues, and other sources of income directly attributable to the mill (Strauss and Bunch 1987). Thus, many Duquesne and other local government officials were supportive of efforts to stop disinvestment in the region. As one local government official commented, "most were for trying anything; without the Steel Valley Authority, nobody was going to try."

With a base of support among many in the Mon Valley, the Steel Valley Authority and Tri-State continued to fight plant closings. In 1986 attention turned to other plant closings in the area, particularly two rail products plants in nearby Swissvale and Wilmerding owned by American Standard Corporation. The Steel Valley Authority challenged the company's plans to close the plants and filed a lawsuit to prevent the closing (U.S. District Court for the Western District of Pennsylvania 1986). Although ultimately unsuccessful, the lawsuit showed both the potential and the limits of this solution to the plant closing problem.

Still, the Steel Valley Authority continued its efforts. A plan to reopen part of a steel mill owned by LTV Corporation failed, but the Steel Valley Authority was more successful in 1992 when it helped a group of workers reopen a Pittsburgh bakery closed in 1989 (Parks 1992). To extend its perspective on plant closings, both the Steel Valley Authority and Tri-State joined a nationwide coalition, the Federation of Industrial Retention and Renewal, dedicated to a similar agenda of preventing plant closings and establishing worker-community control over investment and disinvestment decisions.

PROBLEM DEFINITION AND
EXPLAINING COMMUNITY RESPONSES

Problem definitions of plant closings set the stage for community debate and action. As such, they are important ingredients in our understanding of community responses. As Robert Alford concluded in his study of Wisconsin communities, "the course of conflicts may be partially understood by reference to the ability of groups to establish their definition of the situation as the appropriate one" (Alford 1969: 31). Thus, in Louisville the definition put forth by Brown & Williamson was generally accepted as "appropriate" and the company guided the community response; in Waterloo the feasibility study assumed this role; in the Mon Valley no single definition dominated the response, although U.S. Steel's definition ultimately guided the fate of the Duquesne mill.

But problem definitions do not tell all. Understanding community responses requires a broader look at the political, institutional, and economic characteristics that shape the community. In each case study presented here the characteristics of the local political economy, and indeed, national and international forces as well, played a part in explaining the course of a community response.

The local economy, for example, was critical to our understanding of each response. In Louisville, expanding professional and white-collar employment, along with downtown growth, provided important compensation for the loss of jobs at the Brown & Williamson factory, thereby removing much of the pressure for government action. In Waterloo, the local economy was also relatively strong, although the possible loss of Rath posed dire economic consequences.

In the city of Pittsburgh a growth pattern similar to Louisville's served to deflect some of the criticism of U.S. Steel's plans to close mills in the Mon Valley. However, the near-depression conditions that existed in the smaller Mon Valley communities prompted many local officials and community leaders to consider alternatives to the current pattern of corporate disinvestment, thereby providing an important opening for the Tri-State Conference on Steel. These economic conditions are important in explaining the reception different problem definitions received in each community.

Institutional factors involving key organizations in each community also played an important role. Most importantly, the financial condition and the interests of each company—whether it was Brown & Williamson, Rath Packing Co., or U.S. Steel—were critical in determining the acceptance of different problem definitions. Brown & Williamson's private character and willingness to assume all responsibilities for the closing and its consequences set the tone in Louisville; Rath's search for financial assistance to keep the plant open was critical in Waterloo; and U.S. Steel's adamant opposition to reopening the Duquesne mill was critical in the Mon Valley. These positions were central in determining the staying power of different problem definitions.

The organization of government was also important. Fragmentation of the Mon Valley into different political jurisdictions, for example, greatly complicated Tri-State's goal of a collective response, while the existence of the Black Hawk County Economic Development Committee in Waterloo provided an ideal platform for government action in Waterloo. Other institutional factors, such as labor organizations and community groups, must also be considered.

Nevertheless, problem definitions are critical. As R. J. Lustig reminds us, "it is an old truth of politics that power is revealed not by those who have the ability to provide answers but by those who frame the original questions" (Lustig 1985: 136). Framing the original question is what problem definitions are all about. Success in that endeavor is an important step in moving an issue from the level of general discussion to an agenda for decision and action.

Why is one definition more successful than another in this endeavor? That is, what are the characteristics of definitions most successful in "framing the original question"? While not an exhaustive list, the following characteristics are particularly important. First, political acceptability is critical. The different dimensions of the problem definition—the explanation of causation and the solution for the problem, for example—must be acceptable to key actors in the community. Political acceptability, in turn, is dependent largely on congruence with the existing political economy. As I argued above, definitions most consistent with existing economic conditions and institutional and community interests were most likely to survive.

Thus, Brown & Williamson's definition and actions fit with the current growth of the Louisville economy, and the company recognized the interests of workers by providing a closing benefits package. In Waterloo, the analysis and conclusions of the feasibility study were consistent with the importance of Rath as the second largest employer in the county and the general community support for a labor-management-government solution. And in the Mon Valley case, U.S. Steel's definition was consistent with the nationwide decline in the steel industry, while Tri-State's definition drew support because it spoke to the current economic conditions of many in the area, particularly the mill towns of the Mon Valley.

Perhaps most important was a definition's compatibility with the position of the corporation involved in the closing. Indeed, the power of business to set the agenda and terms of discourse was considerable. Not only does the business exercise legal ownership of the plant, but its control touches all parts of the political economy, creating what Lindblom refers to as the "privileged position of business" (Lindblom 1977 and 1982). Thus, in their respective communities Brown & Williamson and U.S. Steel occupied dominant positions in shaping the problem definition and overall community response. Rath Packing Company, however, occupied a significantly less powerful position. The severe financial problems of the company and the fact that the Waterloo operation was its main plant combined to diminish the company's position. It was the feasibility study, rather than the company, that ultimately won the battle of problem definitions.

A second important feature of successful problem definitions is comprehensiveness. Those definitions that provided a comprehensive understanding of the problem were most likely to survive. In particular, a viable solution was an essential part of the definition if the problem definer expected community support (Kingdon 1984). In this sense, as Rochefort and Cobb put it in Chapter 1, solution availability helped determine problem definition. For example, Brown & Williamson proposed definitions that were quite comprehensive and included viable solutions; the company explained the cause of the problem and provided an acceptable solution in the form of employee benefits and continued presence of the corporate headquarters. The feasibility study in Waterloo was particularly comprehensive and also offered a viable solution. In contrast, Rath workers and management each had definitions of the problem but both definitions were incomplete and lacked a broad-based solution. A definition without a solution was unlikely to garner general support.

In the Mon Valley the definition put forth by Tri-State won considerable support, despite its radical critique of capitalism, for two reasons: because it was so comprehensive in its analysis of the problem and because it proposed a solution that was politically possible, albeit difficult—creation of the Steel Valley Authority. There were several other organizations in the Mon Valley that were also critical of plant closings, such as the Denominational Ministry Strategy, but they garnered less support, in part because their definitions were not as comprehensive and they lacked a coherent solution. The U.S. Steel definition, for its part, won a significant degree of acceptance in Duquesne because it provided solutions in the form of an industrial park and worker reemployment assistance center.

And finally, a claim of authority or knowledge also characterized those problem definitions that shaped the community response. Brown & Williamson, for example, based its definition on economics and the "authority" of the market, in particular the "laws" of supply and demand. This base of authority was generally accepted in the community. In Waterloo, the economists, management specialists, and other consultants who produced the feasibility study were accepted as experts who could speak with authority on the problems and solutions at Rath. The feasibility study received its share of criticisms, but it was generally accepted as the authoritative basis for the community response.

In the Mon Valley, U.S. Steel spoke from a position similar to that of

Brown & Williamson, but economic problems in the Mon Valley raised serious questions about the "authority" of a supposedly self-equilibrating market. Acceptance of U.S. Steel's base of authority was thereby weakened. For Tri-State a base of authority was also problematic, particularly given its general critique of capitalism. However, its position was strengthened based on the organization's detailed analysis of U.S. Steel, its efforts to refute point-for-point U.S. Steel's definition of the problem, and its emphasis on creating the Steel Valley Authority, a legitimate governmental entity incorporated under state law.

A problem definition that possesses these three characteristics—political acceptability, comprehensiveness, and a claim of authority—is not guaranteed success, but it does stand a better chance of shaping the community response. Thus, whether a plant closing definition focuses on ensuring the company's survival, averting the actual closing, or responding to the closing's consequences, the path to success includes matters of political acceptability, comprehensiveness, and authority. Few definitions hold a dominant position on all three measures, but for those that do, the extensive ability to shape the policy process is indeed impressive.

NOTES

1. Based on "Mass Layoff" Reports, Bureau of Labor Statistics, U.S. Department of Labor. According to this definition, a "mass layoff event" occurs when 50 or more workers claim unemployment insurance benefits from one establishment during a three-week period, with at least 50 workers separated for more than 30 days.

2. This quotation and other quotations in the chapter not otherwise attributed are based on anonymous interviews with the author.

REFERENCES

Alford, R. 1969. *Bureaucracy and Participation*. Chicago: Rand McNally.

Baron, M., and C. Martoni. 1985. "Steel Valley Authority: Revitalizing the Industry." *Pennsylvanian*, May, pp. 8–11.

Brown & Williamson Tobacco Corporation. n.d. *The Brown & Williamson Story*. Louisville, Ky.: Corporate Affairs Department.

Cobb, R., and C. Elder. 1983. *Participation in American Politics: The Dynamics of Agenda-Building*. 2nd ed. Baltimore: Johns Hopkins University Press.

Crowdus, V. 1979a. "3,000 at Brown & Williamson Learn They're Losing Their Jobs." *Louisville Courier-Journal*, January 19, p. 1.

_____. 1979b. "Tobacco Firm and Union Reach Pact." *Louisville Courier-Journal*, April 8, p. B7.

Cunningham, J., and P. Martz. 1986. *Trouble in Electric Valley*. Pittsburgh: University of Pittsburgh School of Social Work.

DaParma, R. 1985. "SVA Stipulates Priorities." *Tribune Review*, November 23, p. C1.

Deitch, C. 1984. "Collective Action and Unemployment: Responses to Job Loss by Workers and Community Groups." *International Journal of Mental Health* 13: 139–53.

Deitch, C., and R. Erickson. 1987. "Save Dorothy: A Political Response to Structural Change in the Steel Industry." Pp. 241–279 in *Redundancy, Lay-offs and Plant Closures*, ed. R. Lee. London: Croom Helm.

Development Planning and Research Associates. 1978. *Operation and Management Review and Evaluation, Rath Packing Company, Waterloo, Iowa*. Manhattan, Kans.

Dvorchak, B. 1985. "Tri-state Conference 'Quietly' Working for Jobs." *McKeesport Daily News*, January 7, p. 18.

Garr, R. 1978. "Rumors Not New to Brown & Williamson Workers." *Louisville Times*, November 16, p. A16.

Gusfield, J. 1981. *The Culture of Public Problems: Drinking, Driving and the Symbolic Order*. Chicago: University of Chicago Press.

Hornack, J., and S. Lynd. 1986. "The Steel Valley Authority." Unpublished paper. Pittsburgh: Steel Valley Authority.

Kingdon, J. 1984. *Agendas, Alternatives, and Public Policies*. Boston: Little, Brown.

Lazard Freres and Company. 1986. "Dorothy 6: Financial Feasibility of Reopening the Duquesne Works." New York.

Levin, D. 1992. "G.M. Picks 12 Plants to Be Shut As It Reports a Record U.S. Loss." *New York Times*, February 25, p. A1.

Lindblom, C. 1977. *Politics and Markets*. New York: Basic Books.

———. 1982. The Market as Prison. *Journal of Politics* 44: 324–336.

Lustig, R. J. 1985. "The Politics of Shutdown: Community, Property, Corporatism," *Journal of Economic Issues* 19: 123–152.

Moeller, P. 1979. "B & W Puts Pride Where Pain Is." *Louisville Courier-Journal*, June 17, p. E1.

Overton, J. 1981. "Diversification and International Expansion: The Future of the American Tobacco Manufacturing Industry with Corporate Profiles of the 'Big Six.'" Pp. 156–196 in *The Tobacco Industry in Transition*, ed. W. Finger. Lexington, Mass.: D.C. Heath.

Parks, J. 1992. "Workers' Ingenuity, Pluck Revive Industry, Jobs." *AFL-CIO NEWS*, September 28, p. 9.

Portz, J. 1990. *The Politics of Plant Closings*. Lawrence: University Press of Kansas.

Stout, M. 1983. "Eminent Domain and Boycotts: The Tri-State Strategy in Pittsburgh." *Labor Research Review* 1: 7–22.

———. 1986. "Reindustrialization from Below: The Steel Valley Authority." *Labor Research Review* 5: 19–35.

Strauss, R., and B. Bunch. 1987. *The Fiscal Position of Municipalities in the Steel Valley Conference of Governments*. Pittsburgh: Carnegie-Mellon University School of Urban and Public Affairs.

Teague, C. 1981. "Easing the Pain of Plant Closure: The Brown & Williamson Experience." *Management Review* 70 (April): 23–27.

Tri-State Conference on Steel (Pittsburgh). 1984. "Steel Valley Authority: A Community Plan to Save Pittsburgh's Steel Industry."

United States Steel Corporation. 1985a. "Response to the Locker/Abrecht Duquesne Works Feasibility Report." Pittsburgh.

———. 1985b. *Annual Report*. Pittsburgh.

U.S. Bankruptcy Court for the Northern District of Iowa. 1985. Orders Approving Sale of Trademarks. Rath Packing Company-Debtor.

U.S. Congress. 1980. Senate Committee on Labor and Human Resources. *Hearings on Workers and the Evolving Economy of the Eighties*. 96th Cong., 2d sess.

U.S. Department of Labor. 1985. Brown & Williamson Case Study. *Plant Closing Checklist: A Guide to Best Practice*. Washington D.C.: Bureau of Labor-Management Relations and Cooperative Programs, 37–41.

U.S. District Court for the Western District of Pennsylvania. 1986. Amended Complaint. *Steel Valley Authority v. Union Switch and Signal Division, et al.*

USX. 1986. Brochure. Pittsburgh: USX Corporation.

Waterloo Courier. 1978. "Crisis at Rath Troubling to All. Editorial, May 14, p. 1.

3

Attention, Boundary Effects, and Large-Scale Policy Change in Air Transportation Policy

Frank R. Baumgartner and Bryan D. Jones

Public policies are often redefined through public debate. In this chapter, we focus on three elements of these redefinitions, describing how issues can change, first through the rise and fall of attention to their various component parts. Second, we distinguish between micro- and macroredefinitions, noting how microissues, such as a single bill in Congress or a single cabinet appointment, are often the subject of scholarly attention but that the subject of issue definition can also be studied at a much higher level of abstraction. Finally, we show how high agenda status is related to boundary effects, where innovations or redefinitions from one political issue spill over into other areas where they can have a great impact. We discuss a wide variety of issues to make these points, but we pay special attention to air transportation over the first eighty-five years of the century.

ISSUE COMPONENTS

The topic of issue definition is central to studies of public policy and of politics more generally because different definitions of issues generate different cleavages in society. Public debate and policymaking concerning important policy issues rarely consider all elements of an issue at once; rather, only some parts of an issue become salient at any one time. Since a single issue may be associated with many different, and often conflicting, implications, the definition of the set of issues that come to be associated with a given public policy is probably the most important element in determining its outcome. When an issue, such as air transportation, rises on the public agenda, a single component usually is salient. For example, the primary concern may

Jeff Talbert provided expert research assistance to make this paper possible.

be with safety questions, with technological advances, or with economic regulation of the airlines. As different components of an issue come to the surface, different actors are advantaged or disadvantaged. The definition of the relevant topics in a public policy debate is therefore central to the policy process and, more broadly, to the political process.

Here we show how the process of issue definition shifts the terms of the political debate, as Rochefort and Cobb argue in the introduction to this volume. Further, we demonstrate a method of data collection and empirical illustration that might be used by others to provide quantitative methods in an area where these have proven difficult to develop. We show that as the topic of attention on a given issue changes, the tone of attention inevitably changes as well. Positive attention, or enthusiastic coverage of a given issue, gives way to hostile coverage as attention shifts from one component of an issue to another, equally partial, aspect of the same question. Issue definition has critical policy consequences because different topics of attention generally carry different implications for what government policies, if any, should be adopted. By tracing the emergence and the recession of different components of the same issue over the twentieth century, we show how these redefinitions occur and how they are related to changes in policy.

BOUNDARY EFFECTS

Political issues and public policy debates are constantly redefined and changed through the operations of two related processes: boundary effects, where events in one area of politics affect related areas, and the rise and fall of component parts of a complex issue on the public agenda. These two elements of issue definition are the source of some of the most interesting dynamics in American politics. As various parts of an issue come to the political forefront, or as developments in one issue area affect those in another, issues are redefined and new political forces are given advantage or are hurt.

Since a single policy issue can be associated with a great variety of more specific topics, the particular topics that become the subject of public debate directly influence the allocation of bias and resources in the debate. Further, issues overlap. Tobacco policy, for example, is part of agriculture policy more broadly. But it has important tax consequences, it has important health policy consequences, and it is a major source of foreign earnings for American companies. As taxes, health, and foreign trade questions rise or fall on the national political agenda, tobacco farmers, no matter how they conceive of their work or their industry, are affected. In this way, no industry or political issue exists in a vacuum: there is always the potential of spillover into or from related areas. This could be considered another form, on a macro level, of what Rochefort and Cobb term issue "interconnections."

When such a spillover occurs, the redefinition may have important political consequences (see Jones and Strahan 1985).

ISSUE GENERALITY

There are several levels of generality associated with a given policy issue. At a relatively high degree of generality may be such definitions as "agriculture policy," which can easily be divided into a variety of subtopics, either by crop (dairy, corn, wheat, cotton) or by other criteria (living standards of farmers, international trade, safety, immigrant labor, taxes and subsidies). All of these elements are part of something called "agriculture policy," but at the same time they may be related to other issues as well. As different issues become important elements of the public agenda, agriculture policy is treated in different ways, each a part of the same whole, but each pulled apart and treated separately from the others.

At a lower level of aggregation, particular policy issues are debated. The passage of a single act in Congress, for example, often involves a particular set of topics, often arcane. When issues are considered as part of the public or the governmental agenda, it is seldom obvious ahead of time which components will be seen as salient, because each large issue is made up of smaller ones and because no issue exists in total isolation from others.

The choice of dominant topics of discussion has policy consequences because different topics are typically related to different tones. Americans agree that jobs are good and that environmental degradation is bad, for example. But many issues can be related both to questions of jobs and to questions of environmental degradation; indeed, this debate almost defines the nature of recent politics in many areas. More generally, however, this illustration points to the importance of issue definition. Given the topic of attention on a particular issue, one can almost always tell whether that is "good news" or bad for the industry involved.

Redefinitions of old issues are important for the study of policymaking because agreement on a particular issue definition almost always implies a consensus about what, if anything, government should do. Pesticide makers, for example, can expect governmental actions to help rather than hinder them during periods when the issue is defined as one of agricultural productivity. However, if attention shifts to contamination of drinking water, that is bad news for the same group. Government and private industry will react strongly to this new definition.

It may be obvious that a single issue may have both positive and negative consequences, but there are many examples where only one of these dominates public discussion of an issue during long periods of time. These issue definitions have sustained policy consequences, and they are the means by which strategic policymakers often attempt to push government policies in new directions (or to protect themselves from changes in established government policies that benefit them). Issue definitions are at the heart of the policy process.

The various topics or components of an issue are associated with different tones for a great variety of issues in American politics. As attention in a debate shifts from one possible topic to another, advantage or disadvantage is conferred on different groups. Further, we note that issues sometimes involve simple discussion of social conditions, but at other times governmental actions are called for or discussed. Social conditions, such as bad drinking water, only become public policy concerns if people demand that government intervene to solve the problem (by regulating the use of pesticides, for example). So a given issue can be associated with many topics, and these topics of attention are closely related to the nature of governmental response. The close connection between topic and tone gives policy importance to the study of shifts in media attention, since these shifts are generally accompanied by an implicit message about what the government should be called upon to do. Moreover, when a particular component of an issue becomes salient, it may spill over across issue boundaries, affecting seemingly unrelated issues. As issues are redefined, they become associated with other issues and can have unpredictable but important effects across issue boundaries. For example, emphasis on health consequences of an issue can affect agriculture policy, as in the case of tobacco, just as it might affect municipal water treatment systems; if an issue theme other than health consequences is on the public agenda, then agriculture and water treatment could well be seen as completely separate policy topics.

TONE AND TOPIC

When President Bill Clinton presented his first choice as attorney general for confirmation by the U.S. Senate, he thought that he had found a candidate who would represent diversity: Zoe Baird would be the first female to hold that post. When she was attacked for having hired illegal aliens to help in her childcare needs, her defenders attempted the "motherdefense," arguing that she was looking after the needs of her family, putting their benefits first. This argument was largely ignored as public and media attention focused on a single aspect of the nominee: her high salary and perceived membership in a privileged class of well-to-do lawyers. Her relatively humble beginnings and meritocratic rise to affluence were ignored in the wave of media outrage over her illegal action, especially over what was perceived as her confidence that such illegality would go unpunished. Clinton's first cabinet nominee to fall did so because her backers could not control the focus of attention.

We can find three lessons in the Zoe Baird story. In a heated public debate about a person or an issue, the topics of attention most closely associated will be (1) incomplete, (2) difficult to predict, and (3) heavy with consequence. Media attention during a heated debate is incomplete because only certain parts of a story have appeal. The focus of attention tends to be difficult to predict because it is often in reaction to other things that happen to be on the political agenda at the same time. The consequences of attention can be heavy. These may involve personnel issues of particular concern only to those involved, or major choices of public policy of interest to all.

Strategic Issue Redefinition

There are many examples of particular issues where salient topics rise and fall for reasons that are not readily apparent, but often these redefinitions are the obvious work of strategic policymakers seeking political advantage. William Riker describes a variety of interesting cases of issue redefinition in his book *The Art of Political Manipulation*. For Riker, policymakers are at their strategic best when they artfully link a given issue to a topic they know will gain wide acceptance. In one example, a U.S. senator was opposed to military plans to dispose of nerve gas in his state, but he knew that other senators would be pleased that their states had not been chosen, so his only chance for success was somehow to change the nature of the debate. This he did with great success by arguing that the issue was actually related to the Senate's power to ratify treaties and that acceptance of this plan would in fact indicate the Senate's willingness to abrogate its responsibilities and to capitulate in the face of an arrogant and power-grabbing executive branch. With this happy redefinition of the issue, he was able to avoid a defeat that he would almost certainly have suffered otherwise (Riker 1986: 106–113).

John Kingdon has also provided a variety of examples of issue redefinition in the policy process. For Kingdon, redefinition often involves the attachment of new "solutions" to old "problems," as when proponents of mass transit programs argued successively that their programs represented the solution to a variety of public concerns, from the 1973 oil embargo to the air pollution crisis to the problems of overcrowding in the streets. Kingdon records how one advocate summed it up: "There is a continuing interest in mass transit. The underlying goals exist and continue along. You want to do something, and you ask, 'What will work this year? What's hot this year that I can hang this on?'" (1984: 181). In sum, policymakers seeking particular policy outcomes attempt to redefine issues to suit their needs, taking advantage of circumstances as they can.

Roger Cobb and Charles Elder (1983) built on the insight of E. E. Schattschneider (1960), who argued that the disadvantaged in any political conflict have an interest in expanding the scope of the battle. Cobb and Elder pointed out how rhetorical strategies and symbolic politics often are part of these strategies of either limiting conflict to "experts" or expanding it to include a broader range of participants. Whether these redefinitions are part of a particular policy debate as described by Riker or Kingdon, or part of a much larger societal discussion, they can be equally important.

The "Size" of the Redefinition

There are many examples of issue redefinitions with reference to particular policy issues, and their discussion rightfully merits an important place in the literature of policymaking. Indeed, it is difficult to understand how or why certain issues become controversial without knowing how the issues came to be defined as they were. Certainly, Zoe Baird would like to know why she was seen as a wealthy person rather than a woman and mother, when clearly she was all three. In addition to these day-to-day or week-to-week redefinitions, we can also see that over the long term in American politics, a great variety of public policy problems are redefined. The significance of these changes is often ignored, however, either because they seem to take place gradually or because often policy analysts prefer to explain precise events rather than general trends. In the long run, however, American society and its leaders have shifted their understandings of a great number of public policy issues (see Schulman 1980); these changing issue definitions are just as heavy with political consequences as the storm that blew over Zoe Baird in 1993. That storm, however, had a devastating effect on one individual; these affect us all.

Health care and its financing is an example of a huge social and economic question that over the years has been associated with a variety of social understandings. For many years health care has been considered part of the problem of "big government." Such an issue portrayal gives advantage to defenders of the status quo, so there is no surprise when groups such as the American Medical Association raise the specter of "socialized medicine" each time increased regulation is debated. Over time, however, and despite the best efforts of some of those involved, public, governmental, and media understandings of the problems of health care in the United States have been slowly transformed, in a process that we can see dramatically at play in the first year of the Clinton administration. Health care costs are variously discussed as a major cause of economic strain on small businesses, as a contributor to the federal deficit, as an unfair shackle on workers unable to leave their jobs because of the fear of losing insurance coverage, and in other ways as well. As these different parts of the issue are raised, new groups are advantaged and changes in public policy are implicitly called for. No single political actor can cause a redefinition or new understanding of such a broad issue as health care, but long-term redefinitions nonetheless occur.

Long-term redefinitions of important policy problems are more common than people realize, because many of them occur within the confines of professional communities. For example, Herbert Jacob has described the quiet transformation of professional norms in the legal system concerning family policy and divorce in his book *Silent Revolution* (Jacob 1988). Important changes in divorce patterns from the 1950s to the 1980s have not gone unnoticed, of course, but much of the transformation in our laws and practices covering divorce have come from within the professional communities of experts, not from street demonstrations or media campaigns by interest groups.

Treatment and care of the mentally ill has similarly gone through tremendous transformations over the decades, sometimes with enormous public policy consequences. As those professionals who deal routinely with the mentally ill altered their views about proper treatment, patients were either confined and isolated from society, or encouraged, often prematurely, to attempt to integrate. When fiscal pressures, institutional shortages, and hopeful new medical treatments altered the context of professional judgments, great numbers of mentally ill were taken out of isolation and encouraged to live without supervision. Within a short time, standard accepted treatment shifted from isolation and guarded existence to a new emphasis on personal freedom and integration into society (see Mechanic 1990; Johnson 1990; Isaac and Armat 1990). Clearly, massive social movements are not the only means by which issues may be redefined. Often, redefinitions come about through quiet and often unnoticed transformations of professional norms.

Long-term changes in governmental policy toward drug abuse (see Chapter 5) have stemmed from changes in professional norms as well as from large-scale media campaigns. Official policy has shifted in long trends from harsh enforcement but relatively little attention to the problem (from World War II until the early 1960s), to increased attention and hopes for education and treatment alternatives (from the late 1960s through most of the 1970s), and finally (under Presidents Reagan and Bush) to another massive buildup in attention and spending, but with enforcement, incarceration, and interdiction as the preferred solutions. Long-term changes in how professionals, the media, and politicians discuss and portray the issue have important consequences for the broad direction of governmental policy (see Baumgartner and Jones 1993; Musto 1987; Sharp 1991).

Long-Term Issue Redefinitions in the Popular Press

We have analyzed all the media attention reported in the *Readers' Guide to Periodical Literature* for a number of issues, and we can note systematically how different components of particular issues come to the forefront of media attention at different times (for a complete explanation of this procedure, see Baumgartner and Jones 1993: Appendix A). A few simple statistics make the general point. From 1900 to 1988 there were a total of 2,390 articles reported in the *Guide* on the topic of pesticides. Over the century, positive and negative stories about pesticides have been roughly evenly divided: we coded 46 percent of these articles as positive toward the industry and 54 percent as negative. However, considering only those topics where economic and financial aspects of the industry are discussed, 82 percent of the articles are positive in tone. Among those articles discussing health or environmental questions, on the other hand, 80 percent are negative. Public policy debates are often not contradictory; rather, the tone of the debate is determined by the topic of attention (Baumgartner and Jones 1993: 112).

In media coverage of the smoking and tobacco issue, we reported almost identical findings. Of 2,512 articles coded, there were more negatives (46 percent) than positives (31 percent; the remainder neutral or not codeable). Still, depending on the topic of coverage, these percentages were drastically altered. Considering only those articles on health topics, 79 percent of the articles listed in the *New York Times Index* were coded negative from the point of view of the industry, and only 12 percent positive. We found 588 articles on the topics of economics, finance, overseas trade, and the like; 65 percent of these were good news for the industry, as opposed to only 17 percent negative (Baumgartner and Jones 1983: 115).

There is a clear link between the topic of coverage in a given debate and the tone of that coverage. However, there is also a clear tendency for single topics to dominate media attention at any given time. Over any period of a few years, a single group of similar topics typically dominates all media coverage on an issue. So during the 1980s, the vast bulk of media coverage of nuclear power was negative in tone, because it focused on the topics of safety and health. During the 1940s, media coverage of the same industry focused just as exclusively on potential economic benefits from the industry, on optimistic predictions of scientific advance, and on similar positive topics (see Baumgartner and Jones 1993: chapter 4; Weart 1988).

In each of the cases that we followed in our larger study, we reported periods during which one set of topics dominated media coverage of a particular issue, but these periods of focused attention were not permanent. During rare but surprisingly short periods, the dominant focus of attention in a given public policy debate shifts. Where tobacco had once been king, lung cancer, health-care costs, and other topics industry leaders would rather see ignored can suddenly move to the forefront of media concern. Not surprisingly, we found that government actions tend to follow closely the nature of media attention to a given industry. During periods of fascination with the positives associated with a given industry, agencies attempt to foster its growth. Thus we have the Atomic Energy Commission engaging in every effort to foster the growth of the private nuclear industry in the 1940s and 1950s, or the Agriculture Department encouraging the use of pesticides during the 1950s and 1960s. When social understandings of these industries change, as social, professional, and citizens' groups mobilize to bring other aspects of the same issues to the forefront of media attention, then government policies also change. After the shift in media attention on nuclear power in the 1970s, governmental regulators changed their emphasis; as the media shifted from glamorizing smoking tobacco to vilifying it, those elements of government charged with insuring public health become more active, to the detriment of industry leaders (and to those elements in government charged with aiding farmers, as well).

In sum, topics of attention are related to tones of attention. As these change over time (and they can change very rapidly), tremendous pressures can be brought to bear on governmental institutions, causing dramatic alterations in the directions of governmental policies, even over broad areas of the economy. So the issue-definition process is not only of academic interest, but heavy with political consequence, a point that becomes apparent when we look in greater detail at the history of media attention to the topic of air transportation in the United States. Air transportation has not been subject to any particular vilification in the media, of course. Still, coverage has alternated in its focus on different components of the issue. Governmental policies, always at the center of the industry, have been altered in important ways as social understandings of the prospects and problems of the industry have changed over the years.

AIR TRANSPORTATION

In order to provide a more complete analysis of the relationship between changes in the salience of the various components of a policy issue and the nature of the corresponding policy response, we have conducted a thorough study of the issue of air transportation from 1900 to 1985. Figure 3.1 shows the total number of articles on air transportation topics to appear annually in the *Readers' Guide to Periodical Literature* during that period. There have been a total of 13,951 articles, but the figure shows that these have been distributed very unevenly over the years. Essentially, air transportation questions burst onto the media agenda in this country in the years following the Second World War. Commercial aviation expanded in the postwar years along with an enthusiastic wave of media attention to the new engines, airplanes, and airports that were being built around the country. During the late 1940s and into the early 1950s, there were around three hundred articles on air transportation issues annually in the *Readers' Guide*.

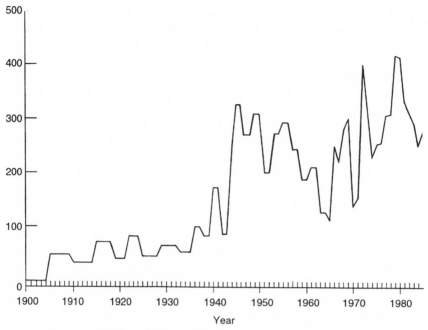

Figure 3.1. Annual Coverage of Air Transportation Issues in the *Reader's Guide to Periodical Literature,* 1900–1985

After the initial postwar surge of enthusiastic interest in the possibilities of air travel, attention to the topic steadily declined until the mid to late 1960s. In the 1970s and 1980s there were some peaks of interest in the topic, but these waves of interest lacked the enthusiasm of the first ones. Attention to the general topic of air transportation rose and fell, as shown in Figure 3.1. However, air transportation is a big issue, made up of a variety of smaller components. Attention to each of these was not equal during these periods.

On the basis of the titles listed in the *Guide*, we have coded each article in Figure 3.1 into one of four categories: technology issues, accounting for 47 percent of the total (generally reports of new aircraft being developed, new types of engines, and other technological advances); rates, routes, regulation, and other issues concerning competition and the marketplace (30 percent of the total); economics and finance (generally business news concerning the financial health of the industry; 17 percent of the total); and safety questions (6 percent of the total).

We have also noted whether each article was positive or negative toward the air transportation industry. The American air transportation industry gets tremendously good press and always has throughout the century. Positive articles, such as hopeful new technologies, the introduction of new airplanes, the building of new airports, and the like, account for 86 percent of the total articles in the study. Negatives, on such topics as crashes, safety lapses, congestion, delays, noise pollution, cost overruns, and the like, account for only 14 percent of the total. The generally positive tone of air transportation articles is by no means self-evident and is in stark contrast to how other issues are covered in the media. The industry in general benefits from a much more rosy public discussion than many other industries we have studied, such as the pesticide, tobacco, or nuclear power industries (see discussion above and Baumgartner and Jones 1993). Media attention almost always has extolled the virtues of the American air transportation system, rather than harping on its negative externalities, as is often the case for other industries (see Vogel 1989: 214 ff.).

In addition to the coding described above, we also noted whether each article mentions anything about government regulation, involvement, or activity, and we found that only eight percent of the articles are related to government activities. Ninety-two percent concern private companies, social problems, or technological advances without any mention of governmental actors. Not only is the air transportation industry remarkable in its positive media image, but also in the paucity of government actions discussed in the media.

We can use the data just described in order to chart changes in how air transportation questions have been discussed in the media during the century. Figure 3.2 shows that different components have dominated media attention to air transportation questions at different times.

Technological advances were the dominant concern of media coverage throughout the first half of the century and remained an important element well into the 1950s. In more recent decades, however, media attention has turned to questions of economic regulation. The development of the jet engine, transatlantic travel, and the jumbo jet once dominated media discussion of air transportation issues. In more recent years, discussion has focused on rate structures, government regulation, and the functioning of the regulated market in air travel. From questions of scientific or technological advance, articles on air transportation have shifted their emphasis to questions of how to manage a controlled and highly regulated market.

From the turn of the century until the Second World War, media attention to air transport issues almost never involved discussion of governmental actions or regulations (see Figure 3.3). Only fourteen titles containing any mention of government activities appeared during this period, despite the fact that the basic subsystems regulating routes, rates, and safety were established during those years and despite the decision to publicly subsidize the system. The subsystem surrounding air transportation was constructed far from the realm of public opinion and from the glare of media attention (see

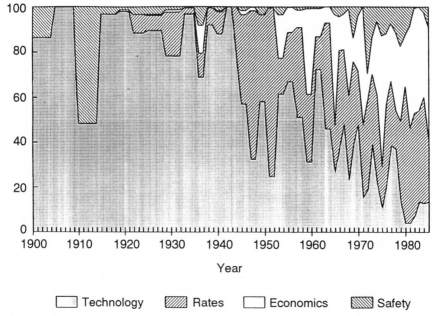

Figure 3.2. Percentage of Annual Coverage Concerning Each of Four Topics, Air Transportation Articles, *Reader's Guide,* 1900–1985

Redford 1960). From 1944 to 1946, however, thirty-four articles mentioning government actions appeared, reflecting a spurt of interest in government involvement in peacetime applications of a technology that had proved itself during the war. (Air traffic was far from the only industry to be subject to such enthusiastic hopes, though it may have been the most successful in this conversion; see Baumgartner and Jones 1993 for a discussion of the nuclear power and pesticide industries in particular.)

A second wave of governmental discussion, this one longer and more intense, came in 1953 and lasted until 1962. During this time a total of 356 titles in the *Readers' Guide* concerned governmental aspects of air transportation, or an average of about thirty-five per year. Finally, a third wave, from 1966 until the end of our series in 1985, shows a consistent background of discussion of governmental actions concerning air transportation questions. While the figure makes clear some peaks and valleys of coverage, 642 articles mentioning government activities have appeared since the mid 1960s, an average of approximately thirty-two per year. Previous discussions of governmental actions were short-lived, but since the 1960s, they have become a permanent part of the topics covered by the media whenever they discuss air transportation.

Government action is usually not called for when industrial leaders tout

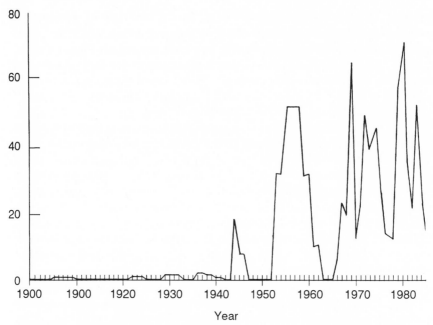

Figure 3.3. Annual Number of Air Transportation Articles Mentioning Government Activities, *Reader's Guide,* 1900–1985

technological breakthroughs. Rather, media attention tends to link an industry to government attention when a social or an economic condition needs attention. We can see this by comparing the topics of attention for those articles that mention governmental activities to those that do not. Table 3.1 presents this simple comparison.

In spite of the role of the government in the development of the civilian

Table 3.1   Topics of Air Transportation Articles Indexed in the *Readers' Guide,*
Articles Mentioning and Not Mentioning Government Actions, 1900–1985 (%)

	Technology	Rates	Economics	Safety	Total
Articles mentioning government actions	4	77	14	5	100 (1,046)
Articles not mentioning government actions	50	27	17	6	100 (12,905)
Total	47	30	17	6	100 (13,951)

aviation industry in the United States, media coverage of government actions focuses overwhelmingly on economic regulation functions. Over three-quarters of all articles concerning government actions focus on rates, routes, and regulation, whereas these topics account for only about one-quarter of nongovernmental coverage. Media attentiveness seems to have followed passively the establishment of the basic regulatory and subsidy structures, rather than led a public debate over them. The biggest difference between government-related and nongovernment stories is that when technological advances are considered in the media, the role of government in helping those along tends to be ignored in the nongovernment stories.

There is no shortage of reports of good things that the government does with regard to the air transportation industry. When we look again only at the 1,046 articles concerning government actions reported in the *Guide*, we can see that fully two-thirds of these report positive actions. Even concerning safety issues, the government is more likely to be linked to positives than to negatives in American media coverage of this industry. Indeed, many government activities reported in the media, such as building new airports, licensing new designs, awarding new transoceanic routes, or even subsidizing the major airplane-building companies through military contracts and research efforts, are good news for the industry. We can see in the case of air transportation what we have termed elsewhere a "mobilization of enthusiasm" in the media. Public authorities, confident in their wartime successes, moved boldly to put to civilian use many of the technologies of World War II. Unlike other industries, the air transportation industry has experienced no significant mobilization of hostility toward it. (The closest we may have come was a wave of protest in the 1970s concerning excessive noise and proposed landing rights for supersonic aircraft.) Most other industries have experienced a wave of criticism in the media at some point during the last fifty years.

As we see in Figures 3.2 and 3.3, a third wave of attention to governmental questions associated with the industry began in the late 1960s and lasted virtually uninterrupted into the 1980s, while at the same time air transportation issues were being redefined. The combination of new topics of interest more relevant to governmental action (or more likely to lead to demands for government intervention) and the spillover of new issues from other areas led to dramatic changes in governmental policies toward the industry in the 1970s.

Government Interest

When we look at congressional attention to the same topics discussed in the media, we find an interesting pattern. Just as the issue surged onto the media agenda during the late 1960s, it also surged onto the congressional agenda. "Congress held only a total of forty-seven hearings [on air transportation] from the turn of the century until 1968" (Baumgartner and Jones 1993: 211). The issue leaped onto the congressional agenda shortly after this date, however, as part of the wave of interest in deregulation. While public safety has long been an important concern, economic issues have also been of paramount interest. In fact, the element of air transportation that sparked congressional interest was deregulation. The airlines followed trucking, telecommunications, savings and loans, and a variety of other industries as Washington policymakers' enthusiasm for deregulation spread (see Baumgartner and Jones 1993: 210–214).

How air traffic was pushed onto the governmental agenda presents an interesting case of spillover from other substantive issue areas. Though certainly air transportation questions had become a standard part of the routine governmental agenda by the 1960s, since various levels of government had become more and more involved in regulating routes and rates, building airports, and investigating safety problems, there was no single surge of safety problems that forced this issue onto the laps of the governmental officials.

The issue of air transportation illustrates three important points. First, it is a large industry with a great variety of public policy concerns. As different parts of the story have gained public and media attention, the nature of public policy response has changed. As in many other technologically complex issues, this once-novel issue has become routinized. As the story moved from the science pages to the business pages, governmental questions exhibited a dramatic change in focus. Whereas people expect the government to promote science, they want protection from big business. Since this issue, like many others, has elements of both technological innovation and business power, its redefinition over the decades is especially interesting, particularly to those in high-technology areas.

Second, like any other issue of public policy, air traffic does not exist in a vacuum. Indeed, governmental response to public policy concerns in this area has been strongly affected by spillovers from other regulated industries. Thus our analysis of air transportation seems to show that this industry shares much with other large areas of the economy—that media attention to the various component parts tends to focus on one or a few and to change over time, thereby leading to changes in governmental response. It also shows that air transportation, like other industries, can be strongly affected by what we have termed boundary effects: spillovers from unrelated events beyond its leaders' control.

Third, the redefinition of air transportation was of a very large scale. It may have involved manipulation at the level of individual bills as illustrated by Riker (1986), but more importantly it affected the ways in which policymakers thought about the entire air transportation system. This type of large-scale and long-lasting redefinition is not easily controlled by any single individual or group of policy actors. Further, it has rarely been studied by political scientists. But these redefinitions, which sometimes occur rapidly, can shape the nature of the entire political debate for years.

THE POLICY CONSEQUENCES OF ISSUE DEFINITION

We have argued in this chapter that issues are rarely considered in their entirety. Rather, their *component parts* rise and fall on the public agenda, and as they do, the nature of governmental response can be expected to change as well. Secondly, sometimes issues are redefined through unintentional and probably uncontrollable *spillovers* from related issue areas. And, finally, the *size* or generality of the issue definition is a critical, and often unrecognized, component of the policy process. A large-scale issue redefinition can determine the fundamental direction of public policy for decades, yet such redefinitions are often unrecognized because they are so large. Whatever its source, the redefinition over time of large public policy issues such as those considered in this chapter is likely to have significant political consequences.

The definition of relevant questions of political debate concerning an industry or area of the economy determines in large part the nature of social response to it. During periods when air transportation is seen as a means to create American jobs building airplanes, government agencies can be expected to do all they can to foster the growth of the industry. But when the same industry is linked to accidents, excessive noise, price gouging, the abandonment of rural areas, or other negatives, governmental officials can be expected to respond accordingly with attempted corrective measures. Issue definitions matter because they determine the nature of public and private mobilization efforts to encourage or to discourage a particular activity. As such, they are at the center of the political debate and should be at the center of political scientists' study of the political process.

REFERENCES

Baumgartner, F. R., and B. D. Jones. 1993. *Agendas and Instability in American Politics*. Chicago: University of Chicago Press.

Cobb, R. W., and C. D. Elder. 1983. *Participation in American Politics: The Dynamics of Agenda-Building*. Baltimore: Johns Hopkins University Press.

Isaac, R. J., and V. C. Armat. 1990. *Madness in the Streets: How Psychiatry and the Law Abandoned the Mentally Ill*. New York: Free Press.

Jacob, H. 1988. *Silent Revolution*. Chicago: University of Chicago Press.

Johnson, A. B. 1990. *Out of Bedlam: The Truth about Deinstitutionalization*. New York: Basic Books.

Jones, C. O., and R. Strahan. 1985. "The Effect of Energy Politics on Congressional and Executive Organization in the 1970s." *Legislative Studies Quarterly* 10: 151–79.

Kingdon, J. W. 1984. *Agendas, Alternatives, and Public Policies*. Boston: Little, Brown.

Mechanic, D. 1990. "Promise Them Everything, Give Them the Streets." *New York Times Book Review*, 16 September.

Musto, D. 1987. *The American Disease*. Exp. ed. New York: Oxford University Press.

Redford, E. S. 1960. "A Case Analysis of Congressional Activity: Civil Aviation, 1957–58." *Journal of Politics* 22: 228–258

Riker, W. H. 1986. *The Art of Political Manipulation*. New Haven, Conn.: Yale University Press.

Schattschneider, E. E. 1960. *The Semi-Sovereign People*. New York: Holt, Rinehart and Winston.

Schulman, P. R. 1980. *Large-Scale Policy Making*. New York: Elsevier North Holland.

Sharp, E. B. 1991. "Interest Groups and Symbolic Policy Formation: The Case of Anti-Drug Policy." Paper presented at the annual meeting of the American Political Science Association, Washington, D.C., August 29–September 1.

Vogel, D. 1989. *Fluctuating Fortunes: The Political Power of Business in America*. New York: Basic Books.

Weart, S. 1988. *Nuclear Fear: A History of Images*. Cambridge, Mass.: Harvard University Press.

4

Sexual Harassment:
A Defining Moment
and Its Repercussions

Ellen Frankel Paul

American popular and political culture lurches from one "crisis" to the next, each trumpeted from the front pages of newspapers, the covers of national newsmagazines, the mouths of nightly news anchors, talk-show guests, and hosts of low-brow "reality" programs. A brief, and by no means complete, list of some of the issues that have blistered the American consciousness in the early 1990s would include Alar sprayed on apples and said to be a human health hazard; electromagnetic waves emitted by high-voltage power transmission lines and computer monitors that allegedly increase the risk of cancer and miscarriages and, more recently, high-frequency electromagnetic waves claimed to cause brain tumors in yuppies addicted to their cellular telephones; contaminated grapes from South America and poisoned over-the-counter medications; undercooked hamburgers infested with a virulent strain of E-coli bacteria that caused the deaths of two children who consumed the product at a Jack-in-the-Box; the diet pill and powder industry, which allegedly produces ineffective potions, fraudulently represented to the public; dangerous medical devices, including silicone breast implants said to cause serious systemic illnesses; and General Motors light trucks said to explode on impact due to poor design of the gas tanks. Each issue's partisans demand a remedy, usually one that would involve government action: regulation, outright prohibition, or expenditure from the public fisc.

In this crisis-of-the-week environment, how does an issue break through the cacophony, seize the imagination of the public, and secure a place on the national agenda? It seems easy enough to procure for almost any issue the fifteen minutes of fame that the late pop-artist Andy Warhol prophesied for each of us, but to emerge from the pack and to have enough staying power to last long enough so that a remedy of some sort can be effected is increasingly problematical. One obstacle is that virtually any concern that any interest group, professional association, plaintiffs' lawyer, politician, academic, newsman, or other public figure might embrace is declaimed at the same decibel level: a stentorian screech. Admittedly, some issues are imperative enough to warrant such treatment, but others clearly are not. Witness the proclamation by researchers that Americans do not get enough sleep, that this constitutes a national crisis, and that the government should form a national commission (no doubt comprising these self-same researchers) to study what can be done about the crisis and make recommendations for federal action.

The issue of sexual harassment has managed to catapult itself above the fray, and for this reason it is an apt candidate for discussion in a collection devoted to problem definition. Sexual harassment offers a particularly graphic illustration of how an issue can emerge from relative obscurity, seize the national imagination, and rise above the other "crises" clamoring for public attention, and that journey will be the focus of the second section of this paper, following a brief, nontechnical discussion of the legal status of sexual harassment as it developed from the mid 1970s. I will also examine how different constituencies frame or define sexual harassment, how they make their disparate cases for its prevalence, and how they variously categorize behavior that may or may not fall under it. Finally, I will examine how the solutions advocated by various partisans emerge from how they define, delimit, and assess the frequency of the problem.

One cautionary note is in order: it would be foolish to think that by examining how sexual harassment attained its notoriety one could achieve easily generalizable results, for few matters in the social sciences—or in human affairs more generally—are so facilely repeatable. Yet by studying the emergence of sexual harassment as a "front-burner" issue on the national agenda, we may identify elements that could also be observed in the rise of other issues.

EMERGING FROM THE CROWD

The modern women's movement emerged in the late 1960s and early 1970s, and in the roughly twenty years of its maturation, sexual harassment has been a simmering issue among feminists. In its more radical form, feminism indicts men as oppressors of women, and one of the principal engines of this domination lies in the realm of sexual prowess. Thus, marriage is often viewed as tantamount to prostitution. Another arena of exploitation is the workplace, where women are subjugated through outright sexual discrimination, lower pay (the oft-cited 70 percent of men's wages), and diminished opportunities through channeling into traditionally female jobs (nursing, teaching, social work, childcare).

Sexual harassment in the workplace, then, is an issue that neatly melds these two strands of feminist doctrine: the sexual exploitation of women by men takes a particularly virulent form when combined with the power of men over women in the office, university, hospital, or factory. Because men usually occupy the more highly paid, prestigious, and privileged ranks in all work venues, they, as supervisors, can exercise their power to exploit women by demanding sexual favors in return for promotion, higher pay, or job retention; or they, as either co-workers or supervisors, can create a sexually charged work environment that makes continued employment for a woman unbearable (MacKinnon 1979). The former behavior by supervisors is now universally acknowledged to be sexual harassment—termed *quid pro quo* sexual harassment by the courts—and was the first type of sexual harassment to be litigated in our federal courts in the mid 1970s (*Williams v. Saxbe* 1976). The latter variety still has its skeptics, but since the early 1980s it has been acknowledged by the lower federal courts and denominated *hostile environment* sexual harassment (*Bundy v. Jackson* 1981). The promulgation by the Equal Employment Opportunity Commission (EEOC) in 1980 of an amendment to its *Guidelines on Discrimination Because of Sex* to include sexual harassment was instrumental in solidifying judicial acceptance of sexual harassment as sex discrimination and was particularly useful in overcoming judicial skepticism about hostile environment sexual harassment (*Guidelines* 1980).

Somewhat belatedly in 1986 the Supreme Court heard its first sexual harassment case, *Meritor Savings Bank v. Vinson* (1986), and gave its official blessing to developments that had been percolating in the lower courts for over a decade. *Meritor* gave almost complete endorsement to the EEOC's *Guidelines* on sexual harassment, placing liability for quid pro quo harassment by a supervisor on the employer on a standard of strict liability. Thus an employer is liable whether or not he knew of the harassment. For hostile environment sexual harassment by a co-worker, the employer is liable under a knowledge or constructive knowledge standard: if an employer knew or should have known of the offending behavior and failed to act appropriately to correct the situation, the employer is liable. *Meritor* left undecided only the standard of liability—whether strict or the weaker standard of knowledge—for hostile environment harassment by supervisors.

Both quid pro quo and hostile environment sexual harassment are now well established as sex discrimination under Title VII of the Civil Rights Act of 1964. Title VII prohibits employers of fifteen or more workers from discriminating in their hiring, promotion, and firing procedures. The EEOC is charged under Title VII with receiving and investigating complaints of sexual discrimination (and thus, of sexual harassment) and engaging in conciliating efforts to resolve disputes. When it cannot otherwise resolve a meritorious complaint, the EEOC can sue the employer, or it can issue a "right to sue" letter to the injured party, who may then pursue the matter in the federal courts.

Prior to the passage of the Civil Rights Act of 1991 in November of that year, the only remedies available for successful plaintiffs were injunctions barring harassment in the future, reinstatement, back pay, or other appropriate equitable relief; full compensatory and punitive damages were not available. With the passage of the new act, a person who prevails in a sexual harassment suit can receive compensatory damages—including damages for past out-of-pocket losses, future monetary losses, and emotional harm—and, in addition, punitive damages are available when the defendant acted with "malice or with reckless indifference to the federally protected rights of an aggrieved individual" (Civil Rights Act 1991; see also *EEOC Policy Guide* 1992). These expanded monetary remedies and the new right to a jury trial make sexual harassment suits more attractive to both those who experience sexual harassment and their attorneys, and EEOC filings and suits have proliferated, as anticipated at the time by opponents of the expanded remedies. However, compensatory and punitive damages were capped under the act—which is seen as a barrier to full justice by many—a compromise that is likely to be overridden by a new Democratic administration and a Congress controlled by the same party.

It is fair to say, then, that before the dawning of the 1990s, sexual harassment had gained a beachhead in the federal courts but had not become what I will call, for lack of a better term, a "front-burner" issue for the general public. True, academic feminists, particularly lawyers, zealously promoted the argument that sexual harassment ought to be viewed as sexual discrimination, and they were very influential in encouraging the courts to go beyond congressional intent and read sexual harassment into Title VII. Beyond the federal courts, however, concern for sexual harassment traveled in fairly narrow circles. Interest was pretty much confined to activist women's groups (such as the National Organization for Women), feminists principally but not exclusively in the universities, occasional stories in the general media, and more frequent coverage in feminist magazines and professional journals. Following startling developments that will be explored in the following section, this picture would change dramatically and within a matter of a few days.

SEXUAL HARASSMENT EXPLODES
ON THE NATIONAL CONSCIENCE

A single incident propelled sexual harassment from the doldrums inhabited by scores of public policy issues, and that incident was the sensational charges brought by law professor Anita Hill against Supreme Court nominee Clarence Thomas. While this incident and its aftermath will be the main focus of this section, there were other less spectacular events both before and after the Hill/Thomas imbroglio that seared the national conscience. Sexual harassment's emergence as a "front-burner" issue might be compared to waves battering a coastline: just as one wave pelted the shore and began its retreat another would come crashing ashore, with Anita Hill's charges surging landward with the force of a tsunami. Poetic license aside, the wave imagery is appropriate, as we will see, with ripples preceding Hill and several substantial waves succeeding her. Without these subsequent reminders, it is doubtful that even with all of the publicity that the Hill charges received, the issue of sexual harassment would have been resilient enough to have staying power in competition with an ever-changing panoply of new "crises." Media and public attention spans are notoriously short, and seemingly getting even shorter, so for any issue to retain its allure the public must receive frequent, graphic, enticing reminders. It did not hurt sexual harassment's prospects that the details of its occurrence are often lurid, titillating, tantalizing. Not every public policy issue, of course, can hope to possess such seamy advantages.

Although instances of sexual harassment and the court cases that accompanied them had received media attention in the past, none had the impact of Anita Hill's charges. One pre-Hill incident did, however, achieve substantial national notoriety. What happened to Lisa Olson on September 17, 1990, is, in retrospect, the first act of what would go on to become a theatrical triumph. Lisa Olson, a sports reporter for the *Boston Herald*, charged five players on the just-defeated New England Patriots football team with sexual harassment for making sexually suggestive and offensive remarks to her when she entered their locker room to conduct a postgame interview. The incident amounted to nothing short of "mind rape," according to Olson. After vociferous denunciations in the media that could not be ignored, the National Football League investigated, found Olson's charges credible, fined the team and three of its players $72,500, and found that one of the players displayed his nude body to the reporter in a lewd and intimidating fashion while the others made sexually suggestive remarks. The National Organization of Women called for a boycott of Remington electric shavers in protest, for the Patriots and Remington have the same owner, Victor Kiam, who allegedly displayed insufficient sensitivity when the episode occurred. Olson sued the owner, three players, two former Patriots officials, and the Patriots for sexual harassment, alleging that the team had not dealt seriously with her allegations (Borges 1991).

The Anita Hill/Clarence Thomas Hearings

Nothing that preceded it, however, would give adequate warning of just how devastating a charge of sexual harassment could be in such a highly charged political atmosphere as the confirmation hearings for Judge Clarence Thomas. With Justice Thurgood Marshall's resignation from the Supreme Court, liberal opinion and the interest groups that advance liberal causes had lost one of their last champions on the highest court in the land. After a decade of Republican control of the White House under the leadership of presidents committed to changing the perceived liberal bent of the Court under Chief Justice Earl Warren and his successor, Warren Burger, liberals had lamented the gradual erosion of what had been an engine for social change. Holding the presidency for only one term since 1968, Democrats and liberal opinion leaders held little hope of influencing the Court, other than to use their hegemony in the Senate to block the confirmation of any nominee whom they could either brand as "out of the mainstream," as they had with President Reagan's nominee, Judge Robert Bork, or as someone with a character flaw or something unseemly in his past behavior.

In the interim between Justice Marshall's resignation on June 27, 1991, and President Bush's nomination four days later of Judge Thomas, who was then serving on the United States Court of Appeals for the District of Columbia, there was considerable pressure on the president to name another black man or minority group member to fill Marshall's shoes. Although President Bush repeatedly contended that he had not named Judge Thomas because of his race, but rather, his qualifications, the nominee was immediately attacked as weakly qualified by some of the same liberal interest groups that had so recently clamored for the appointment of an African-American. In an effort to raise the "character issue," numerous rumors were circulated in Washington, including one that Thomas enjoyed watching pornographic movies while at Yale Law School, rumors that echoed similar charges against Judge Bork. The opposition to Thomas suffered from an impediment that had not hampered unity during the Bork battle, for several influential black groups were reluctant to declare themselves in opposition to a black appointee. They feared that such opposition might alienate their constituencies—indeed, Thomas enjoyed over 50 percent approval among blacks at the time of his appointment (Puddington 1992)—and, even if successful, result in nothing more than the naming of an equally conservative white man, a Pyrrhic victory at best. For example, Benjamin Hooks, the director of the National Association for the Advancement of Colored People (NAACP), the preeminent black civil rights organization, sent out mixed signals on his leanings, delaying the organization's eventual opposition until late in the game, thus blunting its impact. Although Hooks eventually testified against Thomas's confirmation, the tardiness of the group's decision weakened opposition forces and prevented a clear-cut and united front from forming earlier when it might have been more efficacious (Phelps and Winternitz 1992). Hampered by such indecisiveness in the ranks of civil rights groups, the anti-Bork coalition of liberal interest groups reassembled in an attempt to "Bork" Clarence Thomas. The most influential groups in this loose-knit coalition were women's organizations opposed to the repeal of abortion rights (the National Organization of Women, the National Women's Caucus, the National Abortion Rights Action League, the National Women's Law Center), liberal activist groups with a more broadly defined mission (People for the American Way), and civil rights groups (the National Leadership Conference on Civil Rights, the Alliance for Justice).

Beginning on September 10, the Senate Judiciary Committee held eight days of hearings on Judge Thomas's nomination, hearings in which Thomas portrayed himself as a man of humble background—a self-made man from Pinpoint, Georgia—who as a result of his upbringing could empathize with the downtrodden. Thomas attempted to blunt his conservative public image by, for example, waffling on the "litmus test" issue of abortion, claiming that he never discussed the issue or held a firm opinion on it. Such tactics were met with mistrust and cynicism by his political opponents on the committee, in the media, and in the interest groups. Opponents charged that he was being manipulative and that once on the Court he would provide another solid vote for conservative causes, and would, in particular, add the crucial vote for overturning *Roe v. Wade* (1973), the case that had constitutionalized abortion rights for women, and that the Republican party under Reagan and Bush had been dedicated to overruling. Having failed to mollify his liberal opponents, Judge Thomas's performance disappointed many of his conservative supporters, but for different reasons. They felt that he should have defended his beliefs, rather than waffling on them or deflecting questions with the response that he could not answer because the issue would likely come before the Court. Thomas's White House handlers, many commentators speculated, had decided upon this strategy of ducking controversial issues and refusing to comment on particular cases—the traditional response of nominees before the committee prior to Judge Bork—because of the debacle that resulted from Bork's vigorous defense of his beliefs.

Despite reservations on both sides of the ideological divide—stronger, of course, on the liberal side—on September 27 the Judiciary Committee, on a seven to seven vote, sent the nomination to the full Senate without recommendation. One Democrat on the committee, Chairman Joseph Biden, voted in the affirmative along with the six Republicans. The full Senate began debate on the nomination October 3, with the vote scheduled for six o'clock on the evening of October 8. Although the vote would be tight, opponents had all but conceded that Thomas would be taking his seat on the high court (Spencer 1991; *Wall Street Journal* 1991).

Unbeknownst to the public or to the Senate at large (except for the committee members and some of their staff, the Democratic majority leader, and probably a few other key senators), a bombshell was about to be dropped that would explode all expectations. On Sunday, October 6, Timothy Phelps of *Newsday* and Nina Totenberg on National Public Radio's "Weekend Edition" broke the story of University of Oklahoma law professor Anita Hill's charges of sexual harassment. She had lodged her complaint to the Judiciary Committee under the cloak of confidentiality, which had now been breached by what Totenberg said were multiple sources. The following day, Hill held a news conference in which she aired her charges of sexual harassment against Thomas, alleging that in her nine months as his special assistant at the Department of Education, where he served as assistant secretary for civil rights, and at the Equal Employment Opportunity Commission, where he was chairman and where she transferred with him, Thomas made sexually explicit comments to her about X-rated movies and repeatedly asked her for dates. Skeptics were quick to point out the irony of the charges: that the former chairman of the EEOC—the very organization that shortly before Thomas's ascension had promoted guidelines on sexual harassment and that under his leadership helped legalize the notion that sexual harassment is prohibited under Title VII's ban on sex discrimination, and the man who reportedly encouraged the Reagan administration to support that position before the Supreme Court in *Meritor v. Vinson*—would now stand accused of this same offense (Gigot 1991).

As the story of Anita Hill's charges gradually emerged, it became clear that they had been circulating in the opposition and among Senate staff opposed to Thomas as early as the end of August. After repeated importuning by aides to Senators Kennedy (D. Mass.) and Metzenbaum (D. Ohio), Hill agreed to discuss her charges with Judiciary Committee staff members in confidence, and after several contacts throughout the month of September she eventually consented to the release of her name to the FBI for investigation and the submission of a "personal statement" on September 23 to the committee. Democratic committee members were informed of the charges and the FBI report as was the ranking Republican on the committee, Senator Strom Thurmond, who apparently did a less than complete briefing of his Republican colleagues. On September 27 the committee members voted, after receiving Hill's statement and the FBI report, but no mention of either was made in public, and the committee chairman attempted to honor Hill's wishes for anonymity by collecting all copies of the documents. A subsequent investigation conducted for the Senate by a New York lawyer, Peter E. Fleming, Jr., whose report appeared the following May, failed to identify the source of the leak to the two reporters, although he did find that the leak originated from the Senate. The trail seemed to point to an aide to Senator Metzenbaum. Perhaps the most intriguing finding in Fleming's report was the intimate connection between certain interest groups that opposed the Thomas nomination and Senate staffers who likewise had an interest in torpedoing his confirmation. The Alliance for Justice fastened upon a rumor of sexual harassment back in July, and its director passed the tip on to a Metzenbaum aide. Another Senate aide, of one of Senator Kennedy's committees, was also very active in contacting Hill and encouraging her to proceed with charges; this individual was a former employee of People for the American Way.

By the time of the scheduled vote on October 8, pressure from senators, interest groups, female House members, and the press proved too compelling to ignore. Thomas requested a delay in the vote, and it was postponed for a week in order to give the Judiciary Committee time to investigate the charges. From October 11 to the wee hours of October 14, what ensued was nothing less than a national teach-in on sexual harassment, carried live by the major networks and the cable news outlets. Americans in huge numbers remained glued to their tubes, mesmerized by the unfolding spectacle of sleaziness in high places. Judge Thomas flatly denied everything, relating the torment and bewilderment that Hill's charges had caused him.

> I have suffered immensely, as these very serious charges were leveled against me. I have been racking my brains and eating my insides out trying to think of what I could have said or done to Anita Hill to lead her to allege that I was interested in her in more than a professional way, and that I talked with her about pornographic or X-rated films. . . .
> This is a person I have helped at every turn in the road since we met. . . .
> I have never, in all my life, felt such hurt, such pain, such agony. . . .
> My family and I have been done a grave and irreparable injustice. (Reuters 1991: 10)

Thomas was followed by a cool Anita Hill recounting lurid details of her former boss's alleged remarks about pubic hair in a Coke can, his own physical endowments, and those of porno star Long Dong Silver.

> One of the oddest episodes I remember was an occasion in which Thomas was drinking a Coke in his office. He got up from the table at which we were working, went over to his desk to get the Coke, looked at the can and said, "Who has put pubic hair on my Coke?" On other occasions he referred to the size of his own penis as larger than normal, and he also spoke on some occasions of the pleasures he had given to women with oral sex. (*New York Times* 1991: 11)

Thomas reappeared that night to again declare his complete innocence, professing to the startled Judiciary panel and nation that he had not deigned to listen to Hill's testimony. Charging that he was the true victim, Thomas played what his opponents would charge was the "race card," stirring deeply entrenched emotions among blacks and summoning racial solidarity for his cause. In a ringing declaration of disgust with the proceedings, Thomas declaimed:

And from my standpoint, as a black American, it is a high-tech lynching for uppity blacks who in anyway deign to think for themselves, to do for themselves, to have different ideas, and it is a message that unless you kowtow to an old order, this is what will happen to you. You will be lynched, destroyed, caricatured by a committee of the U.S. Senate rather than hung from a tree. (Reuters 1991: 14)

As Thomas returned for six hours of grilling by the committee on October 12, Hill's attorneys and handlers, fearing that the tide was turning against them, arranged for a lie detector test to be administered and announced on the following day that she had passed. This stratagem failed, for public support had swung solidly in Thomas's favor, with polls showing 2 to 1 support among blacks, the general population, and women as well as men (Kolbert 1991). The hearings ended at two o'clock on the morning of October 14, and they ended inconclusively, with neither side landing a knockout blow. Hill's witnesses—four friends who maintained that she had mentioned sexual harassment to them at the time—were imprecise in their recollections of dates under questioning and could not deliver the coup de grace because none of them had observed the incidents. Thomas's character witnesses, most notably women from the EEOC (seventeen of whom were clamoring to testify on his behalf), could not prove that the incidents had never occurred, although they did burnish his image, attest to his never having harassed them, and question Hill's motives.

What all sides could agree upon was the impossibility of reconciling Hill's and Thomas's contradictory stories, for Thomas flatly denied that any of the lurid events that Hill had so meticulously related had ever occurred. Clearly, someone was lying, but opinion was divided over who the prevaricator was. Many analysts have since commented that those who favored Thomas before Hill's charges tended to believe him, and those who opposed Thomas tended to credit her (Tushnet 1992)—not very surprising given human nature's ineluctable bias. Also, many have pondered the reason for the dichotomy between elite opinion (as represented in the print and electronic media, by experts, academics, and liberal interest groups) and the perception of the Hill/Thomas hearings by the American public. Although elite opinion wrote and spoke in great excess bewailing the prevalence of sexual exploitation and harassment of women throughout American society and by overwhelming numbers believed Hill's charges, the public seemed remarkably immune to their imprecations. One analyst concluded that here was a case in which the public had direct access to a highly charged news event, and they drew their own conclusions, relying little if at all on the usual bevy of "talking heads" to interpret events for them (Boot 1992). Thus, it is not very surprising that on the first anniversary of the hearings, this pervasive elite opinion had begun to reshape the public's image of the hearings, and Hill's believability had increased with time while Thomas's had receded under the onslaught of continued media condemnation. Polls in October 1992 showed Hill and Thomas either neck-and-neck in credibility or with Hill enjoying a 4 to 10 percent lead (Reed 1992). Ishmael Reed, a black magazine editor, writing in the *Washington Post*, attributes the shift in public opinion to "a year of pro–Anita Hill effusions from white media feminists, including the producers of popular sitcoms. In the media, Hill is now portrayed as something of a saint" (Reed 1992: C1).

The drama came to an end, officially at least, when the Senate voted on October 16 to confirm Thomas to the Supreme Court by a 52–48 margin, the closest contest ever for a successful nominee. But the public debate on Anita Hill's charges and her credibility, and the larger outcry over sexual harassment in the workplace would continue.

Recriminations and second thoughts have abounded, with both Thomas's partisans and opponents reappraising the tumultuous event. In attempting to comprehend why the general public failed to credit Hill's charges, many of her supporters have flagged what they perceived as a weak defense by the Democrats on the committee in the face of vigorous, unrelenting assaults on her credibility by Republican senators Arlen Specter (Penn.), Oren Hatch (Utah), and Alan Simpson (Wyo.) (Chemerinsky 1992). Republican strategy revolved around several key elements: (1) attempting to discredit Hill's veracity by fastening upon inconsistencies in her story, including the much more graphic description of the events at the hearings than in her prior statement to the committee or her news conference after the story broke in the press; (2) questioning why she waited a decade to raise these charges when Thomas had withstood two previous Senate confirmations after the alleged episodes; (3) probing why she followed her alleged harasser from the Department of Education to the EEOC after he had harassed her in her first position, which they portrayed variously as opportunism or careerism, if her account of events were true, or evidence that she fabricated the tale; (4) scrutinizing her motives to explain why she might have a vendetta against Thomas, variously attributed to her disappointment at not receiving a promotion at the EEOC or her secret, unrequited passion for Thomas, or her outrage at Thomas having wed a white woman; (5) raising the question of why she continued to have contact over the years with Thomas, using him as a reference for jobs, inviting him to speak at her university, calling him for a chat while in Washington; (6) searching for political differences that she may have had with Thomas over affirmative action or other policies; (7) interrogating Hill on her connection to Democratic Senate staffers and liberal interest groups that had opposed Thomas's confirmation, with the implication that some of these people played a nefarious role in forcing her to come forward and in tailoring her charges for maximum effect; and (8) emphasizing that there were no contemporaneous witnesses to the events that Hill portrayed, nor was there a pattern of sexual harassment of other women whom Thomas supervised. This last point was particularly telling, since there was nothing tangible by which to judge the veracity of the two combatants, nothing to get beyond "he said, she said." (Although one woman might have testified to similar behavior towards her by Thomas, she declined to appear.) The lack of corroboration for Hill's charges, coupled with the appearance of female EEOC employees who gave heartfelt testimonials to Thomas's exemplary character, served to weaken Hill's case in the public mind, and the committee's Republicans capitalized on this.

Hill's supporters have since argued that the Democrats erred in conceding a trial-like standard of "presumption of innocence" when other nominees had been withdrawn for far less damaging peccadillos. The committee's chairman, Senator Joseph Biden (D. Del.), already under assault for having not pursued Hill's charges more vigorously prior to the committee's vote, repeatedly assured the nominee that he should be accorded this presumption. Thus, Thomas's detractors maintain that when the Senate finally voted, many senators argued that since they could not discern who was telling the truth, they would vote for Thomas, giving him the benefit of the doubt. The committee's Democrats, too, are faulted for a weak defense of Hill, for tolerating the unrelenting Republican interrogation with barely a whimper of protest, and for acquiescing to Thomas's insistence in his opening statement that his private life was off limits to questioning. Many point to the fact that several of the key Democrats on the committee were hobbled with scandals of their own that prevented them from being more assertive or seizing the high moral ground. Thus, Hill's partisans tend to focus on errors in strategy committed by the Democratic senators and what they see as the underhanded, deceptive, cold-hearted strategy employed by the administration and the Republican committee members—rather than on any fundamental weakness in Hill's account—to explain why Thomas ultimately prevailed in the court of public opinion. If only the Democrats had tamed the Republican inquisitors, they argue, matters would have been resolved quite differently and Clarence Thomas would not be a Supreme Court justice (Hertzberg 1991; *New Republic* 1991).

Hill skeptics define the problem very differently. They focused from the beginning on the unsubstantiated nature of her charges and on the unholy, back-alley alliance between liberal Senate staffers and activists in liberal interest groups who together badgered Hill into coming to the committee with her charges and then violated her privacy by leaking the story to the press, thus circumventing the legitimate political process by a "dirty trick."

The skeptics have focused also on the substance of Hill's charges of sexual harassment to question both their seriousness and, more generally, the ever expanding parameters of sexual harassment as promoted by feminist activists. Even if Hill were telling the absolute truth, which they doubt, Thomas's indiscretions amounted to nothing more serious than a flair for telling off-color jokes and social obtuseness in pressing an indifferent female for dates (Amiel 1991). Such behavior would in no way constitute sexual harassment of the sort that the skeptics concede is illegal: Thomas never pressed Hill for sexual favors under threat of retaliation, demotion, or loss of employment, nor did he impair her advancement in any way. Thus, her charges did not amount to anything like quid pro quo sexual harassment, and they doubt whether the actions of which he stood accused would constitute hostile environment sexual harassment, since she followed him on his upward career path to the EEOC, not a plausible action for someone who found his overtures unwelcome or the work environment, therefore, unbearable.

The more general lesson that most Thomas believers draw from the imbroglio is that sexual harassment boundaries have been too greatly extended, so that even casual, yet to some women offensive, sexual jesting in the workplace is a federal issue. Most argue that sexual harassment of the hostile environment sort needs to be much more clearly and narrowly defined to cover only egregious behavior well beyond the pale of anything Hill charged against Clarence Thomas. As for Hill herself, they see a calculating careerist, riding on Thomas's rising star until he could do her no more good and then throwing in her lot with the liberal interest groups bent on his destruction when that would be more advantageous to her own advancement. They regard her honors, awards, cover stories in *Time* and *Newsweek*, and her munificent speaking engagement fees since the hearings as further evidence of this opportunism; they call her "the new national postergirl for sexual harassment" (*National Review* 1991), a woman who made her name and fortune by besmirching the reputation of an entirely innocent man.

The Hill/Thomas hearings raised the issue of sexual harassment to national consciousness, and its tangible effects were immediate: more sexual harassment filings with the EEOC; an increase in the numbers of women running for high political office in 1992, particularly the Senate, because, they said, of the Anita Hill incident (Smolowe 1992); and a plethora of newspaper, magazine, and television stories on sexual harassment, highlighting both the Hill charges and those of other women around the country. The intangible effects are more difficult to assess, but certainly the visibility of the hearings afforded the women's movement the opportunity to advance one of their key issues as never before. This national "consciousness raising" put men on their guard that scenarios which seemed much less serious to them than the typical quid pro quo offense could nevertheless destroy their careers should a woman pursue sexual harassment charges against them; the workplace became a tenser environment, no doubt. Depending on the perspective of the commentator, victimized women were either encouraged to pursue sexual harassment charges because of the increased notoriety of the issue or discouraged due to the unwanted spotlight cast upon Anita Hill.

In the aftermath of the hearings, Congress enacted the Civil Rights Act of 1991 which made available for the first time full compensatory and punitive damages to victorious plaintiffs in sexual harassment suits. Employers throughout the country issued or refined rules against sexual harassment, and the consulting industry enjoyed a bonanza as businesses rushed to hold sexual harassment seminars for their employees. The Hill/Thomas hearings were nothing less than the defining moment for sexual harassment. As Judge Stephen Reinhardt, of the United States Court of Appeals for the Ninth Circuit, wrote: "The sexual harassment issue will never again be the same in America. As the Army-McCarthy hearings changed the nation's view of red-baiting and the Watergate hearings changed our view of politics, the Judge Thomas–Professor Hill hearings transfixed America and will inevitably deeply affect our nation's views of sexual harassment" (Reinhardt 1992: 1431).

Tailhook

As enthralling as the Hill/Thomas hearings were, it is likely that sexual harassment would have faded from the public mind had not fresh instances played themselves out on the national stage. When navy Lieutenant Paula Coughlin complained to her boss of an assault upon her and other women at the navy aviators' Tailhook Association (a private organization) convention on the night of September 17, 1991, it is likely that had it not been for Anita Hill's charges one month later, the navy's old-boy network would have swept her complaint under the table, and indeed that was the initial reaction of those to whom she complained. Instead, Coughlin, frustrated by the dilatory navy investigation, decided to go to the press, and on June 24, 1992, the Tailhook scandal took on national proportions. The story reverberated in the press for over two years and cost the secretary of the navy and several admirals their jobs for ignoring or attempting to downplay the incident.

Lieutenant Coughlin's position as an aide to Rear Admiral Jack Snyder did not protect her when she took what turned out to be a wrong turn down a hallway at the Las Vegas Hilton. She met drunken aviators and their tradition of the "gantlet," as several of them pushed her to the ground and tried to pry her clothes off. At least twenty-six women, fourteen of whom were naval officers, would face the gantlet, as the drunken pilots grabbed the women's breasts and buttocks, attempting to strip them of their clothes. Some of them would voluntarily come forward after Coughlin's interviews with "World News Tonight" and the *Washington Post*; others told their stories reluctantly to Pentagon investigators. A report by the inspector general of the Pentagon, issued a year later, faulted senior navy officials for undermining their own investigation in order to curtail negative publicity (Schmitt 1992). In the wake of Tailhook, the navy ordered all personnel to undergo one-day training on sexual harassment and the navy's rules proscribing it.

A marked difference between the Tailhook incident and Anita Hill's charges was the nearly universal condemnation of both the navy's handling of the investigation and its culture that had bred such contempt for women. Conservative voices distinguished Hill's charges, the veracity of which they in any case doubted, from the kind of physical assaults and lewd behavior that the women endured at the hands of the inebriated fliers (*Wall Street Journal* 1992). Activist voices viewed the incident as confirmation of their worst fears about the pervasiveness of sexual harassment throughout society, the indifference of male authorities to female whistle blowers courageous enough to put their careers in jeopardy, and the need to place more women in positions of leadership to ensure that harassers will face speedy retribution. Thus, the public debate that followed the Tailhook disclosure was far less acrimonious and more narrowly drawn than the controversy that raged in the aftermath of the Hill/Thomas hearings. A few conservative voices did quarrel with the "scapegoating" of senior navy officers for the bungled Tailhook investigation (Cropsey 1992), and they warned of possible overreaction in the form of lifting all bans on women in combat. Yet on the key issue of whether or not Tailhook crossed the line from tasteless behavior to sexual harassment, they agreed with the activists that it had.

Senator Packwood's Indiscretions

While sexual harassment accusations against two influential senators had surfaced after the Anita Hill revelations—Senator Brock Adams (D. Wash.) declined to run for reelection after eight women charged him with sexual harassment, and Senator Daniel Inouye (D. Hawaii) was accused of molesting a female barber seventeen years before—nothing quite compares to the controversy that has swirled around the claims of ten female former employees of liberal Republican Senator Bob Packwood of Oregon. With the public revelation of the charges coming just weeks after a tough reelection campaign, and a year after the Hill/Thomas hearings, the women's allegations produced much agonizing on the part of women's groups, for Senator Packwood had been one of the few voices on the Republican side of the aisle sympathetic to women's issues during the twelve years of Republican control of the White House. Many women activists were reluctant to denounce a man who had rallied to their side on the key issues of abortion rights, family leave, and the Equal Rights Amendment and who had an excellent reputation for promoting women to positions of authority on his staff. Indeed, at the time of the charges women held the top positions. The senator had close ties to the National Abortion Rights Action League (NARAL) and had been one of the first backers of the Capitol Hill Women's Political Caucus's sexual harassment statement, signing on in the spring of 1991 to a document that included unsolicited flirtations and dirty jokes under the banner of sexual harassment.

Gossip had percolated for years, both in Washington and Oregon about the senator's groping of female employees, but never publicly. However, in the closing days of the campaign rumors circulated about these sexual harassment claims, but the senator managed to deflect them with an outright denial. He raised questions with *Washington Post* reporters about the women's credibility (including innuendoes about their sexual proclivities) after he was notified on October 31 that the *Post*'s story would not be ready for publication until after the election. This was a break for Packwood (and a cause for later defensiveness by the *Post*), who won reelection over another liberal, Democratic Representative Les AuCoin, by only a 52–48 percent margin.

None of the women, former and would-be employees and lobbyists, alleged that the senator had inflicted retribution on them for turning down his advances. Their stories were roughly similar: of Packwood grabbing them, trying to kiss them, and trying to loosen their clothes. Some said that they had felt uncomfortable enough to leave his employment in the months that followed. The *Post* found several friends of each of the women who stated that they had been told of the incident soon after it occurred. None of the women filed formal complaints at the time, fearing that they would not be believed or that their careers would be put in jeopardy. (Congress, in any case, had exempted itself from Title VII sexual harassment charges.) Shortly after the election, when the *Washington Post* gave the senator details of the allegations of six of the women, he responded, "I will not make an issue of any specific allegation." He offered a backhanded apology: "If any of my comments or actions have indeed been unwelcome or if I have conducted myself in any way that has caused any individual discomfort or embarrassment, for that I am sincerely sorry" (Graves and Shepard 1992: A1)

Immediately after the story broke, calls for a Senate investigation and for Packwood's resignation erupted back in Oregon from representatives of women's groups and the Oregon Democratic party. The state coordinator for the National Organization for Women came out strongly for an investigation, stating that "sexism and misogyny come in all forms and it's important to catch all perpetrators. . . . Packwood is supposed to be a role model. As an individual, I would be very happy if he resigned." The executive director of the Oregon Coalition of Women said, "It would be only fair and courageous for Packwood to recognize he has outlived his usefulness and resign" (Pianin and Graves 1992: A14). The reactions among representatives of national women's organizations—including Eleanor Smeal of the Fund for a Feminist Majority, Harriet Woods of the National Women's Political Caucus, Judith L. Lichtman of the Women's Legal Defense Fund, and Kate Michelman of NARAL—were more tempered, with expressions of outrage and calls for an investigation, but stopping short of demands for Packwood's resignation.

A few days later, under this intense political pressure, and after Gloria Allred, head of the Women's Equal Rights Legal Defense and Education Fund in Los Angeles, wrote to the Senate Select Committee on Ethics demanding a prompt inquiry, Senator Packwood announced that he would request and cooperate with a Senate Ethics Committee probe. He also declared that he would seek counseling for an alcohol problem, a problem that several of the women had associated with his sexual importunings. In his statement he claimed not to know whether alcohol contributed to the occurrence of these episodes, and he asserted that when the *Post* had first interviewed him, he "honestly believed these events had never occurred" (Barr 1992: A12). This statement, coupled with a more sincere-sounding apology, failed to placate a coalition of Oregon groups that had formed to seek Packwood's removal from office. They saw his latest apology as political maneuvering or an attempt to excuse his behavior as alcohol induced, rather than as an act of genuine contrition, an interpretation that seemed plausible in light of a Packwood spokesman's admonition that the senator's statement should not be read as a confession of guilt. On November 30, 1992, Senator Packwood entered an alcohol clinic, one day after a story broke that one of the women had been pressured by a friend of the senator's not to come forward with her allegations.

The Senate Ethics Committee instituted a preliminary investigation into the accusations on December 2. Senator Packwood returned to his home state of Oregon on January 29, 1993, and met with a firestorm of protest, some of it violent, from those seeking his resignation. As he met with small groups of supporters throughout the state, the senator assured them that he would not resign, that the stories of the women would appear "in quite a different light" when he mounted his defense, and that he would not rule out using information about their sexual backgrounds in his defense (Egan 1993). Perhaps in reaction to these assertions, the Ethics Committee on February 4 announced that it would broaden its investigation to include an additional charge of intimidation and that it would shield witnesses from questions about their sexual histories.

Packwood's history as a strong supporter of women's professional advancement and "women's issues" divided women's groups in a way that had never occurred during the Anita Hill fracas, particularly estranging local Oregon branches of women's groups from their national hierarchies. It is undoubtedly true, too, that the seeds of this dissension were sown earlier, during the election season. When the National Abortion Rights Action League had endorsed Senator Packwood over his similarly liberal and profeminist opponent, Representative Les AuCoin, the local chapter had balked, citing the senator's recent overtures to their bitter adversaries, the anti-abortion group, Oregon Citizens Alliance. They claimed that the senator had made peace with this group in order to forestall a third-party challenge from the right to his reelection bid; a similar candidacy in 1990 had garnered 13 percent of the vote and helped defeat a Republican gubernatorial contender (*Washington Post* 1991).

Liberal opinion on the Packwood allegations was virtually unanimous in calling for the Senate to eliminate the exemption that it had granted itself from federal sexual harassment suits (*New Republic* 1992; *New York Times* 1992), in demanding an investigation of the charges, and in viewing the allegations as the essence of sexual harassment. Many activists, nevertheless, felt torn between their admiration and indebtedness to Packwood-the-defender-of-feminist-causes and their repugnance at Packwood-the-sexual-predator. The most aggressive in calling for Packwood's resignation was an organization formed for that purpose, comprising several groups, the most influential of which were the Oregon chapters of NARAL, NOW, Planned Parenthood, and the Oregon Commission for Women (Smith 1992). Many of these Oregonian activists expressed annoyance with their national leadership's waffling on Packwood.

Conservatives have been relatively quiet on the Packwood scandal, preferring, one suspects, to let the liberals fight it out and unwilling to come to the defense of a Republican not much to their liking. Lisa Schiffren, an aide to Vice-President Dan Quayle, departed from this general indifference by pointing out that Senator Packwood's actions did not meet the older definition of sexual harassment—that of using power and the threat of reprisal to obtain sex—and that when he was rebuffed the senator relented. Although she stopped short of a defense of the senator's actions, Schiffren pondered a paradox of the newer, "politically correct" concept of sexual harassment (other than the one explored repeatedly in the media of the senator's liberal record versus his sexual appetite): now successful seducers are blameless while their inept fellows are "guilty of the new crime—sexual harassment" (Schiffren 1992: A23). She also faulted "prominent feminists" for assiduously courting the senator despite persistent rumors over the years of his sexual importuning of women, which she saw as "tacitly covering for him." Schiffren speculated that with the election of a Democratic president coupled with Democratic control of both houses of Congress, these activists no longer needed Packwood as a liberal conduit to the Republican White House, so they are now willing to "throw him overboard." Most conservative opinion makers lay pretty low on this one, preferring to watch the spectacle of recriminations between the national women's organizations and their Oregon associates.

Sexual Harassment and the National Agenda

One must always be skeptical of too facile generalizations, but it might be plausible to conclude that if any issue is to stay on the national agenda for more than a brief moment, it must benefit from repeated incidents that remind the harried citizens of its urgency. Sexual harassment as a national issue built upon the phenomenal publicity it received during the Hill/Thomas hearings; nine out of ten people interviewed by pollsters reported having viewed at least part of the hearings, and the networks' coverage received higher Nielsen ratings than a play-off game. With the Tailhook and Packwood charges reverberating in the media, citizens were regularly reminded of the salience of the issue. With each new instance, too, memories of Anita Hill were reinforced, with commentators trying to justify some of her lapses—such as not complaining at the time or following her boss to a better job—by citing the similar behavior of other accusers.

Sexual harassment benefited from another element that most other "crisis" issues cannot summon, and that is the synergy between it and other recent scandals involving date rape, incest, child molestation at daycare centers, and priests molesting children. The date rape trials of the boxer Mike Tyson and a nephew of Senator Ted Kennedy (D. Mass.) added to the public anxiety over the prevalence of rape and violence against women in our society. Thus, all of these examples of sexual impropriety helped to produce heightened public awareness of these "women's issues."

Other instances of sexual harassment of more localized impact also served to keep the issue before the public:

- When Randy Daniels was about to be appointed a deputy mayor of New York City, a former employee, Barbara Wood, came forward to tell of a night that he walked her to a subway station and made advances to her with crude remarks of a sexual nature and of his retaliation on the job after she rebuffed him. Daniels denied the charges, withdrew from the deputy mayor's position, and filed a libel suit against his accuser. (Sontag 1992)
- A New York state assemblywoman charged three of her colleagues with sexual harassment. Two of them offered abject apologies and the third did not come forward. One of the repentants was accused of misspeaking the word "sex" for "six" at a gathering of hundreds at a Chamber of Commerce meeting and then looking at her and saying, "Whenever I think of Earlene, I think of sex." The second penitent admitted to making Assemblywoman Hill climb over him in order to reach her seat in

the Assembly chamber. The third was charged with following her into her office and threatening to throw her from the window when she declined his advances. (Lyall 1993)

- A prominent female neurosurgeon at Stanford Medical School resigned to protest the appointment as department chair of a professor whom she accused of sexism and sexual harassment. Dr. Frances Conley rescinded her resignation when the university promised to investigate, and the accused professor was eventually forced by the university to resign his chairmanship. (*Chronicle of Higher Education* 1992)

These examples are only the tip of the iceberg, the instances that received some notoriety in media that have a national circulation, but more localized stories also helped to keep sexual harassment a viable issue long beyond the usual life span of a "crisis-of-the-week" issue. Thus, we may conjecture that with other policy issues as well, repeated instances—preferably of a shocking or horrifying nature—will be an advantage in insuring that public attention continues to focus on that issue. At the very least, the "wave phenomenon" that we observed with the ascendancy of sexual harassment is something to look for when examining other political issues.

DEFINING, DELIMITING, AND ASSESSING
THE PREVALENCE OF SEXUAL HARASSMENT

As we observed earlier, opinions differed over these notorious examples of sexual harassment, with opinion divided most intensely over Anita Hill's charges against Clarence Thomas. For both the Tailhook convention incident and the charges against Senator Packwood, the range of debate was far narrower because virtually all observers concurred that the acts complained about were indeed egregious, and that they did constitute sexual harassment. Probing a bit deeper, we will see that there is a very good reason why the Anita Hill charges proved so much more divisive than the other two episodes, and that reason revolves around conflicting definitions of what constitutes sexual harassment and, thus, differing assessments of its pervasiveness and severity.

Sexual harassment is a notoriously ill defined and almost infinitely expansible concept, including everything from rape (a dastardly crime by every sane person's standards) to (and I take these examples from actual court cases) unwelcome neck massaging, discomfiture upon witnessing sexual overtures directed at others, yelling at and blowing smoke in the ears of female subordinates, and displays of pornographic pictures in the workplace. Defining sexual harassment as the United Methodist Church council did—as "any sexually related behavior that is unwelcome, offensive or which fails to respect the rights of others"—the concept becomes broad enough to include everything from "unsolicited suggestive looks or leers [or] pressures for dates" to "actual sexual assaults or rapes." Categorizing everything from rape to "looks" as sexual harassment widens the concept as far as it will stretch.

Many definitions advanced by feminists share this feature of expansiveness with the United Methodists' approach. They also, typically, import an assumption of male malfeasance into the definition of sexual harassment, an assumption that in the majority of cases is perfectly reasonable, in the sense that it describes the archetypal transgression, but all concede that it is possible for a woman to sexually harass a man or that a member of one sex could harass another of the same sex. Most assume, also, that sexual harassment is not essentially about sex, but rather, *power*. Since men have traditionally held positions of power in business, and women have entered the workplace in large numbers and with lofty ambitions only during the last quarter century, it is mostly men who abuse their authority by harassing women for sexual favors or otherwise contaminating their working environment with inappropriate sexually laden comments or gestures. Law professor Catharine A. MacKinnon was an early and hugely influential force in shaping the feminist notion of sexual harassment, and her definition makes precisely these assumptions: of male malfeasance, of sexual harassment as an exercise of male power and domination over women.

> Intimate violation of women by men is sufficiently pervasive in American society as to be nearly invisible. Contained by internalized and structural forms of power, it has been nearly inaudible. Conjoined with men's control over women's material survival . . . it has become institutionalized. . . . *Sexual harassment, most broadly defined, refers to the unwanted imposition of sexual requirements in the context of a relationship of unequal power.* Central to the concept is the use of power derived from one social sphere to lever benefits or impose deprivations in another. . . . American society legitimizes male sexual dominance of women and employer's control of workers. . . . Sexual harassment of women in employment is particularly clear when male superiors on the job coercively initiate unwanted sexual advances to women employees (emphasis added). (MacKinnon 1979: 1–2; see also Farley 1978)

Other pioneers in defining sexual harassment share MacKinnon's theses. "This is the heart of the issue," Billie Dziech and Linda Weiner write. " 'Sexual harassment' implies misuse of power and role" (Dziech and Weiner 199: 21). Other commentators endorse this assessment: "Sexual harassment is the exploitation of a powerful position to impose sexual demands or pressures on an unwilling but less powerful person" (Note 1984: 1451). "Sexual harassment is really about power. It is the abuse of power by those who have it towards those without it. It is using sex to intimidate, humiliate, or force specific workplace behavior against the will of those with whom you work" (Leibmann 1992: 1443).

The EEOC's *Guidelines* offers a more neutral definition, one that does not import the activist's assumption of sexual harassment as an expression of male dominance over women:

> Unwelcome sexual advances, requests for sexual favors, and other verbal or physical conduct of a sexual nature constitute sexual harassment when (1) submission to such conduct is made either explicitly or implicitly a term or condition of an individual's employment, (2) submission to or rejection of such conduct by an individual is used as the basis for employment decisions affecting such individual, or (3) such conduct has the purpose or effect of unreasonably interfering with an individual's work performance or creating an intimidating, hostile, or offensive working environment. (*Guidelines* 1980: 925)

Many conservative voices find even the EEOC's definition too expansive, preferring to confine sexual harassment exclusively or almost exclusively to quid pro quo situations in which a supervisor threatens job-related reprisals if a woman employee (or, theoretically, a man) declines to submit to his (or her) sexual advances. The essential element, as they see it, is *extortion* rather than *power*. The supervisor abuses his authority by extorting sexual favors under threat of reprisals. Barbara Amiel captures the spirit of this more restrictive approach: "There is such a thing as sexual harassment in the workplace. It involves a person demanding sexual favors in return for job security or promotion. *That is extortion*" (emphasis added) (Amiel 1991: 15).

Some extend the argument further, claiming that the supervisor's act, which exceeds the bounds of his position, also defrauds his employer by disrupting the work environment by importing elements that are no part of the employer's marketplace function (Paul 1990). Sexual harassment by a supervisor, on this account, is a flagrant abuse of trust, using company resources in an entirely unauthorized manner for the perpetrator's own satisfaction. Regarding what many conservatives see as lesser offenses—for example, Justice Thomas's alleged telling of sexual jokes, reprising of X-rated movies, and requesting dates—there is a tendency to limit rather than expand the concept of sexual harassment. Amiel puts this position succinctly:

> Let us assume that every word Professor Hill is saying is true. What on earth does this have to do with Judge Thomas's fitness for the Supreme Court? As I understand it, feminism not withstanding, we have not yet made it illegal to discuss sex. *If he [Thomas] did what she [Hill] alleges,*

we can convict him at worst of bad taste and possible poor judgment of another person's reactions (emphasis added). (Amiel 1991: 14)

Hence, if the extortion element is missing, and neither a threat nor a reprisal ensues, the conservative is likely to view the incident as an act of social ineptness, bad taste, gaucherie, but not a Title VII federal offense. Many of the allegations against Senator Packwood would, in their view, fall into the gauche rather than the civil-rights-violating category. The senator was offensive in his actions, but he backed off when the women resisted, and he did not exact retribution.

Conservatives tend to be even more skeptical of *hostile environment* scenarios in which co-workers create an uncomfortable work environment for female employees. They are quite bothered by the expansibility of the concept of sexual harassment in the hands of activists and some federal judges, worrying that if every off-color joke is potentially a federal suit for which the employer is liable, the workplace will become an unbearable place, one in which normal relations between men and women will become so tense as to be insufferable. Conversely, conservatives worry that by expanding sexual harassment in the other direction—that is, to encompass criminal activity such as rape, molestation, or sexual assault—important distinctions will be lost, as a concept that embraces everything from displaying *Playboy*'s centerfold on the outside of one's locker to rape accompanied by bludgeoning tends to lose its usefulness. To lump the rapist with the pin-up fancier is to trivialize the former and exaggerate the significance of the latter. In the words of Amitai Etzioni, here arguing a conservative position:

Sociologists will be quick to recognize that such stretching of the concept of sexual harassment has an opposite effect from the one intended: it undercuts those who seek to stamp out unwanted sexual advances and pressures. Every society has a limited store of moral indignation; if one squanders it by lumping serious offenses with marginal ones, it will soon be depleted. (Etzioni 1992/1993: 54)

Thus, conservatives find what happened at the Tailhook convention unacceptable but they would make distinctions among the offenders. For those involved in jeering the victims, moral censure is appropriate. Criminal liability, perhaps, is fitting for those who undressed an inebriated seventeen-year-old girl.

A useful set of incidents to distinguish the feminists' tendency to expand the concept of sexual harassment from the conservatives' propensity to constrict it is the three incidents of which the New York assemblywoman protested—the verbal gaffe of "sex" for "six" and then the remark that in her presence he cannot help thinking about sex, being forced to leap over an assemblyman to get to her seat, and being threatened with defenestration for resisting the sexual advances of another assemblyman. The activists would view all three events as sexual harassment, while the conservatives only the third. The conservative would view the first two as social faux pas; they would see in the activists' categorization of these events as sexual harassment precisely the sort of expansiveness in the concept that they had predicted and feared.

Assessing the Prevalence of Sexual Harassment

It should come as no surprise that the two camps view the extent of the problem of sexual harassment differently. Activists—particularly those who equate all heterosexual sex as analogous to rape (Koven and St. John 1992), but even many with a more charitable view of consensual sexual acts between members of the opposite sex—tend to perceive sexual harassment as a pervasive problem, one that virtually every woman will experience during her working years. Skeptics, naturally, find the surveys on the prevalence of sexual harassment flawed, for, they argue, their results depend upon the acceptance of the feminists' sweeping definition of sexual harassment.

When feminists uncritically cite surveys on the extent of sexual harassment, they do so as activists in behalf of a cause, and like activists on any issue, they know that in order to make their case to a national audience, they have to trumpet startling figures of "crisis" proportions. In this realization they are no different from those equally zealous partisans of other causes. This is the way the policy game is played, and in making this observation, I do not mean to detract from the seriousness of the activists' intentions, nor from their sincere belief in the pervasiveness of sexual harassment in the workplace. When conservatives cast doubt on the feminists' numbers, they likewise have a political motive: to rein in the activists, to defend traditional office flirtations, to limit employer liability to sexual harassment suits.

Polls on the extent of sexual harassment lead to the conclusion that women in overwhelming numbers are the victims of workplace sexual predators:

- A poll by the *Albuquerque Tribune* found that nearly 80 percent of the respondents reported that they or someone they knew had been the victim of sexual harassment.
- The United States Merit Systems Protection Board, in a study commissioned by Congress, found that 42 percent of women (and 14 percent of men) working for the federal government had experienced a form of unwanted sexual attention between 1985 and 1987, with unwanted sexual teasing identified as the most prevalent form. ("Sexual" 1987)
- A Defense Department survey found that 62 percent of women in the military (and 17 percent of men) suffered "uninvited and unwanted sex-

ual attention" within the previous year compared to 40 percent of female civilian federal employees. (Lancaster 1992)

- A *New York Times*/CBS News poll found that 38 percent of women had been the "object of sexual advances, propositions, or unwanted sexual discussion" from men, while 53 percent of men reported that at some time in their careers they had said or done something that could have been construed as sexual harassment.

- A study of the workforce in Los Angeles found that 54 percent of the women interviewed had experienced what they considered acts of sexual harassment, including 7.6 percent who complained that sex was expected of them as a condition of their job. (Gutek 1985)

- The American Astronomical Society found that of the 250 women members of the association who responded to a survey, 70 percent reported that they had experienced sexual discrimination or harassment sometime in their careers, with 42 percent having experienced verbal harassment. (McDonald 1991)

- A *Washington Post*/ABC News poll conducted about a year after the Hill/Thomas hearings found that 32 percent of women had been sexually harassed, compared with only 23 percent who had reported having been harassed in October 1991; 85 percent of men and women said that sexual harassment was a problem in the workplace, up from 74 percent in the immediate aftermath of the hearings. (Morin 1992)

- An International Labor Organization report covering twenty-three countries found that sexual harassment is a worldwide problem. (Abrams 1993)

The activists deploy these studies, usually without any caveats about the parameters of the concept of sexual harassment employed in each study. For example, Professor Anita Hill herself remarked that "statistics show that anywhere from forty-two to ninety percent of women will experience some form of harassment during their working lives" (Hill 1992: 1445). In the wake of Anita Hill's charges, filings of sexual harassment complaints with the EEOC increased by over 50 percent for the first half of 1992 as compared to the same period the year before. Commentators attribute the increase to a heightened awareness of sexual harassment as a result of the Hill/Thomas hearings, rather than a proliferation of harassment itself (Gross 1992).

There do exist, however, polling results that cast some doubt on the extent and severity of sexual harassment in the workplace. A poll of 1,026 men and women conducted by the Roper Organization in December 1991 (some two months after the Anita Hill accusations) found that 51 percent of the respondents said there was no sexual harassment at their own place of employment, and 22 percent said there was "not much." Sixty-one percent said they were completely satisfied and 23 percent mostly satisfied with the way their employer "is dealing with the issue of sexual harassment in the workplace." Only 6 percent said they were totally dissatisfied or "not too satisfied." The responses of men and women were almost identical ("Current Developments" 1992).

Conservative opinion tends to be highly skeptical of the polls that show high rates of prevalence and widespread concern about sexual harassment. For example, *Forbes* Senior Editor Gretchen Morgenson, writing shortly after the Hill/Thomas showdown, argued that sexual harassment is not the ever-present, costly problem that the activists perceive, rather it is "largely a product of hype and hysteria." The Supreme Court's *Meritor v. Vinson* decision, she argued, is little more than an "employment act for sex harassment consultants." Doubting the activists' argument that private tort suits emerging from sexual harassment incidents have proliferated, she cites a study by a San Francisco law firm that found only fifteen cases litigated to a verdict in California from 1984 to 1989 (Morgenson 1991). She also mentions the opinion of Ralph H. Baxter, Jr., management cochairman of the American Bar Association's Labor Law Committee on Employee Rights and Responsibilities, who believes that the number of private sexual harassment suits filed each year is greatly exaggerated by the activists.

Morgenson doubts the activists' argument that women complain about only a tiny percentage (the usual figure quoted is between 5 and 10 percent) of sexual harassment episodes. Why then, she asks, did the New York State Human Rights Commission dismiss "for no probable cause" almost two-thirds of the complaints it received over a five-year period? She means to imply by this that incidents that women do not complain about are neither legion in number nor egregious in character. For Morgenson, the future on the sexual harassment battleground looks bright: she predicts that by the year 2000, when the Bureau of Labor Statistics estimates that men will only outnumber women in the workplace by some seven million workers, harassment will dissipate. More women will be in positions of authority, and more departments will hit a threshold of 30 percent women, at which point she states, sexual harassment "goes away."

For activists who define sexual harassment in the broadest terms, the natural tendency is to credit those studies that find it a rampant and growing problem throughout society. Conversely, conservatives who adhere to a much narrower definition of sexual harassment tend to believe research that flags a much diminished problem and one that is much nearer to eradication. Thus, problem definition unmistakably colors one's perspective on the extent and severity of sexual harassment.

SOLUTIONS

Just as problem definition dictates one's judgment of the pervasiveness of sexual harassment, it likewise directs the two camps to markedly different solutions. Activists champion the proliferation of consulting groups to educate employees on the issue and to assist companies in fashioning and implementing sexual harassment policies. Following the Supreme Court's decision in *Meritor v. Vinson* in 1986, in which the Court said that employers may limit their liability by having such policies in force and tailoring a suitable enforcement mechanism, consulting firms flocked to accommodate companies' newly found interest in sexual harassment. Estimates are that three out of four companies now have such policies in place.

On the legal front, the activists endorse an updated standard of reasonableness in assessing sexual harassment, one no longer based on the traditional tort standard of the "reasonable man," but instead on a "reasonable woman." They argue that what should count in court is the sensitivity of an average woman, rather than what a male judge or juror might find acceptable. Recently, both the Ninth Circuit Court of Appeals at San Francisco and a Florida federal district court endorsed this "reasonable woman" standard (*Ellison v. Brady* 1991; *Robinson v. Jacksonville Shipyards* 1991). In the same spirit, activists endorsed the provisions of the Civil Rights Act of 1991 that made the legal landscape more appealing for plaintiffs by providing for jury trials and compensatory and punitive damages, and they are working for the abolition of the $300,000 cap that this legislation placed on monetary damages in sexual harassment suits. They favor, too, allowing class action suits (*Jenson v. Eveleth* 1991) and the extension of employer liability to instances in which third parties sexually harass the employer's workers during the course of business.

Predictably, the conservative skeptics disapprove of these legal trends towards expanding the scope and remedies for sexual harassment suits. Their instincts run in the opposite direction: narrowing the scope of sexual harassment to the classic quid pro quo scenario, thus limiting employer liability. As for the "reasonable woman" standard championed by the activists, one critic wrote that what is really meant is "the response of the pathologically neurotic woman" (Amiel 1991: 15). Since they surmise that the problem is greatly exaggerated, the concept ill-defined and much too encompassing, they resisted the expansion of remedies in the 1991 Civil Rights Act. That is one reason why the cap was imposed, as a compromise to get the bill passed and secure President Bush's signature. Some conservatives, as we have seen, expect that demographic changes in the near future will greatly diminish a problem whose extent and severity they doubt in the first place.

CONCLUSION

As we have seen, problem definition plays a decisive role in how both partisans and critics conceptualize sexual harassment, how they assess its scope and severity, and how they fashion their competing solutions to the problem. Activists defined sexual harassment in broad, sweeping terms, capturing under its banner everything from quid pro quo demands for sexual favors to sexist jokes and pin-ups. Even more extreme partisans include rape within sexual harassment's purview. Naturally, then, activists—as with any policy issue—trumpet sexual harassment's magnitude and proliferation throughout society, and they endorse appropriately dramatic remedies, both legal and social. Men, they think, need to be reformed, consultants need to be hired, films and workshops on sexual harassment must be attended. Critics define sexual harassment much more narrowly, usually to quid pro quo with, for some, inclusion of only the most outrageous hostile environment scenarios. As they look at society through this narrowed lens, they find sexual harassment far from rampant, and dwindling through natural demographic changes. Quite logically, their proposed solutions range in the opposite direction from those of the enthusiasts, preferring to circumscribe the legal definition of sexual harassment, limit rather than extend employer liability, and, more generally, diffuse what they see as the hysteria that has built up around this issue.

In the ascension of sexual harassment onto the national policy stage, we discovered the importance of having a "postergirl for sexual harassment," as one of Anita Hill's detractors called her. Putting it less tendentiously, a policy issue, in order to emerge from a throng of competitors, needs a crystallizing moment: a dramatic incident, a catastrophe of some kind, or perhaps a scandal, that causes the national media spotlight to shine upon it. In the immediate aftermath of this initial earthquake, it helps immensely if other aftershocks of a lesser but still compelling nature ensue in order to refocus media attention on the issue and trigger recollections and reflections on the original incident. Sexual harassment, we found, enjoyed two other advantages that most competitors might not: it benefitted from synergy with related shocking events, particularly two date rape trials involving prominent individuals; and it titillated the public, ever attentive to salacious gossip about people in high places.

Generalizing from these findings on sexual harassment to other policy issues must be undertaken with extreme caution. However, commentators on other issues might look for the phenomenon of the *tsunami* (or the earthquake, depending on one's preference for one analogy or the other) followed by lesser waves (or aftershocks). It would be interesting to see whether this pattern that we observed with sexual harassment's ascendancy can be found in the rise of other issues to the national agenda. It would be interesting, also, to see whether other issues exhibit such a strong relationship between problem definition and assessments of pervasiveness. Sexual harassment seems to be one of those issues, like abortion or permitting homosexuals in the military, about which opinion tends to be dichotomized, and in which rapprochement—reaching some middle ground—is particularly difficult.

REFERENCES

Abrams, J. 1993. "Harassment Is a Problem around World." *Blade,* January 10, p. 2.

Amiel, B. 1991. "Senatorial Harassment." *National Review,* November 4, pp. 14–15.

Barr, S. 1992. "Packwood Seeks Probe of Conduct." *Washington Post,* November 28, pp. A1, A12.

Boot, W. 1992. "The Clarence Thomas Hearings." *Columbia Journalism Review* 30 (January–February): 25–29.

Borges, R. 1991. "Herald Writer Olson Sues Patriots, Leaves City." *Boston Globe,* April 26, p. 1.

Bundy v. Jackson, 641 F.2d 934 (1981).

Chemerinsky, E. 1992. "October Tragedy." *Southern California Law Review* 65: 1497–1516.

Chronicle of Higher Education. 1992. "Stanford Said to Ask Physician to Quit Neurosurgery Post." March 4, pp. A17, A18.

Civil Rights Act of 1991, Title 1, Sec. 102(b).

Cropsey, S. 1992. "Tailhook: Let the Military Discipline Its Own." *Washington Post,* October 20, p. A19.

"Current Developments." 1992. *Daily Labor Report* 58 (March 25): A7–A8.

Dziech, B., and L. Weiner. 1990. *The Lecherous Professor: Sexual Harassment on Campus.* 2d ed. Urbana: University of Illinois Press.

EEOC Policy Guide on Compensatory and Punitive Damages under 1991 Civil Rights Act. July 7, 1992.

Egan, T. 1993. "Harsh Homecoming for Senator Accused of Harassment." *New York Times,* January 29, p. A6.

Ellison v. Brady, 924 F.2d 872 (CA 9 1991).

Etzioni, A. 1992/93. "Sexual Harassment, Second Degree." *Responsive Community* 3 (Winter): 54–56.

Farley, L. 1978. *Sexual Shakedown: The Sexual Harassment of Women on the Job.* New York: McGraw-Hill.

Gigot, P. 1991. "Scandal Machine May, at Last, Have Gone Too Far." *Wall Street Journal,* October 11, p. A8.

Graves, F., and C. Shepard. 1992. "Packwood Accused of Sexual Advances." *Washington Post,* November 22, p. A1.

Gross, J. 1992. "Suffering in Silence No More: Fighting Sexual Harassment." *New York Times,* July 13, p. A1.

Guidelines on Discrimination Because of Sex. 1980. Equal Employment Opportunity Commission, 29 CFR Sec. 1604.11, p. 921–931.

Gutek, B. 1985. *Sex and the Workplace.* San Francisco: Jossey-Bass.

Hertzberg, H. 1991. "What a Whopper." *New Republic,* November 4, p. 42.

Hill, A. 1992. "Sexual Harassment: The Nature of the Beast." *Southern California Law Review* 65: 1445–1449.

Jenson v. Eveleth Taconite Co., 139 F.R.D. 657 (1991).

Kolbert, E. 1991. "Most in National Survey Say Judge Is More Believable." *New York Times,* October 15, pp. A1, A20.

Koven, L., and R. St. John. 1992. "Sexual Assault at Stanford: Who Defines It, and What Are the Implications for Student Life?" *Stanford Review*, pp. 4–5. (Reporting on a lecture by C. MacKinnon.)

Lancaster, J. 1992. "The Sex Life of the Navy: After 'Tailhook' Scandal, an Attempt to Reform." *Washington Post*, May 17, pp. C1, C2.

Leibman, A. 1992. "Doubting Thomas: Sexual Harassment Truth or Consequences." *Southern California Law Review* 65: 1441–1444.

Lyall, S. 1993. "2 Men Apologize for Harassment." *New York Times*, January 14, p. B8.

MacKinnon, C. 1979. *Sexual Harassment of Working Women: A Case of Sex Discrimination*. New Haven, Conn.: Yale University Press.

McDonald, K. 1991. "Many Female Astronomers Say They Face Sex Harassment and Bias." *Chronicle of Higher Education*, February 13, p. A11.

Meritor Savings Bank v. Vinson, 477 U.S. 57 (1986).

Morgenson, G. 1991. "May I Have the Pleasure. . ." *National Review*, November 18, p. 36.

Morin, R. 1992. "Consensus on Harassment Grows." *Evening Bulletin*, December 18, p. 1.

National Review. 1991. "Senatorial Harassment." November 4, p. 12.

New Republic. 1991. "Mr. Thomas Goes A-Courting." October 28, pp. 7–8.

New Republic. 1992. "Resign, Bob Packwood." December 21, p. 7.

New York Times. 1991. "Prof. Anita F. Hill: 'I Felt That I Had to Tell the Truth.'" October 12, p. 11.

New York Times. 1992. "Sexual Harassment in the Senate." November 24, p. A14.

Note. 1984. "Sexual Harassment Claims of Abusive Work Environment under Title VII." *Harvard Law Review* 97: 1449–1467.

Paul, E. 1990. "Sexual Harassment as Sex Discrimination." *Yale Law and Policy Review* 8: 333–365.

Phelps, T., and H. Winternitz. 1992. *Capitol Games: Clarence Thomas, Anita Hill, and the Story of a Supreme Court Nomination*. Westport, Conn.: Hyperion Press.

Pianin, E., and F. Graves. 1992. "Senate Urged to Probe Packwood Allegations." *Washington Post*, November 24, pp. A1, A14.

Puddington, A. 1992. "Clarence Thomas and the Blacks." *Commentary* 93: 28–33.

Reed, I. 1992. "Feminists v. Thomas." *Washington Post*, October 18, p. C1.

Reinhardt, S. 1992. "The End of the Age of Ignorance." *Southern California Law Review* 65: 1431–1439.

Reuter's transcript. 1991. "Judge Clarence Thomas: 'My Name Has Been Harmed.'" *New York Times*, October 12, pp. 10, 14.

Robinson v. Jacksonville Shipyards, 760 F.Supp. 1486 (PC MFla 1991).

Roe v. Wade, 410 U.S. 113 (1973).

Schmitt, E. 1992. "Senior Navy Officers Suppressed Sex Investigation, Pentagon Says." *New York Times*, September 25, p. 1.

"Sexual Harassment of Federal Workers: An Update." 1987. U.S. Merit Systems Protection Board.

Schiffren, L. 1992. "Sexual Politics, the Real Thing." *New York Times*, December 2, p. A23.

Smith, L. 1992. "Groups Seek Ethics Probe of Packwood." *Washington Post*, November 25, p. A4.

Smolowe, J. 1992. "Politics: The Feminist Machine." *Time*, May 4, pp. 34–36.

Sontag, D. 1992. "City Hall Sex: 'So Why Am I Here? Because My Character Is Up for Grabs.'" *New York Times*, November 8, p. 22.

Spencer, C. 1991. "The Chronology of the Clarence Thomas Confirmation." *Black Scholar* 22: 1–3.

Tushnet, M. 1992. "The Degradation of Constitutional Discourse." *Georgetown Law Review* 81: 251–311.

Wall Street Journal. 1991. "The Anita Hill Chronology." October 10, p. A14.

Wall Street Journal. 1992. "Conduct Unbecoming." July 7, p. A14.

Washington Post. 1991. "State Abortion-Rights Group Undecided about Packwood." July 7, p. A17.

Williams v. Saxbe, 413 F.Supp. 654 (D.D.C. 1976).

5

Paradoxes of National Antidrug Policymaking

Elaine B. Sharp

To the casual observer, it may seem that we are waging an endless battle against drugs. The contemporary war on drugs, initiated in the early years of the Reagan administration, would certainly give such an impression. It has occupied much of the 1980s and, in the hands of the Bush administration, continued into the 1990s. This war on drugs has featured unprecedented uses of the U.S. military for drug interdiction purposes; the creation of a network of regional task forces (beginning with one in south Florida in 1982) designed to concentrate federal, state, and local arresting and case-making resources; televised, prime-time addresses from the Oval Office focused exclusively on the drug problem; the spread of drug education and substance abuse prevention programs throughout America's schools; new laws empowering the government to seize assets of alleged drug traffickers and to deny bail to such individuals; the clogging of the American criminal justice system with drug-related cases; and much more.

In fact, dramatic as it seems, the contemporary war on drugs is simply the latest of a number of episodes of policymaking directed at one version or another of "the drug problem." Drug policymaking in this country dates from the Harrison Narcotics Act of 1914, which created a special tax on producers, importers, and manufacturers of opium and coca products and required that all who sold these products register with the local internal revenue office and pay the tax. Aggressive enforcement of this act, including Treasury Department crackdowns on physicians who were prescribing regular doses of drugs to addicted patients, constitutes the first "war on drugs" in the United States (Trebach 1982: 120–125).

The drug issue has reemerged several times since. In the 1930s, for example, Harry Anslinger, head of the Bureau of Narcotics and Dangerous Drugs within the Treasury Department, pressed for passage of legislation to effectively outlaw marijuana use by imposing extremely high taxes on marijuana sales. Using scare tactics, such as claims that marijuana use could cause people to become violently aggressive and crime prone, Anslinger effectively spearheaded the campaign that resulted in the passage in 1937 of the Marihuana Tax Act (McWilliams 1990: 70). In the 1950s, Anslinger was instrumental twice more in raising the drug issue to prominence, leading to the passage of the Boggs Act of 1951, which increased the severity of penalties for drug law violations, and the Narcotics Control Act of 1956, which established still more severe penalties. For example, suspended sentences and probation were ruled out for drug violators, and the death penalty was permitted for those convicted of selling heroin to minors (McWilliams 1990: 116).

The Nixon administration featured a dramatic "war on drugs" focused on heroin use. In that episode, the electoral imperatives facing Nixon, who had been elected on a "law and order" platform, led to a search for a dramatic gesture that could allow for credit-claiming on the law and order front. Discovery that heroin addicts could be maintained on stable doses of the experimental drug methadone provided an irresistible opportunity for Nixon staffers. The result was a campaign designed to introduce this "magic bullet" solution after initially raising public alarm about the dangers of heroin abuse, in part through publicity about the drug use of returning Vietnam veterans (Epstein 1977). Introduction of a major federal treatment initiative focused on methadone maintenance, combined with enhanced drug law enforcement measures, constituted Nixon's war on drugs (Epstein 1977: 123–137).

In the later 1970s, the Carter administration called attention to abuse of prescription drugs, emphasized the need for research on legitimate medical uses of illicit drugs, and, most importantly, began an initiative to decriminalize possession of marijuana in small amounts. These efforts to reorient drug policy were extremely short-lived, in part because the president's health policy adviser, Peter Bourne, had to step down after reports that he had written a prescription for a staff member under a fictitious name and rumors of cocaine use at a Washington party destroyed his credibility (Anderson 1981: 21–22; Trebach 1982: 240).

These various episodes hint at the continuity and change in the definition of the drug problem in this country as drugs have repeatedly come onto the governmental agenda, the public agenda, or both during the twentieth century. In a number of ways, the Reagan/Bush episode of drug policy is simply a continuation of that pattern. But the history of the drug issue in the 1980s and early 1990s is characterized by two especially intriguing features—the length of the issue attention cycle and the disjunction between popular and governmental attention to the issue on the one hand and objective indicators of problem severity on the other. In this chapter I will consider these twin peculiarities of the contemporary version of "the drug problem" and attempt to show how important concepts of problem definition make these peculiarities understandable.

THE CONTEMPORARY WAR ON DRUGS:
THE PECULIARITIES

Students of problem definition and agenda setting have long agreed that "problems" or "issues" have a distinctly limited life. This is so because of the plethora of matters competing for the attention of the public and for space on the governmental agenda, because of the limited capacity of the governmental agenda, and because the public readily loses interest in issues, especially those that seem irresolvable. Thus concepts such as "issue saturation" (Hilgartner and Bosk 1988) and the "issue attention cycle" (Downs 1973) are key themes in the study of problem definition. In the normal course of events, issues are expected to fade quickly from the scene as citizens become saturated with coverage of them and as political opportunities for capitalizing upon them elapse.

From this perspective, contemporary experience with the drug issue is notable for its longevity. This can be illustrated by examining empirical evidence of both popular attention to the drug issue and of the presence of drugs on the governmental agenda. Throughout the 1980s there was an escalation in popular concern with drugs, beginning with a gradual increase in media attention in the early 1980s followed by a dramatic upswing in both media attention and mass public concern, as evidenced by a surge in articles on drugs in popular magazines and increasing numbers of Gallup Poll respondents indicating that drugs are the most important problem facing the country (see Figure 5.1). By contrast, the life cycle of the drug issue during President Nixon's "war on drugs" better approximated standard expectations concerning issue attention cycles. That episode of popular attention was limited to three years.

Evidence of the drug issue on the governmental agenda also illustrates its comparative longevity in the contemporary phase (Figure 5.2). After Nixon's relatively brief but dramatic war on drugs and the even briefer round of attention to the issue in the Carter administration, governmental attention to the issue reached a low point in 1980, as evidenced by the number of congressional hearings relating to drugs and the number of presidential mentions of drugs in *New York Times*-indexed coverage of the president. For the entire decade after that, however, congressional and presidential attention to the issue ratcheted upward.

In short, the drug issue has rarely in the last twenty years been completely out of sight. But after two episodes that approximate the notion of an abbreviated issue attention cycle, the latest episode of concern and policymak-

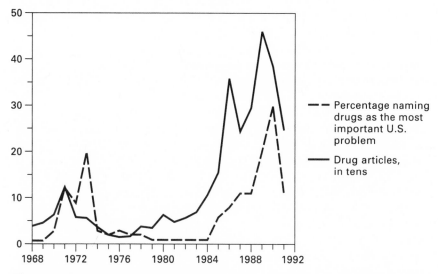

Figure 5.1. Drugs on the Popular Agenda

Sources: Gallup Poll and the author's original coding of relevant years of the *Reader's Guide to Periodical Literature;* reprinted from Elaine B. Sharp, *The Dilemma of Drug Policy in the United States* (New York: HarperCollins, 1994), p. 15.

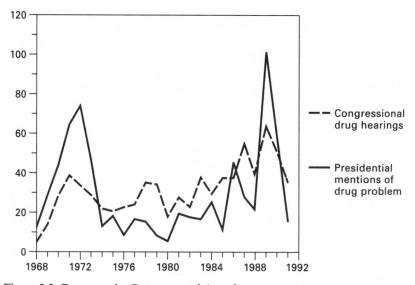

Figure 5.2. Drugs on the Governmental Agenda

Source: Author's original coding of hearings using Congressional Information Service on compact disc and the *New York Times Index* for the years represented; reprinted from Elaine B. Sharp, *The Dilemma of Drug Policy in the United States* (New York: HarperCollins, 1994), p. 36.

ing about drugs shows that the issue has achieved a level of staying power that belies notions of an attenuated life-span on the agenda.

Ironically, escalating attention to the drug issue has corresponded with declining drug use, at least as evidenced by some official indicators. Measuring the "actual" scope of drug use or abuse is fraught with difficulty. In response to our knowledge gap on this matter, the National Institute on Drug Abuse established in the early 1970s a program of survey research designed to monitor trends in drug use. This effort consists of an annual survey of a random sample of high school seniors and a nationwide survey of a representative sample of households, conducted every two or three years since 1972. Both surveys show substantially the same thing—that from a high point in 1979 there has been a steady and dramatic decline in reported use of illicit drugs. For 18-to-25-year-olds in the household survey, for example, marijuana use has been halved since 1979, cocaine use has declined by more than 50 percent, and hallucinogens, never used even experimentally by more than 10 percent of young adults, are now used by negligible numbers.

Of course, these survey results can be and have been roundly criticized as invalid indicators of the "real" scope of illicit drug use in America. Alternative indicators, such as information on the price and purity level of street drugs or on drug-related hospital emergency cases, seem to contradict the reassuring findings in the survey data and to suggest a surge in the drug problem in the mid to late 1980s (NNICC 1988: 7 and 27).

Still other critics might argue that survey research on levels of illicit drug use misses the point—that the real drug problem is not simply one of illicit drug use by individuals accessible to survey research but the violence and social disruption that stem from the trafficking of drugs, or the lost productivity that results from the abuse of either illicit drugs or legal drugs such as alcohol, or the family tragedies that result from heavy drug use by one family member, or the societal tragedies that crack babies represent. Numerous other images and interpretations of the drug problem can be offered. And this variety in definitions of the problem offers the first important clue to the durability of the drug issue.

As Hilgartner and Bosk (1988: 63) argue, issues fade from view when they become saturated. Saturation occurs when a large number of issue entrepreneurs "simultaneously elect to produce material on a particular problem, thus flooding the public arenas with redundant messages and driving down their dramatic value." As a result, editors, researchers, politicians, talk show hosts, and other opinion leaders begin to look for new topics, and the saturated issue loses its privileged place of attention. However, an issue can be saved from saturation if it can be transformed in a way that sustains its novelty and hence its dramatic value. That is, if a problem can be recast or repackaged in a different light, it can continue to capture attention.

Although it is important to acknowledge, as Rochefort and Cobb in this volume have, that problem conceptions are, in this sense, malleable, they are neither infinitely malleable nor equally malleable. Some issue areas have characteristics that are particularly amenable to issue transformation, while others do not. In the following section I will consider what some of these characteristics might be and the role they have played in transformation of the drug issue.

Of course, objective conditions and new social phenomena such as crack babies do not automatically constitute themselves into new and compelling versions of social problems. Such new versions of a problem must be constructed by issue entrepreneurs with a stake in keeping popular attention focused on the core problem that is being transformed. Just as some problems are likely to be more amenable to issue transformation than others, so are there likely to be differences in the propensity of a network of policy specialists to seek continuing popular attention. Popular attention to a problem is not, after all, invariably an advantage. As scholars of interest groups have long noted, powerful "iron triangles" composed of congressional subcommittees, bureaucratic agencies, and interest groups linked to a particular policy area, which once controlled policy formation and implementation, sustained their power largely through their ability to function in a closed fashion, with little public visibility or public attention to the functioning of the group.

In short, durability of an issue on the popular agenda requires, on the one hand, problem characteristics that readily lend themselves to issue transformation and hence to novelty and, on the other hand, political actors with a stake in sustaining public attention to a problem. The following sections outline the characteristics that have been important in ensuring novelty of the drug problem and the features of the drug policy issue network that ensure there will be individuals with stakes in maintaining issue visibility.

CHARACTERISTICS OF THE DRUG ISSUE

Dramatic Potential

One key to the durability of the drug issue is its dramatic character. As Downs argues (1973: 41), problems tend to fade from the scene if they have no intrinsically exciting qualities, or if they lose those qualities when nightly news coverage of the problem ceases. Similarly, Hilgartner and Bosk (1988: 61) emphasize the importance of drama in problem definition.

Virtually any problem might be viewed as having some dramatic potential. For example, while agricultural issues might seem less than exciting to many Americans, the economic problems of the small family-owned farm were given considerable drama in the late 1970s and early 1980s as the American Agricultural Movement staged tractorcades on Washington and films featuring the desperate struggles of the small farmer were developed in Hollywood. The drug problem, however, is inherently and highly dramatic. News editors, congressional hearings convenors, and movie makers have their choice of dramatic angles, including the activities of undercover narcotics officers and drug traffickers in the cities of America, the military drama and international intrigue of U.S. antidrug efforts in Central and South America, the alien yet fascinating world of crack houses, and much more. Each of these varied images of the drug problem has substantial dramatic value; taken as a set, they provide such a range of tragedy, excitement, and life-threatening episodes that audience interest can be maintained over long periods.

The inherent drama of the drug issue means that a wide variety of incidents can serve as "triggering events"—that is, those occurrences that galvanize attention and provide instant raw material for those who would characterize a topical area as a crisis. The cocaine-related death of basketball star Len Bias in 1986 is the classic example of such a triggering event, but the drug issue is littered with many others as well. The introduction of two new terms into American parlance—"drive-by shootings" and "crack babies" suggests two of these.

Proximity

One reason for the dramatic potential of the drug issue is the personal relevance of the topic to so many individuals, or what Rochefort and Cobb call "proximity." Objectively speaking, it might seem that drugs are not personally relevant to that many Americans. If the data reported from the surveys of the National Institute on Drug Abuse are even close to accurate, drug use, and especially regular drug use, is a matter for a very small minority of Americans; presumably an even smaller percentage are seriously addicted. The situation would seem to fit one of Downs's (1973: 41) specifications for an issue that will suffer from a short attention cycle: "The number of persons suffering from each of these ills is very large *absolutely*—in the millions. But the numbers are small relatively—usually less than 15 percent of the entire population."

However, the drug topic is personally relevant to many individuals despite the fact that relatively small numbers of individuals abuse drugs, have family members abusing drugs or caught up in the world of drug trafficking, or are exposed to the dangers of urban crossfire in drug trafficking zones. Proximity, or personal relevance, derives not just from objective exposure to the problem but from the salience and centrality of the values that are embodied in a problem topic. With respect to drugs, a wide variety of core values are at stake. The drug issue can be characterized as touching upon one's children's health, personal safety in the streets, and the moral fabric of society, among others. Because such core values are involved, the topic of drugs is highly proximal to the personal lives of individuals.

Novelty

Perhaps more important than its inherent dramatic value is the fact that the drug problem lends itself to transformation, and hence to novelty. Transformability is enhanced by the complex and contradictory nature of the problem. This is evident when one considers a feature of problem description already highlighted by Rochefort and Cobb—the characteristics of the problem population. With respect to drugs, there has not been a single problem population. Instead, two competing images of the problem population have moved into and out of prominence. Consistent with Musto's (1973) interpretation, the drug problem has most often been defined in terms of the threat posed by the drug use of groups, such as racial and ethnic minorities, who were already viewed as among the "dangerous classes." This tradition includes early views of the drug problem as the use of opium by Chinese and the spreading fear that cocaine use would energize blacks to rebel against white society's restrictions on them (Musto 1973: 5–8). The Nixon administration's association of the drug problem with returning Vietnam vets, who were disproportionately black and tainted by their involvement in a war that had generated images such as that of the My Lai massacre, was a continuation of this theme.

However, such "dangerous classes" are not the only problem population that has served to define the drug problem. The sustained novelty of the drug issue arose in part because it has alternated between this view and a second view that defines the problem in terms of the corruption of mainstream American youth. From this point of view, the real problem is the fact that young people, who tend to be experimental and rebellious, will be drawn into activities such as marijuana use that are gateways for an inevitable slide into harder drug use and ruined lives. In the 1970s, such a changed image of drug users led to the "embourgeoisment" of the drug problem and hence opened the way for the topic of decriminalization of marijuana on the agendas of state legislatures across America (Himmelstein 1983: 98–120).

Thus, differing definitions of the drug problem hinge on two different problem populations, with contrasting characteristics (Rochefort and Cobb, this volume). On one hand, the drug users are strange, threatening, and undeserving of sympathy; on the other hand, drug users are the most familiar, sympathetic, and deserving characters of all—our children. For much of the history of the drug issue, alternate definitions of the problem based on alternating emphases on each of these problem populations have coexisted. Although these alternate problem definitions compete with each other, they also reinforce each other by allowing for novelty in media coverage, thus reducing the chance that the issue will become boring.

Equally important for understanding the length of the issue attention cycle for drugs is the variety in the causal stories that can be used to define the drug problem. As Stone (1989) persuasively argues, political actors use causal stories in a process of strategic image-making for their focal issue. Depending upon the goals of the political actor, a matter might be characterized as (1) an accident, (2) the intentional outcome of purposeful action, (3) an inadvertent result of purposeful action, or (4) an intended but mechanical consequence of unguided forces. Stone is primarily concerned with the ways in which these different causal theories can shape policy outcomes and hence in how political actors struggle to push the problem definition from one category to another. But her typology of causal theories suggests something else as well. If a particular matter is readily definable in several of these categories, it is likely to have a longer halflife on the policy agenda. This is so for two reasons. On the one hand, the varying images of the problem help to prevent issue saturation for the mass public. On the other hand, an issue with good prospects for image transformation will attract a larger number of political players, many of whom will have a stake in a competing interpretation of the problem and hence a stake in preventing the matter from fading into settled policy.

An examination of the contemporary history of the drug issue shows precisely this process. Perhaps the dominant causal story about drugs is one of "intentional cause." That is, the drug problem is characterized as one of evil drug traffickers intentionally perpetuating and extending drug consumption for purpose of maximizing their own profits. In the most basic version of this scenario, drug users and society in general are victims and drug traffickers are villains. The resulting criminal model defines the problem as one requiring law enforcement responses to catch villains and mete out suitably stiff penalties. During the Reagan administration, the intentional cause explanation was extended to include adult drug users as villains rather than victims. Addressing a White House conference on drugs in 1988, First Lady Nancy Reagan clearly articulates this causal story:

> The casual user may think when he takes a line of cocaine or smokes a joint in the privacy of his nice condo, listening to his expensive stereo, that he's somehow not bothering anyone. But there is a trail of death and destruction that leads directly to his door. The casual user cannot morally escape responsibility for the action of drug traffickers and dealings. I'm saying that if you're a casual drug user you're an accomplice to murder. (*Public Papers of the Presidents* 1990: 269)

This dominant image of the drug problem has been challenged regularly by an alternate view, frequently referred to as the medical model of the drug problem. Proponents of this problem definition emphasize that drug abuse is a disease requiring treatment. From this perspective, it is not helpful to blame drug abuse on anyone. Because of the difficulties of the human condition and inevitable human frailties in dealing with those difficulties, it is inevitable that some will succumb to the psychoactive alternative. Note that this problem definition moves drugs from the realm of intentional cause to the realm that Stone calls accidental cause, that is, a realm of natural events that are neither intended nor purposefully guided.

Proponents of drug abuse prevention programming have also made use of this problem definition. Contemporary drug abuse prevention programs such as Project DARE are based upon the work of a group of University of Houston researchers who, in the late 1970s, promulgated a theory of "psychological inoculation." According to this theory, people are regularly exposed to societal pressures for substance abuse, just as they are exposed to disease-causing germs. Consequently, they must be "inoculated" through exposure to artificial versions of these societal pressures, so that they can build resistance to the "disease" of substance abuse (Botvin 1990). The result, in programs such as Project DARE, is "resistance skills training" consisting of exercises that help students cope with stress, identify situations in which there will be peer pressures for drug or alcohol use, and practice effective responses to those situations.

Much of the history of drug abuse policy consists of an interplay between the two causal theories articulated so far—the criminal model of intentional cause and the medical model of accidental or natural cause. Although the criminal model has been by far the more dominant problem definition, the existence of the medical interpretation has been an important factor in keeping drugs on the agenda, both because of the institutionalized interests (treatment professionals, education and prevention specialists) that have rallied around that definition and because the medical alternative offers competing images of the drug problem that prevent popular boredom with the issue. The news media and the entertainment industry can develop stories of lives ruined or of families rallying to overcome a member's substance abuse problem as well as stories of high-level trafficking and undercover policing.

If this interplay were not enough, there is yet a third problem definition, based upon a causal theory that Stone calls "inadvertent cause." Causal stories in this realm emphasize unintended consequences of purposeful action. With respect to drug policy, the relatively small but vocal set of participants who have been pressing for legalization of drugs base their definition of the problem upon just such a causal theory. From this perspective, the "real" drug problem is the illegal status of drugs and the set of unintended side effects that this inevitably yields. Making drugs illegal creates a black market for drugs, and in this black market drug prices and profits are much higher than they would be in a legal market. Consequently, the attractiveness of drug trafficking as an enterprise is enhanced (Ostrowski 1991: 304–305). Furthermore, because drugs are sold in black market transactions, violence, rather than a framework of contract law and other forms of legal protection, constitutes the methodology for enhancing and protecting market share (Glasser 1991: 274). The result is the street violence, such as drive-by shootings of rival crack-dealing gang members, that has helped to destroy the social fabric of many urban neighborhoods. Finally, legalization proponents contend that the illegal status of drugs creates unintended dangers for drug users. Since the purity and dosage of illegal drugs cannot be effectively controlled in the fashion of legal pharmaceuticals, drug users are subjected to unnecessary health risks (Zeese 1991: 260). And, legalization proponents contend, the health risks posed by many drugs, if properly administered, are negligible compared to the substantial direct costs to the user and indirect costs to society that result from the illegal status of the drug. For example, a felony conviction for drug possession can damage an individual's future prospects for legitimate employment and therefore makes a life of crime more likely.

The legalization argument, with its claim that the drug problem is really an inadvertent cause of failed drug control, has been far less influential in problem definition for this issue than has the intentional cause theory of criminal model proponents or the natural cause theory of medical model proponents. Although congressional hearings on drug legalization have been held and although a number of notable individuals have served as spokespersons for legalization, the concept is still outside the mainstream of policy thinking in the United States and viewed as acceptable by only a minority of the public. Despite its fringe status—or perhaps even because of it—the drug legalization perspective has played an important role in keeping the drug issue on the agenda for a sustained period of time. Like the medical model, the legalization argument offers a counter to the dominant, criminal model of the drug problem. The fact that it has little political viability does not necessarily detract from its interest value. Indeed, the radical nature of the drug legalization argument gives it an exotic flavor, which heightens its interest value. As a high school and college debate issue, as a talk show topic, as an occasional discussion piece in the news, and as an argument among the drug policy intelligentsia, legalization is irresistible. Its lack of political viability tends to give the discussion of legalization something of the flavor of a "pseudo-academic and entertainment exercise" (Peterson 1991: 324). But, at the same time, it serves the purpose of keeping the drug issue alive, interesting, and on the agenda.

THE DRUG POLICY ISSUE NETWORK AND PROBLEM DEFINITION

As the preceding sections show, the drug topic has a number of important characteristics that make it less susceptible to a short issue attention cycle than other topics. It has substantial dramatic potential. And it has a high potential for diverse problem definition, and hence for staying power on the agenda, does not automatically mean that the issue will be pursued in that way. Only if there are policy entrepreneurs and groups with appropriate stakes in the issue will the rich raw material of drug problem definition be extensively mined.

Indeed, even if there are groups with substantial stakes in the drug problem, it may *not* be in their interest to attempt to generate sustained popular concern with the problem. There are, in fact, at least two situations in which those with a stake in a particular problem will want to either keep the matter out of the hands of the mass public or divert existing popular concern from the topic. Each of these situations has occurred with respect to the drug problem.

The first situation is a case of symbolic politics. Symbolic politics refers to the powerful dynamic of first raising public concerns about an issue, then offering an apparently effective policy response that assuages public concerns. According to Edelman (1977: 4), this threat-reassurance dynamic plays off of the public's predisposition to be psychologically dependent upon authorities for problem solution:

Knowing that they are often helpless to control their own fate, people resort to religion and to government to cope with anxieties they cannot otherwise ward off. . . . Eagerness to believe that government will ward off evils and threats renders us susceptible to political language that both intensifies and eases anxiety at least as powerfully as the language of religion does.

The initial phase of the threat-reassurance scenario obviously requires that public concern about a problem be mobilized. But in order for symbolic politics to be effective, this phase must be followed by demobilization of concern, as the public is reassured by government action. Even if that action involves only rhetoric rather than the commitment and effective use of resources, reassurance can often be generated. And when such a threat-reassurance scenario is successful, the result is enhanced power and legitimacy for the political authorities that managed the mobilization and demobilization of popular concern. Such is the essence of symbolic politics.

The history of drug policymaking in the United States offers at least one clear example of the deliberate demobilization of popular concern about drugs as part of a threat-reassurance cycle. As noted in the first section of this chapter, the heroin problem was the focal point of an effort by Nixon's domestic policy staff to whip up fears about drugs, which could then be allayed by claims that the government's new commitment to methadone treatment had resolved the crisis. Shortly after his successful reelection bid, Nixon gave a speech in which he claimed that the nation had indeed "turned the corner" on drug addiction. This reassurance rhetoric was followed by further disengagement from the "war on drugs," including dramatically diminished presidential attention to the issue and the end of pressures for budgetary increases for treatment (Goldberg 1980: 42). The threat-reassurance cycle was complete.

Symbolic politics, with its pattern of deliberate defusing of an issue relatively quickly after placing it on the agenda, is fully consistent with the natural shortness of the issue attention cycle. The unusually long period of attention to the drug issue in the 1980s, therefore, cannot be understood in terms of symbolic politics, except perhaps as an instance in which policy entrepreneurs lost control over an attempt at symbolic issue management.

The second situation in which those with substantial stakes in a policy problem wish to keep it off the popular agenda is that of iron triangle policymaking. When a small number of interest groups, in conjunction with specialized administrative agencies and congressional subcommittees, have been able to address a problem in a way that gives them hegemony over a particular problem area, that "subgovernment" will rarely have an interest in mobilizing public concern over the problem area. Instead, any necessary improvements in policy can be quietly handled through incremental adjustments to existing programs. The mobilization of the general public is disadvantageous to such subgovernments, because it might stir alternative problem definitions and the activity of new groups with different stakes in the issue. Avoiding such disruptions to settled policy through controlled, low-visibility negotiation among entrenched interests is the hallmark of iron triangles (Cobb and Elder 1983). Of course, hegemonic subgovernments cannot be maintained indefinitely. In fact, one of the chief developments in U.S. politics over the past 20 years or so has been the demise of established subgovernments as excluded interests have found ways to successfully challenge their dominance (Baumgartner and Jones 1991).

The drug policy domain has witnessed just such a transformation from a closed system of dominance by a very small number of interests representing the criminal model of the problem to a much more differentiated issue network composed of many different organized interests with variegated stakes and problem definitions (Sharp 1991). In particular, a diverse array of organized interests with stakes in the treatment and prevention of drug abuse has emerged to champion the medical model of the drug problem. These include drug treatment experts based at university medical schools, directors of drug treatment programs, and various governmental, private, or nonprofit organizations such as the National Association of Prevention Professionals, the National Association of State Drug Abuse Coordinators, the National Association of City Drug Coordinators, the American Public Health Association, the National Institute on Drug Abuse, the Alcohol, Mental Health, and Drug Abuse Administration, and many more.

There is no evidence that the activation of multiple competing interests in the drug policy area has substantially altered the nation's priorities for dealing with the drug problem. Instead, except for the brief period of Nixon's emphasis on a methadone-focused treatment initiative, drug policy funding at the national level has always been primarily focused on interrupting the supply of drugs through interdiction at the border and enforcement of drug control laws internally, with many fewer resources devoted to interruption of demand through treatment and prevention efforts. If anything, this emphasis on supply-side efforts has intensified in the past decade despite the presence of treatment and prevention interests (Falco 1989: 25–28).

However, the emergence of an issue network has had a substantial impact on the life cycle of the drug issue. It has given the drug problem a seemingly permanent place on the government agenda, and this continuous governmental attention sustains popular concern as well. The nearly constant congressional attention to the drug issue stems not only from the proliferation of organized interests with stakes in challenging the dominance of the criminal model, but also from the fact that there are now so many different venues for proponents of one or another interpretation of the drug problem to air their views. In contrast with the earlier period of subgovernment hegemony, in which subcommittees of the Senate Judiciary Committee or special committees on organized crime were virtually the sole venues for consideration of the drug problem, a diverse array of congressional committees and subcommittees is now engaged in drug policy-related hearings. These include the House Select Committee on Narcotics Abuse and Control, the Senate Committee on Labor and Human Resources, the House Committee on Education and Labor, the House Committee on Interstate and Foreign Commerce, as well as the House and Senate committees on the Judiciary and the House Select Committee on Crime (Sharp 1991).

In one respect, the contemporary pattern of problem definition and policymaking for drugs epitomizes Browne's (1990) description of "issue niches": The policy domain (here, drug policy) is populated with a variety of organized interests, but direct conflict among the groups is rare; instead, such organized interests focus on a narrow band of issues that do not necessarily bring them into direct conflict with other interests on matters of broad relevance to the domain. Even the least powerful of organized interests in a domain have at least some issue terrain in which they are indisputably dominant, and a congressional venue receptive to their stakes in the issue.

What Browne's analysis overlooks, however, are the implications of such issue niches for indirect conflicts that keep an issue alive. The institutionalization of issue niches occupied by organized interests with competing definitions of the drug problem means that drug policymaking is never fully settled. While groups with stakes in treatment or prevention approaches may not directly confront law enforcement interests over central policy issues, they nevertheless have an institutionalized niche from which to press repeatedly and indirectly for changes in the status quo. As Baumgartner and Jones (1991) show, use of the mass media to alter popular images of the issue is a key to such attempts. Meanwhile, organized interests with stakes in the dominant problem definition and the policy status quo are prompted to regularly mount image-management efforts of their own. The result is buffered but institutionalized skirmishing over problem definition—a process that keeps one or more versions of the drug problem constantly on the public agenda.

This institutionalized skirmishing of organized interests is coupled with another form of institutionalized conflict over drugs. By the mid 1980s, partisan conflict over the drug issue had become thoroughly institutionalized. In this regard, it is not surprising that each of the major pieces of drug-related legislation in the 1980s was passed in an election year. Elections in the 1980s became occasions for Republicans to dramatize the drug issue as a means of forcing Democrats' hands for tougher crime legislation, occasions for Democrats to critique the limitations of Reagan administration drug-fighting efforts, and occasions for the parties to joust over the details of comprehensive legislation timed to maximize credit-claiming in election years.

Consistent with Polsby's (1984) arguments about the building of partisan conflict when policy issues incubate over a substantial period of time, this partisan wrangling appears to have increased over the course of the decade. In 1984 and 1986, partisan skirmishing was largely confined to Democrats' critiques of the ineffectual symbolism of Nancy Reagan's "just say no" campaign and partisan one-upmanship over the harshness of provisions in two major pieces of legislation. Thus, in 1984, Congress passed major anticrime legislation (Public Law 98–473), which increased penalties for drug law offenders, created bail and preventive detention requirements that virtually eliminated pretrial release for those accused of drug law violations, and enhanced the government's ability to use forfeiture as a weapon against drug traffickers by permitting officials to seize and keep, without a hearing, assets worth more than $10,000 that were claimed to result from criminal activity (*CQ Almanac* 1984: 216). The Anti-Drug Abuse Act of 1986 again increased penalties for drug trafficking and provided federal grants to states for drug law enforcement and education programs. Although not included in the final bill, the initial provisions, the result of partisan one-upmanship, would have allowed prosecutors some use of illegally seized evidence and established the death penalty for major drug traffickers (Greenhouse 1986: 33).

In 1988, when a comprehensive antidrug bill (Public Law 100–690) was enacted, the influence of a presidential election year was evident. Spokespersons for both parties accused their opponents of inadequate efforts with respect to the drug problem. Presidential candidate Jesse Jackson elevated the drug problem to a very high level of prominence in his campaign, critiquing the Reagan-Bush administration for inadequate funding of treatment, antidrug education, and local law enforcement assistance. In response, George Bush pressed for tougher law enforcement measures for both dealers and users (*CQ Almanac* 1988: 85–86).

Given the high levels of public concern about drugs in 1988 (see Fig. 5.1), neither party could afford to be portrayed as preventing action on the issue. Consequently, despite considerable wrangling, Public Law 100–690 finally cleared Congress in November of 1988 and was signed by the president. That comprehensive legislation contains provisions for a cabinet-level position to coordinate drug policy (the "drug czar"), stiffer penalties for drug dealers, more funding for drug law enforcement, treatment, and education, provisions that would require federally funded institutions to take steps to guarantee that the workplace is drug-free, and provisions that would penalize users of drugs by permitting their ejection from public housing or denial of certain federal benefits to them (*CQ Almanac* 1988: 86–89).

However, the sweeping authorizations in the 1988 legislation did not resolve the question of strategy and priorities, particularly in a time of severe budget constraint. By 1989, when newly elected President Bush announced a major new drug control strategy, partisan conflict over the issue was in full swing. The president's plan, which would have provided funds for the antidrug effort by cutting from existing federal programs, was assailed by Democratic congressmen such as Charles Rangel, Thomas Foley, and George Mitchell as an inadequate, unrealistic, nickle-and-dime effort (Berke 1989: 12). As one commentator noted: "It remains to be seen whether the Democrats will gain any meaningful partisan advantage from the drug war . . . but they are clearly going to try" (Apple 1989: 12). Not surprisingly, then, the drug issue was chronically on the congressional agenda during the Bush administration.

CONCLUSION

There is an important interplay between problem definition and agenda setting. In the case of drugs, important features of problem definition help to account for the presence of the issue on the popular and governmental agendas. However, many of these features, such as the inherent dramatic potential of the drug issue, its proximity to core values, and the novelty that stems from its multiple causal images and problem populations, are generally true of the drug issue. They help to account for the frequency with which drugs have appeared on the agenda since 1914, but do not, in and of themselves, account for the especially long issue attention cycle of the contemporary episode of concern with drugs.

However, the institutional context in which problem definition occurs does provide crucial insights about this. The institutional context for drug problem definition has become a congested policy space filled with a multitude of organized interests having diverse stakes and problem definitions. Furthermore, that policy space includes institutionalized patterns of behavior, such as partisan wrangling over the drug issue and the interjection of drug policymaking into the election cycle.

The result is a scenario that contrasts in an important way with Kingdon's (1984) characterization. In Kingdon's well-known formulation, the policy-making process consists of three separate streams of activity: (1) a problem stream, consisting of the objective circumstances, symbolic interpretations, institutionalized indicators, and crisis events that have the potential to capture attention; (2) a policy stream, consisting of the ideas and initiatives of the interest groups, officials, and experts who constitute policy issue networks; and (3) the political stream, consisting of the partisan and electoral activities of government officials and the resulting balance of organized political forces. "Policy windows," opportunities for attention to a particular problem, occur when there is a convergence of the three streams, either by accident or through the efforts of a policy entrepreneur. Most important, the opening of a policy window is characterized by Kingdon as a relatively rare event, and the duration of such a window of opportunity Kingdon characterizes as quite limited. In this sense, Kingdon extends more basic concepts such as the "issue attention cycle" by emphasizing the importance, and rarity, of occasions in which objective circumstances make an issue ripe for attention and relevant and compelling policy solutions are available from the issue networks concerned about the topic *and* political circumstances are favorable for such initiatives.

In contrast with Kingdon's characterization, the policy window for drugs seems to be chronically open, at least for the past dozen years or so. But the developments traced in this chapter, coupled with Kingdon's analysis, suggest why this might be so. In each of the streams described by Kingdon, the drug problem has become more continuously activated. In the policy stream, for example, we find a proliferation of organized interests, which virtually ensures a constant flow of varied yet expertly based diagnoses and prescriptions concerning the drug problem. In the political stream, we find a variety of issue niches within which these varied organized interests can develop their policy proposals, and we find that partisan conflict over the drug issue has caused it to be regularly attached to the election cycle. Finally, because of inherent features of the drug issue, such as its transformability and dramatic potential, we find that the problem stream is regularly activated by triggering events involving drugs. With respect to the drug issue, then, it is by no means rare for the three streams to be confluent.

REFERENCES

Anderson, P. 1981. *High in America: The True Story behind NORML and the Politics of Marijuana.* New York: Viking Press.

Apple, R.W. 1989. "Short of the Mark." *New York Times*, September 7, p. 12.

Baumgartner, F., and B. D. Jones. 1991. "Agenda Dynamics and Policy Subsystems." *Journal of Politics* 53: 1044–1074.

Berke, R. L. 1989. "Parties Skirmish about Strategy in War on Drugs." *New York Times*, September 7, p. 12.

Botvin, G. J. 1990. "Substance Abuse Prevention: Theory, Practice, and Effectiveness." Pp. 461–520 in *Drugs and Crime*, ed. M. Tonry and J. Q. Wilson. Chicago: University of Chicago Press.

Browne, W. P. 1990. "Organized Interests and Their Issue Niches: A Search for Pluralism in a Policy Domain." *Journal of Politics* 52 (May): 477–509.

CQ Almanac. 1984. "Major Crime Package Cleared by Congress." Washington, D.C.: Congressional Quarterly, pp. 215–229.

CQ Almanac. 1988. "Election-Year Anti-Drug Bill Enacted." Washington, D.C.: Congressional Quarterly Inc., pp. 85–112.

Cobb, R. W., and C. D. Elder. 1983. *Participation in American Politics: The Dynamics of Agenda-Building.* 2d ed. Baltimore: Johns Hopkins University Press.

Downs, A. 1973. "Up and Down with Ecology—the 'Issue-Attention Cycle.'" *Public Interest* 32: 38–50.

Edelman, M. 1977. *Political Language: Words That Succeed and Policies That Fail.* New York: Academic Press.

Epstein, J. 1977. *Agency of Fear.* New York: Putnam.

Falco, M. 1989. *Winning the Drug War: A National Strategy.* New York: Priority Press.

Glasser, I. 1991. "Drug Prohibition: An Engine for Crime." Pp. 271–282 in *Searching for Alternatives: Drug Control Policy in the United States*, M. B. Krauss and E. P. Lazear, ed. Stanford, Calif.: Hoover Institution Press.

Goldberg, P. 1980. "The Federal Government's Response to Illicit Drugs, 1969–1978," Pp. 20–62 in *The Drug Abuse Council, The Facts About "Drug Abuse."* New York: Free Press.

Greenhouse, L. 1986. "Congress Approves Anti-Drug Bill as Senate Bars a Death Provision," *New York Times*, October 18, p. 33.

Hilgartner, S. and C. L. Bosk. 1988. "The Rise and Fall of Social Problems: A Public Arenas Model." *American Journal of Sociology* 94: 53–78.

Himmelstein, J. 1983. *The Strange Career of Marihuana.* Westport, Conn.: Greenwood Press.

Kingdon, J. W. 1984. *Agendas, Alternatives, and Public Policies.* Boston: Little, Brown.

McWilliams, J. C. 1990. *The Protectors: Harry J. Anslinger and the Federal Bureau of Narcotics, 1930-1962.* Newark: University of Delaware Press.

Musto, D. F. 1973. *The American Disease: Origins of Narcotic Control.* New Haven, Conn.: Yale University Press.

National Institute on Drug Abuse. 1991. *National Household Survey on Drug*

Abuse: Main Findings 1990. Washington, D.C.: U.S. Government Printing Office, pp. 25, 29.

National Narcotics Intelligence Consumers Committee (NNICC). 1988. *The NNICC Report 1987: The Supply of Illicit Drugs to the United States*. Washington, D.C.: NNICC.

Ostrowski, J. 1991. "Answering the Critics of Drug Legalization." Pp. 296–323 in *Searching for Alternatives: Drug Control Policy in the United States*, ed. M. B. Krauss and E. P. Lazear. Stanford, Calif.: Hoover Institution Press.

Peterson, R. E. 1991. "Legalization: The Myth Exposed." Pp. 324–355 in *Searching for Alternatives: Drug Control Policy in the United States*, ed. M. B. Krauss and E. P. Lazear. Stanford, Calif.: Hoover Institution Press.

Polsby, N. 1984. *Political Innovation in America: The Politics of Policy Initiation*. New Haven, Conn.: Yale University Press.

Public Papers of the Presidents, Ronald Reagan, Book I, 1988. 1990. Washington, D.C.: U.S. Government Printing Office.

Sharp, E. B. 1991. "Interest Groups and Symbolic Policy Formation: The Case of Anti-Drug Policy." Paper prepared for the annual meeting of the American Political Science Association, August 29–September 1, 1991, Washington, D.C.

Sharp, E. B. 1994. *The Dilemma of Drug Policy in the United States*. New York: HarperCollins.

Stone, D. A. 1989. "Causal Stories and the Formation of Policy Agendas." *Political Science Quarterly* 104: 281–300.

Trebach, A. 1982. *The Heroin Solution*. New Haven, Conn.: Yale University Press.

Zeese, K. B. 1991. "Drug War Forever?" Pp. 251–270 in *Searching for Alternatives: Drug Control Policy in the United States*, ed. M. B. Krauss and E. P. Lazear. Stanford, Calif.: Hoover Institution Press, 1991.

6

Problem Definition and Special Interest Politics in Tax Policy and Agriculture

Gary Mucciaroni

The Reagan administration's attempts to reduce the scope and scale of government sometimes entailed confronting reputedly powerful "producer groups" that represent industries or sectors of the economy that produce goods and services. They include some of the most highly organized and resourceful lobbies in Washington. Two areas where such groups were challenged were tax policy and agriculture. In the former case, the administration and its allies attempted to curtail or eliminate tax expenditure provisions, while in the latter case their target was farm subsidies. In each case they faced an identical obstacle: the political advantages enjoyed by coalitions of relatively narrow and exclusive groups over broad and inclusive interests, including the ability of producer groups to overcome obstacles to collective action (Olson 1982). Because both tax incentives and farm subsidies channel most of their benefits to these groups and distribute their costs widely among very large (and difficult to organize) groups of taxpayers and consumers, the political incentives favored retaining the status quo. The producer groups in both cases were mobilized, vocally opposed to the reforms, while the general public remained unorganized and inert.

Nevertheless, reform efforts largely succeeded in tax policy but failed in agriculture.[1] Much of the reason reform was possible in one case but not in the other, I will argue, has to do with differences in the kinds of problems that became salient and reached the agenda and the way those problems were defined. The soaring cost of farm subsidies was at least as salient as the costs associated with the growth of tax expenditures, but a proreform issue definition emerged and took hold only in the latter case. In both cases fairness was the dominant issue. But in farm policy fairness came to mean relief for farmers themselves, while in tax policy it meant rate reductions and a more equitable distribution of the tax burden by ending corporate tax "abuses." Differences in both objective conditions and the subjective predispositions of participants in the policymaking process gave rise to these different contexts.

TAX EXPENDITURES AND FARM SUBSIDIES

Tax expenditures reduce the amount of income taxes industries and individuals owe the government and provide incentives for investing in particular kinds of economic activities. They include provisions in the tax law that allow a special exclusion, exemption, or deduction from gross income or that provide a credit, a preferential rate, or deferral of tax liability. They are called tax "expenditures" because they are the fiscal equivalent of spending programs: As revenue losses, they affect the government's balance sheet in the same manner. To be sure, many of the most important provisions are intended to benefit the broad American middle class. But beneficiaries have also included a wide range of producer groups—from steel companies and real estate developers to kiwi fruit growers and horse breeders.

Tax expenditures were added and expanded over several decades. These increments added up to massive change, especially since 1970, when revenue losses due to tax expenditures expanded dramatically (Conlan et al. 1990: 23; Witte 1985: 289). They rose as a proportion of income tax receipts from 38 percent in 1967 to about 74 percent in 1982, and they almost doubled as a proportion of GNP, increasing from 4.4 to 8.2 percent (Witte 1985: 291-95; McGinley 1985: 27). Tax expenditures rose from $159 billion in 1975 to $486 billion in 1985, from 21 percent to 45 percent of federal budget outlays (Stewart 1989: 153).

Tax expenditures seemed to have become permanent fixtures on the nation's policy landscape. Scholars, politicians, and pundits alike viewed prospects for reform as about as likely as the fall of the Soviet Union. In lieu of major institutional change, the incentives of the political marketplace dictated that politicians would be unable or unwilling to revoke all but perhaps the most abusive tax preferences (Davies 1986: 287; Freeman 1973: 90; Witte 1985: 380). Reforms of a sort were legislated in 1969 and 1976, but they were modest in both cases; either they made little progress in removing tax loopholes or they added as many new provisions as existing ones they eliminated (Conlan et al. 1990: 29-30).

The Tax Reform Act of 1986 reversed the growth of tax preferences. Numerous provisions benefiting businesses and individuals were either eliminated or made less generous (Murray 1986a: 6-10; Murray 1986b: 6-8; U.S. Congress 1987). Roughly $400 billion in "loophole closing" over five years was accomplished. Tax expenditures fell from $486 billion in 1985 to $373 billion in 1989, or from over 45 percent of budget outlays to about 33 percent of outlays (Stewart 1989: 153). These aggregate figures understate the impact of the act on tax expenditures that were of primary benefit to producer groups. Provisions favoring business and other organized sectors of the economy bore the brunt of the loophole-closing. Provisions benefiting individuals fared much better, especially those whose benefits were highly diffuse. Corporations, taken as a whole, were major losers, having to pay about $120 billion more in taxes (individual taxpayers paid an equivalent amount less).

Farm subsidies are intended to benefit farmers either by increasing the prices they receive for their products in the market (price supports) or by supplementing their income (income supports) (Gardner 1981: chap. 2). The chief price-setting mechanism is the "nonrecourse loan," which farmers obtain from the Commodity Credit Corporation (CCC) at a level specified by the government with the commodity used as collateral. If the market price remains higher than the loan rate, farmers sell the crop, repay the loan, and keep the profit. Alternatively, if the market price remains below the loan rate, farmers turn over the crop to the government to close out their obligations, with the CCC effectively purchasing the product. Hence, the loan rate sets the minimum price in the market. "Deficiency payments," intended to support incomes rather than prices, supplement loans. Farmers are entitled to collect deficiency payments when market prices fail to reach "target prices" set by Congress, which are set higher than loan rates and are calculated to reflect the national average cost of producing a crop. The deficiency payment represents the difference between the target price and the market price or between the target price and the loan rate, whichever is smaller.

The most serious efforts to move toward a market-oriented farm policy were undertaken in the 1980s. When the Reagan administration took office in 1981 farm programs were scheduled for reauthorization, an exercise Congress undertakes regularly every four or five years. Its budget and farm proposals called for eliminating income supports. In addition, the Secretary of Agriculture would be given broad discretion to set price supports. If he chose to set price support levels below market prices, farmers would be forced to get what they could for their crops in the market. Hence, the two linchpins of agricultural policy—income and price supports—essentially would be jettisoned. The Reagan administration renewed its efforts at the beginning of its second term in 1985 by putting forward a proposal similar to the one in 1981. It called for eliminating deficiency payments, this time by phasing them out over five years. The amount of subsidy each farmer could receive would be capped at $20,000 in 1986 and decline to $10,000 by 1988. It also proposed setting the price support level below the average free market price, effectively clearing the market, and limiting the amount that farmers could borrow from the government.

Both of Reagan's proposals were dead on arrival in Congress. Members of the House and Senate committees, who would have to approve them first, were not about to overhaul farm programs in such a radical fashion. They marked up their bills in the traditional manner, with each committee member seeking to enhance the subsidy programs for the principal farm interests in his or her state or district. The administration largely abandoned its efforts at comprehensive reform and entered into extended negotiations with Congress that centered more on where to set price and income supports and overall budgetary levels than on major policy changes. Not only was fundamental, market-oriented reform rejected, but ironically, the 1980s witnessed sharp increases in spending for price and income supports. The amount spent on subsidies fluctuates from year to year, depending in large measure upon economic conditions. Spending has declined somewhat in the 1990s, but the basic contours of farm policy remain rooted in the 1930s and 1940s. Producer group influence remains alive and well in the agricultural arena.

How did a bold tax reform proposal reach the agenda and eventually become adopted, while no serious consideration was given to proposals to reduce government involvement in agriculture? Much of the answer lies in the kinds of problems that became salient in each arena and how those problems were defined. Problem salience means the degree to which people are aware of a problem and care about it. Problem definitions refer to the meanings and interpretations people attach to problems. Problem salience and definition are crucial because they create widely shared perceptions of the producer groups and the legitimacy of their claims. Certain problems and problem definitions will place producer groups and their claims in a positive light, others in a negative light. What matters is the perception of groups as either victims, or alternatively, as victimizers. As Rochefort and Cobb note in chapter 1, how a problem gets defined often depends upon where the cause of a problem is located and who gets assigned the blame—the question of culpability. Whether producer groups will be defeated or not, then, depends upon whether they are perceived as victims of economic misfortune beyond their control or instead, as greedy claimants feeding at the public trough.

PROBLEM DEFINITION AND
THE TRIUMPH OF TAX REFORM

During the period of tax expenditure growth, two problems dominated the policymaking arena—middle-class restiveness with "high taxes" and the presumed need for capital formation. In the first instance, expanding tax expenditures was seen as a way to reduce tax burdens on the middle class. In the second, tax expenditures were legislated to spur investment and economic growth overall and in particular industries.

But by the mid 1980s, the context of the problems had changed. The U.S.

economy was in the midst of its longest peacetime boom in decades, and attention shifted from the needs of business to invest in the economy to the equity of a tax system that allowed many profitable companies to escape paying their "fair share." In the debate over tax reform, middle-class tax relief remained an important issue, but it was married to the problem of fairness in terms of stemming "special interest tax abuses." It became apparent that both fairness and tax relief could be achieved, not by expanding tax expenditures, but by reducing them. If those provisions that benefited producer groups were reduced, the resultant revenue gains could be transferred into rate reductions for taxpayers as a whole. Other issues compatible with reform (though less salient than relief and fairness) also came to the fore: the impacts of tax expenditures on economic efficiency and growth, and the increasing complexity of a tax code crammed with special provisions.

These changes were principally the result of economic conditions, the impact of previous policy choices, and the interaction between the two. Immediately after World War II, more and more personal income became subject to taxation. The broadening of the tax base, plus expanding incomes during the prosperity of the 1950s and 1960s, created a great fiscal dividend for the federal government. Not only was it possible to increase government spending, but also to legislate tax cuts, increases in exemptions, standard deductions, and more narrowly based tax expenditures.

But with the increase in incomes, first from real growth and then from inflation, exemptions and standard deductions began to lose their sheltering effect on middle-class incomes. At the same time, because tax rates were not indexed for inflation, taxpayers moved into higher tax brackets. This "bracket creep" was a boon to Congress, because it automatically increased revenue, avoiding the political pain of legislating tax increases. Instead, Congress could take the popular action of tax reduction. Between 1954 and 1981 Congress adopted fifteen major tax bills. Of these, eleven reduced taxes, only three increased them, and one left revenues unchanged (Witte 1985: 251, 175).

During the 1970s the growth in real disposable income slowed, inflation accelerated, and bracket creep worsened. In inflation-adjusted dollars, the median after-federal-tax (including Social Security) income of one-earner families dropped from $7,743 in 1972 to $6,523 in 1981. This decline in real disposable incomes was accompanied by rising tax burdens. By 1981 individual income tax receipts had reached a record high of 9.6 percent of gross national product. Between 1965 and 1980 taxpayers in all income categories saw their average and marginal tax rates jump (Schick 1990: 139–40).

The squeeze on middle-class incomes generated considerable political pressure for tax reduction through rate cuts and expanded tax expenditures (Witte 1985: 236). Late in the decade, tax revolts erupted in several states, most notably California. The immediate target of Proposition 13 was the property tax, but the grass roots campaign signaled a broader voter distemper with their financial situation. If people were frustrated with their own tax burdens, they were also becoming more sympathetic with complaints from the business community. Contributing to taxpayers' frustration with the income tax was the shift of an increasing proportion of the income tax burden away from corporations and toward individuals. Corporate tax payments had fallen from 25 percent in the 1950s to less than half of that by the early 1980s (Birnbaum and Murray 1987: 11). Despite this trend, business argued that taxes and other forms of government intervention discouraged investment and raised the cost of doing business. Not only could individual taxpayers identify with corporations' complaints about high taxes, but they, like the policymakers, were increasingly concerned with long-term economic performance (Vogel 1989: 193–239). Hence, business's demand for tax relief and incentives appeared less as a special interest demand and more as a reasoned argument to stimulate economic growth.

The fever for rate cuts and expanding tax incentives resulted in the Revenue Act of 1978 and then culminated in 1981 with the passage of the Economic Recovery Tax Act (ERTA). The 1978 legislation began as a proposal to reform the tax code by cutting back on tax expenditures, but it became, instead, an exercise in lowering taxes. President Carter, who called the tax code a "disgrace to the human race" and campaigned on a pledge to overhaul it, floated a plan to eliminate the preferential treatment for capital gains and several other provisions. But Carter's final proposal boiled down to a modest attempt at cutting back such notorious loopholes as the "three-martini lunch." Even this mild reform was ignored by Congress, which proceeded to enact new tax benefits and generously expand many existing ones. Debated in the midst of the furor surrounding Proposition 13, and after almost a decade of academic and official concern with the nation's long-term economic decline, the Revenue Act was crammed with new tax credits and exemptions intended to spur capital formation (Witte 1985: 204–217).

ERTA began in 1981 as the Reagan administration's proposal for substantial tax rate cuts for corporations and individuals. Added to the rate cuts were a series of costly new and expanded tax incentives, the result of a bidding war between congressional Democrats and the Republican administration. Huge revenue losses resulted from liberalized depreciation allowances, the sale of tax credits through leasing, oil tax reductions, and other provisions (Witte 1985: chapter 11). As David Stockman, the administration's budget director, put it: "The hogs were really feeding. The greed level, the level of opportunism, was just out of control" (quoted in Greider 1981: 5).

Rather than diminishing public discontent with federal tax policy, ERTA exacerbated already prevalent perceptions of unfairness. Tax expenditures, including those created by this legislation, diminish both "vertical" and "horizontal" equity. Proponents of the first (progressivity) argue that special tax provisions benefit mainly affluent persons and corporations who are able to take advantage of them. The result is that while marginal (statutory) rates may be progressive, effective rates (what is actually paid) reflected essentially a flat tax rate. Horizontal equity is the notion that those with the same income should pay the same taxes; tax expenditures permit taxpayers at the same income levels to pay widely varying effective rates. By the late 1970s a majority of the public felt that the federal income tax was "unfair," and "unfairness" was cited as the major problem almost to the exclusion of other tax issues (Roper 1978: 45; Roper 1979: 37). Perceptions of unfairness had worsened over time. Since 1972 the federal income tax and the property tax had contended closely for the label "the worst tax—the least fair," but by 1980 the income tax had become the least popular. The public, not surprisingly, felt that income taxes were "too high" for "middle-income families," for "people whose incomes all come from salaries," for those "who own their homes," and for "low-income families." By contrast, large majorities felt that income taxes were "too low" for two groups—"high-income families" and "large business corporations" (Witte 1985: 341–342).

Probably no single person did more to heighten the visibility of the fairness issue than Robert McIntyre, director of the "public interest" lobby group, Citizens for Tax Justice. A little-known disciple of Ralph Nader, McIntyre spent endless hours ferreting out corporate tax abuses and publicizing them. McIntyre's efforts were important because they dramatized and reinforced preexisting perceptions of the system's lack of fairness.

Nothing provided more grist for McIntyre's mill than the aftermath of ERTA. In its wake, corporations and the rich engaged in a tax-sheltering frenzy. Perceptions of unfairness grew sharply with a stream of reports of corporations and affluent individuals paying little or no tax (Shribman 1985: 20). ERTA practically ended corporate taxpaying, with business paying just over 6 percent of the income tax in 1983. Corporate tax avoidance set off a storm of protest in Congress in 1982, when a provision of ERTA allowing profitless firms to sell their tax breaks to profitable ones in a transaction called "safe harbor leasing" led to a flurry of bizarre deals that helped both buyers and sellers. McIntyre found that 128 out of 250 large and profitable companies, many among the best known in the nation, paid no federal income taxes in at least one year between 1981 and 1983. Seventeen paid no taxes in all three years. According to McIntyre, whose findings were widely reported in the press, "Americans are wondering why the federal government is incurring the largest deficits in history even while they are paying the highest taxes ever. This study documents one important answer: the demise of the corporate income tax" (Birnbaum and Murray 1987: 12). Predictably, the findings served as a club for corporation-bashing in Washington. On national television Senator Byrd of West Virginia, for instance, told of a woman raising three children in Milwaukee on an income of $12,000 who paid more taxes than Boeing, General Electric, DuPont, and Texaco, all put together.

While fairness was the issue with the greatest political impact in the tax reform debate,[2] another problem was that the growth in tax expenditures coincided with, and some argued contributed to, the decline in economic growth and productivity in the United States. At the very least, their record of stimulating investment was dubious. By distorting investment decisions, tax expenditures discouraged efficient capital allocation. The expansion of such provisions as the investment tax credit and accelerated depreciation write-offs coincided with declining investment and competitiveness in many of the same industries (such as steel and auto) for which the provisions were enacted. ERTA's impacts confirmed arguments that tax expenditures misallocated resources. Generous shelters for investing in commercial real estate led to an oversupply of office space, prompting press reports of new office buildings standing empty in metropolitan areas.[3]

The American public in general reveals an ambivalence toward the income tax: while they support many of the most expensive tax expenditures that provide middle-class benefits (such as the home mortgage interest deduction), they consider the overall system deeply flawed and endorse tax reform in the abstract. It is plausible to think that one or the other side of this opinion dichotomy becomes more pronounced at different times. When the issue context is filled by a stream of media reports that point out abuse and unfairness, it serves to amplify the discontent with the system generally. The passage of ERTA, as well as its troublesome excesses and the publicity that attended them, reinforced the preexisting perception of unfairness, waste, and complexity. It served as a focusing event, creating the impression of a policy in severe crisis and fueling the perception in Washington that "things had gotten out-of-hand."[4] When this happened, a policy window opened. Reform proponents, waiting for an auspicious moment to push their issue onto the agenda, now had an opportunity to do so before attention was shifted to other issues.[5]

Reformers not only called attention to fairness and other issues, they also framed them in ways guaranteed to augment the political appeal of tax expenditure elimination as a solution to the problem. They focused the policy debate on the unfairness and irrationality of the system *as a whole* rather than on whether this or that particular tax credit or deduction should be eliminated. Their problem definition was couched in broad principles and a blanket indictment of the income tax rather than the merits (political or otherwise) of specific provisions. Second, they focused their efforts on provisions that benefited *producer groups*, while leaving largely untouched the more popular provisions that benefited the middle class.

With tax reform framed as a struggle between specific and diffuse interests, members of Congress who were tempted to vote against reform risked having their challengers at the next election point out (1) that they had denied their constituents a diffuse benefit; and (2) that they were the captive of privileged interests—that when they had the opportunity to vote for greater fairness and efficiency, and less government, they shrank from it.[6] In the media glare that attended their vote, this fear helped to compel a substantial number of members to support reform.

The potency of the problems and problem definitions associated with tax reform could also be seen in the impressive coalition that embraced reform. In an age of divided government, the only kind of coalition capable of defeating a score of producer groups had two key characteristics: (1) it had to be broad-based and diverse, extending across the ideological spectrum, the two political parties, and branches of government; and (2) it had to include committed leaders at the highest levels of government. The coalition that brought about tax reform included the labor-funded Citizens for Tax Justice, Democrats Tip O'Neill, Bill Bradley, and Richard Gephardt, conservative Republicans such as President Ronald Reagan and Jack Kemp, the Treasury Department, and several major corporations.

Reform appealed to many Democrats because of the fairness issue. Democrats had long advocated curtailing tax breaks for corporations and the rich. Neoliberals like Senator Bill Bradley deemphasized the traditional liberal goal of progressivity but did stress the principle of horizontal equity in Bradley's "Fair Tax" plan. Rather than defining fairness in terms of redistributing the tax burden between income classes, he saw it as shifting the burden toward the organized and away from unorganized groups in society. Bradley's plan, which served as the basis for the final legislation, thus avoided being painted as the kind of radical "Robin Hood" redistribution that in the past had engendered conservative opposition to reform. He also stressed the market-distorting inefficiencies of tax expenditures. He wanted a return to an earlier time when the Democratic party had taken the lead on economic growth and was not identified with high taxes and pandering to organized interests. Reform was an issue that he thought could recapture middle-class support for the Democrats.

Key Republicans like President Reagan and Congressman Jack Kemp were attracted to the problem of high taxes. They believed in the supply-side doctrine that emphasized tax rate cuts rather than incentives. They realized that savings from eliminating tax expenditures would allow for rates to be cut further, thus avoiding any worsening of the budget deficit. Kemp also sought to transform the Republicans into a majority party by shedding the Republican image as a party of the rich and big business. Like Bradley, he believed in the superiority of market incentives and rejected social engineering through the tax code. And like Bradley, he had ambitions for the White House and saw tax reform as an issue with diffuse appeal. Kemp and Bradley framed the tax reform issue in populist terms, stressing that eliminating tax expenditures would make the tax code clearer, fairer, and also more productive for the average citizen by removal of distorting market incentives that create economic efficiencies.

Tax reform became the top priority of the president, committee chairmen, and the Treasury secretary. It was they who pushed and persuaded reluctant majorities in Congress to address the issue and approve the measure. Leaders habitually face a number of incentives that might lead them to attack producer groups and embrace problem definitions like those in tax reform. The president and party leaders may be expected to direct their reelection appeals to broad national audiences (Derthick and Quirk 1985: 103). The presidency and parties are held responsible for the general state of the economy and represent broad, inclusive interests. Thus, unlike interest group politics, presidential and party politics tends to expand the scope of conflict (Schattschneider 1960). By tapping into public disillusionment with the income tax and special interest privileges, then, the president succeeded in framing reform as a "white hat issue" that was difficult to oppose openly (Roberts 1986: 20). Congressman Dan Rostenkowski, the Ways and Means Committee chairman, supported reform in part because he knew that if he did not, the Democrats would be open to Reagan's accusation that they were wedded to the past and the captive of special interests. In addition, by fundamentally redirecting policy in a way that entailed defeating reputedly powerful interests, tax reform made it possible for leaders to demonstrate superior political skills, thereby enhancing their reputations.

PROBLEM DEFINITION AND THE FAILURE
OF REFORM IN AGRICULTURE

As with tax policy, the diffuse burdens of farm subsidies became a salient issue in the 1980s, setting the stage for launching a major attack on existing policy. For a long time there had been the criticism that farm programs wasted resources by encouraging overproduction. The dramatic jump in the cost of subsidies during the 1980s reinforced the perception of a policy that had gotten out of control. At the same time, the federal deficit climbed to unprecedented levels, making subsidy costs all the more salient. Even when adjusted for annual rates of inflation, federal outlays for farm subsidies averaged almost five times higher in the 1980s than in the 1970s, increasing from almost $4 billion to about $17 billion. Especially striking is the rise from the mid-1970s to the mid-1980s. In 1975 subsidies were less than $1 billion, but by 1986 they had reached almost $30 billion (U.S. Office of Management and Budget, various years). As a proportion of the federal budget, the level of subsidies appears fairly modest, averaging less than 2 percent of total federal spending and just over 2 percent of nondefense spending from

1970 to 1988. Indeed, despite their substantial growth, farm subsidies grew only slightly faster than the total budget and nondefense spending as a whole. Still, annual farm subsidies in the 1980s averaged 54 percent higher as a proportion of the budget (and 44 percent higher as a proportion of nondefense spending) than in the previous decade (U.S. Office of Management and Budget, various years).[7]

Not only were the inefficiency and cost of farm programs becoming more apparent, but they seemed increasingly unjustified in terms of the dwindling number of farmers in the population and the inequitable distribution of the programs' benefits. There existed fewer and fewer eligible recipients of federal agricultural largesse, and the benefits were skewed in favor of the largest farms. In 1900 there were almost 30 million farmers, 42 percent of the U.S. population, but by 1980 there were just over 6 million farmers, 2.7 percent of the population. Total farm employment declined from 11 million workers in 1950 to 3.5 million in 1982. The average farm in 1982 was three times larger than in 1910, with about 13 percent of all farms accounting for about 73 percent of total sales (Albrecht and Murdock 1988: 29–44). In terms of the distribution of program benefits, payments to farmers in 1983 were $9.4 billion, $4.1 billion of which went to farms with sales of $100,000 or more. These large farms were 12 percent of the total number of farms, but they received 44 percent of payments. The 72 percent of the farmers with the lowest level of sales received only 22 percent of the direct payments. The largest 12 percent of the farms had average net incomes from farming of $97,000 and received direct payments from the government averaging more than $14,000. They also had off-farm income averaging $14,000 (Johnson et al. 1985: 79). Furthermore, a significant fraction of these benefits went to landlords, not to farm operators. Obviously, many of these trends were long-standing, but combined with the explosion in subsidy costs in the 1980s, they highlighted the narrowness of agriculture as an interest and the inequity of farm subsidies.

Certain elements of the kind of broad coalition that brought about tax reform also emerged in the agricultural arena during the 1980s. The Reagan administration proposed radical reform. In Congress a group of urban liberal Democrats joined with some suburban conservative Republicans in favor of reform. By late in the decade, this coalition had gained what seemed to be considerable strength. Farm subsidies have always been more popular among liberals than among conservatives and Republicans, whose objections are rooted in the principles of free markets and less government. In this case, however, the key change occurred among urban liberal Democrats who had supported subsidies in the past. They reasoned that if spending on programs for the poor and the cities were being cut, rural interests should share the pain. Both camps saw reform as benefiting consumers, taxpayers, and deficit reduction.

In sum, a strong case could be made, and was made, that like tax expenditures, farm subsidies contributed to diffuse economic burdens and inequity. The cost, inefficiency, and inequity of farm programs had worsened over time and become highly conspicuous in the 1980s, particularly in the context of high budget deficits and the resulting pressures to reduce spending. And in response to these issues, a broad-based coalition had begun to coalesce around the cause of reform.

A Competing Issue Definition: The Farmer as Victim

Unlike the tax case, however, the problems associated with the diffuse costs of farm subsidies were overshadowed and displaced by the greater salience of another issue: the economic distress in the farm economy itself (Long 1987). What distinguishes agriculture from the tax case, then, is the *simultaneous emergence of a more salient concern* that overshadowed the problems reformers wanted to stress. As a result, instead of being painted as greedy claimants on the public purse, farmers were more sympathetically portrayed as victims valiantly fighting for survival. This issue blunted arguments against subsidies and deflected attention away from their costs. If the rising cost and other undesirable consequences of farm subsidies were viewed as a severe problem, the farmers' own condition seemed even more so. Moreover, the cost of the programs could as easily be interpreted as another indication of the desperate plight of many farmers as it could be of uncontrollable government spending per se.

One reason for the prominence of the farm crisis was its agreed-upon severity. Reagan's 1981 proposal came on the heels of the third consecutive year in which farmers' incomes declined below the level of the previous year. Net farm income declined by about 31 percent in 1980 and reached its lowest point since 1964 (adjusted for inflation). It rose by 26 percent in 1981, but did not reach the levels it had enjoyed throughout most of the 1970s. When the administration put forward its 1985 proposal, the farm economy had worsened further. Land values plummeted beginning in 1981 as inflation receded. Farm productivity peaked in 1982 and 1983 with bumper crops, just at the time that export markets contracted, so net farm income fell considerably in 1982 and 1983 to its lowest level since 1959 (McKinzie et al. 1987: 61). Caught between falling land values, declining crop prices, and rising real interest rates, farmers found it difficult to repay loans taken out during the boom years of the 1970s when production and exports were rising.

Not only were farmers perceived as fighting for their economic survival but as not exclusively or primarily to blame for their situation. Policymakers in the 1970s, such as Nixon's Agriculture Secretary Earl Butz, urged farmers to plant "fencerow to fencerow." Bankers made low interest loans readily available to expand production, and many farmers went into considerable debt buying land and equipment in anticipation of growing world demand. The assumption in the agriculture community was that the world would continue to buy as much as American farmers produced and that inflation would continue making it financially possible for farmers to accrue large debts. With U.S. agricultural productivity outpacing growth in the domestic population, American farmers grew increasingly dependent upon export markets (U.S. Department of Commerce, various years). Exports accounted for about a quarter of gross farm product at the start of the 1970s but about half by the end of the decade. The volume of farm exports increased in that decade by more than 150 percent (*Congressional Quarterly* 1984: 16). By the early 1980s almost two-thirds of total U.S. farm production was sold abroad.

As inflation became intolerable in the late 1970s, the Federal Reserve Board tightened monetary policy, boosting real interest rates and thus slowing economic activity in the United States and abroad. The global recession dampened demand in developing countries, which had gone heavily into debt to fuel domestic expansion and finance imports. Now they were financially strapped trying to meet their loan payments. Aggravated by unprecedented U.S. budget deficits, high interest rates also attracted foreign capital, driving up the value of the dollar in currency markets and making U.S. exports less attractive. Even though huge surpluses had pushed the prices of American farm products down considerably, these prices were still high and uncompetitive in foreign currencies. The drop-off in demand for American products was exacerbated by the grain embargo imposed by President Carter in retaliation for the Soviet invasion of Afghanistan. Finally, competition from highly subsidized European Market countries and the emergence of Australia and Argentina as major grain exporters made it more difficult to expand exports when the embargo was lifted. In 1982, for the first time in a decade, exports declined to $36.6 billion from a record level of $43.3 billion in the previous year. The productive capacity of American agriculture exceeded demand by about 10 percent.

The sense of a farm crisis was never stronger than in 1985 when Reagan put forward his second reform proposal. And with many farmers desperate and needy it was difficult to depict them as privileged and powerful feeders at the public trough. Though Reagan's budget director, David Stockman, argued that the government had no responsibility to relieve farmers of their debt because it "was willingly incurred by consenting adults" (quoted in *Congressional Quarterly Almanac* 1985: 515), few could ignore the role of government, banking, and impersonal national and international economic forces that had led to overproduction and shrinking demand for U.S. farm products. Clearly, the administration's aim was to locate the cause of the farm problem at the individual level, with the voluntary economic choices made by the farmers themselves. But for much of the rest of the policy community it was the larger impersonal causes that were more plausibly to blame.

The sympathy among politicians and the public that farmers evoked in the 1980s was based upon more than objective economic circumstances. The reason the farmers' situation resonated with Americans is the persistence of the agrarian myth. Ideas that emerge and take hold in one historical period, under one set of social and economic conditions, often persist for generations after the original conditions that gave rise to them have passed. The agrarian myth is a holdover from America's rural past when farmers were seen as a yeomanry devoted to tilling the land, as rugged individuals safeguarding Jeffersonian democracy, and as populist masses exploited by greedy Eastern economic interests in the nineteenth century. Films and news broadcasts about the travails of farm life in the 1980s tapped into these widely shared perceptions of virtuous family farmers, and of farming as a way of life that are embedded in American history and mythology. As a result, farmers are not perceived in the same negative light as other special interests. They are considered neither affluent individuals (even though many are) nor heads of powerful corporate organizations.[8]

This mythology is important in politically sustaining farm interests. According to two observers (Bonnen and Browne 1989: 10; see also Thompson 1988; Tweeten and Jordon 1988: 26–27):

> Today, with a farm-based political majority long gone, this agrarian myth persists. It persists precisely because most people have limited experience with agriculture and its economic issues and because those in agriculture have an important stake in romanticizing its social role and seeking widespread public support. . . . The broadcast and print media are the prime purveyors of images. Messages are transmitted that reinforce a type of simple . . . learning. These features of modern communication make it possible for an active minority to proselytize and keep an agrarian myth vital and supportable even when its basic tenets are disputable and under constant intellectual attack.

Once the farm crisis seized Congress's attention, calls for eliminating subsidies seemed callously indifferent to the farmers' plight. Media attention accompanied the crisis, including Hollywood movies like *Country*, *Places in the Heart*, and *The River*, which depicted valiant struggles waged by family farmers in the face of economic exploitation and natural disasters. According to a congressman from South Dakota, the films "shed the stigma" of economic failure for farmers (Roberts 1985; Browne 1988: 86–88). Clearly, in the media and in Congress, far from being faulted for their circumstances, the farmers were seen as almost blameless victims. Talk show host Phil Donahue featured farmers in a two-day telecast from Iowa, and CBS News anchor Dan Rather toured the farm belt in a series of broadcasts. Not surprisingly, the salience of the farmers' plight to the public was exceptionally high. By early 1986, a CBS News poll revealed that 83 percent of respondents nationally thought that at least half of all farmers were experiencing financial difficulty. In addition, only 18 percent blamed the government for the farmers' condition, with 50 percent feeling that additional public financial support of farmers was needed (CBS News/*New York Times* Poll 1986).

"There was a shift [in the salience of problems]," said one lobbyist, "from having the primary objective be movement toward the market, to how do we maintain the income of the farmer" (Rauch 1985: 2538). Calls for reforms that would deprive farmers of government help lost whatever appeal they had, and the reform issue evaporated from public discourse. Broad public support for increasing farm spending persisted into 1988, despite the fact that by that time there were news reports that the debt crisis had bottomed out, the political activism of farmers had died out, and the public expressed concern that government spending on many defense and domestic programs should be cut (Bonnen and Browne 1988: 12; see also *Los Angeles Times* 1988: 3157; Plissner 1987).

The farm crisis breathed new life into the populist appeal of subsidies, undercutting any possibility of the kind of strong bipartisan, liberal-conservative alliance that emerged in favor of tax reform. Almost daily during the deliberations over the 1985 farm bill, members of Congress made speeches and issued press releases and proposals addressing the crisis. The House Agriculture Committee staged highly publicized hearings with famous actresses who starred in the "farm genre" films testifying as people with special insights into the crisis. Republicans criticized these as public relations tactics, a crass bid for electoral advantage by the Democrats. But by the end of the summer many Republicans themselves had joined the Democrats in another media event—the "Farm Aid" concert that featured country music recording artists. The concert was intended as a fundraiser for farmers in trouble, and the musicians visited Capitol Hill on the pretext of seeking "advice" on how to spend the money. According to *Congressional Quarterly*, "members of both parties were being drawn into a political cyclone of having to prove their commitment to farmers" (*Congressional Quarterly Almanac* 1985: 515).

Democrats found the issue enticing because it put the Republicans on the defensive. Party competition to secure the votes of rural interests is particularly intense in the Senate for three reasons. First, rural interests are overrepresented in the Senate, where relatively unpopulated states like the Dakotas are given equal representation with states that have much larger populations. Second, unlike the House, party competition for control of the Senate has been sharp for the past decade or more, with shifts of a few seats between the parties determining which party is in the majority. Finally, virtually every state has some agricultural component to its economy. Unlike the

House, where farm interests are geographically concentrated in 70 or 80 rural districts, in the Senate their numbers are more diffuse. All of this means that farm interests are able to exert greater and more direct pressure on electoral outcomes in the Senate.

Since at least the New Deal, debate over farm bills has raised fundamental issues of principle for Republicans and Democrats (Wilson 1977: 147–153). The former have viewed them as fostering inefficiency, creating dependency, contributing to high taxes and bloated government, while the latter regard subsidies and market controls as necessary to stabilize farm incomes and prices against the volatility and harsh effects of the free market. Particularly in the postwar era when big business and labor unions were able to protect their incomes, Democrats have viewed farmers as deserving similar protection. Thus farm benefits draw a key part of their political support from the notion, rooted in the populist agrarian revolt of the late nineteenth century, that farmers represent a dispossessed and exploited segment of the population deserving of assistance.

In 1984 two Republican senators from the farm belt, Roger Jepsen of Iowa and Charles Percy of Illinois were defeated. Republicans, who held a tenuous 53–47 majority in 1985, were torn between the Reagan administration and the conservative mandate of fiscal responsibility, on the one hand, and the pressures to maintain at least existing levels of farm benefits. In the spring, farm-state Republicans defected from party ranks by approving an emergency credit measure designed to help debt-ridden farmers through another planting season. Reagan, claiming that the credit bill was an unwarranted bailout for bankers who had made unwise loans to farmers, vetoed the bill. But the entire, predominantly Republican South Dakota legislature, along with large groups from Nebraska, Kansas, and North Dakota, came to Washington to lobby for the legislation in a well-publicized media event. Then on major votes on the 1985 farm bill, the administration suffered substantial Republican defections in the House and Senate.[9] Twenty-two GOP Senators were up for reelection in 1986, seven of them from farm states. As the economic slump persisted into the fall campaign, their Democratic opponents accused them of being tied to Reagan's reform efforts. This tactic seemed to pay off in the election, with the GOP losing a net of eight seats, including losses in several midwestern and southern farm states. These losses provided the margin needed for the Democrats to take back control of the chamber. Three of the successful Democratic challengers sat on the Agriculture Committee.

The salience and definition of farm policy problems not only affected coalition-building in Congress, they also discouraged the kind of bold and committed leadership that was so crucial to bringing about tax reform. Leadership was in short supply when it came to reforming farm policy. A major reason for the lack of reform leadership in agriculture was the salience of the prolonged farm crisis and the sympathy that was evoked for the plight of farmers. These circumstances were likely to deter potential reform leaders, who decided that the chances of achieving their ends would be slim and the risks of a political backlash great. In 1981 and 1985 the well-recognized farm crisis and the sympathetic portrayal of farmers as victims effectively kept reform off the agenda, blocking and eventually discouraging the Reagan administration from pushing its proposed policy changes. Rather than challenge key members of Congress to join his effort, as occurred in the tax case, the president abandoned agricultural reform when he met with resistance.

By 1990, the issue context turned more hospitable to reform. A proposal to "means-test" farm benefits reached the agenda that year. By that time, the farm economy had recovered, exports had risen, and commodity prices were healthy. Though the farm crisis was over, its political impacts were still being felt. Several farm states again emerged as key battlegrounds for the GOP's efforts to retake the Senate in 1990. The Republicans, including the Bush administration, had been chastened by their experience in the 1980s. They believed that Reagan's radical proposals and tough bargaining over the farm budget had played into the hands of Democrats. Therefore the administration neglected to send Congress a reform proposal. Furthermore, in seeking to avoid taking a rigid position it might have to abandon (as its predecessor had), it remained disengaged from the policy debate until the very end.

CONCLUSION

This chapter has examined how and why farm interests escaped the defeats that producer groups suffered in the tax arena. In both cases the groups were challenged by reformers at the highest levels of government, in both the groups were widely considered resourceful and influential, and in both they were adamantly and vigorously opposed to reform. Yet, the salient problems that emerged in each arena and how those problems came to be defined played a decisive role in getting tax reform on the agenda and eventually adopted, while they effectively kept large-scale farm policy reform off the agenda.

In both the tax and agricultural cases, existing policies favored producer groups at the expense of diffuse middle-class, taxpayer/consumer interests. In both, plausible proreform problem definitions were articulated regarding the fairness and the costs of existing policies. And there were emergent coalitions that embraced those definitions. But in farm policy, fairness came to mean relief for farmers themselves, while in tax policy it meant rate reductions and a more equitable distribution of the tax burden by ending corporate tax "abuses." In the former, producer groups were portrayed as sympathetic victims of circumstances for which they were not to blame; in the latter, the groups themselves, along with their privileges and claims, were defined as the problem.

Both objective and subjective factors influenced the outcomes. Clearly the most important objective difference was the economic condition of the various economic sectors that the groups represented. The most obvious problem in farm policy was the short-term economic distress experienced by many farmers. In the context of hard economic times on the farm, the rising cost of subsidies could be justified or overlooked. Farm interests were thus accorded a presumption of need. The producer groups in the tax policy, by contrast, either were not experiencing acute economic distress (if they were, they were often spared elimination of their tax preferences) or were in sectors experiencing long-term economic decline for which existing policy was believed to be ineffective. By the mid 1980s the U.S. economy was enjoying its longest peacetime boom in decades. It turned out that the expansion of particularized tax benefits in 1978 and 1981 enabled powerful industries and investors to escape taxation. Attention now shifted from the investment needs of business, which had been the conspicuous problem when the provisions were enacted, to the equity of a tax system that allowed many profitable companies to escape paying their "fair share." Antecedent choices in tax policy created a scandalous atmosphere that proved highly hospitable to agitation for reform.

Moreover, the farmers could be portrayed as genuine victims and not to blame for their plight; instead, impersonal economic and governmental forces were at fault. On the other hand, the average taxpayers could argue that they were paying higher taxes (or saddled with larger budget deficits) because of nefarious, greedy business lobbyists.

In addition to economic conditions, more subjective factors were also important. If, as Rochefort and Cobb argue in chapter 1, political willingness to provide resources to groups in society is "conditioned by societal perceptions of the people who are going to benefit," then farm groups had a clear advantage compared to the business groups that lobbied to keep their tax breaks. Farmers benefited from highly favorable media coverage and entertainment that placed them in a sympathetic light, evoking powerful images of the agrarian myth that is grounded in American history and culture. While business interests are accorded a high degree of legitimacy in the United States, the myth surrounding free enterprise places their claims for government assistance in a much more ambiguous status. Once implemented, incentives to generate growth could as easily be perceived as concessions to big business and wealthy special interests trying to evade paying their fair share of taxes. The media reported the abuses spawned by ERTA and dramatized tax reform as a struggle between public-spirited reformers and Gucci-shod lobbyists. The combination of objective and subjective factors thus resulted in the emergence of problem definitions that were quite different and that resulted in divergent outcomes.

If these definitions of the problem had not emerged and captured the imagination of policymakers, tax reform would not have come about. Likewise, the dominant problem definition that emerged in agriculture made it virtually certain that market-oriented reform would be blocked from reaching the agenda. This does not mean, however, that the emergence of problem definitions conducive to tax reform inevitably led to its triumph. Nor does it mean that if the dominant problem definition in agriculture had been one conducive to reform, then reform would have been achieved, or that the only reason for the defeat of reform was a problem definition hospitable to farm groups' interests. Obviously, problem salience and definition by themselves do not account for the different outcomes. Such a monocausal explanation ignores the influence of the coalitions and institutional actors whose actions and structural features served to block reform in one case and facilitate it in another.

Yet, one measure of the salience and potency of the problems and definitions that took hold in each arena is the way in which they attracted political support and shaped the kinds of coalitions that emerged as dominant. The problem of tax fairness and middle-class tax burdens appealed to a broad-based and diverse coalition, extending across the two political parties and branches of government, and gained the commitment to reform from those who occupied strategic leadership positions in government. While elements of the kind of broad coalition that brought about tax reform also emerged in the agricultural arena during the 1980s (combining conservative Republicans and urban liberal Democrats), it was overwhelmed by the salience and impact of the farm crisis. That issue undercut the nascent proreform coalition, turning the policy debate into a partisan battle in which Democrats had the upper hand, and discouraged bold leadership in the cause of reform.

NOTES

1. When I speak of successful reform in the tax case I simply mean accomplishing a change in policy, regardless of whether the reforms turned out actually to work.

2. When asked which problem they thought carried the most weight with policymakers generally, almost all of those officials, experts, and other policy actors interviewed for this study ranked fairness as the most important.

3. Critics of tax expenditures long complained of other undesirable consequences of their growth as well: the complexity of the tax code, the erosion of the tax base, and an increase in the deficit if their revenue losses are not offset by tax increases or spending cuts.

4. This perception was reiterated frequently by those interviewed.

5. On the importance of focusing events, policy windows and political entrepreneurs, see Kingdon (1984).

6. Responses from interviews invariably pointed to the role of anticipated voter reactions in getting members to decide in favor of taxpayers' diffuse interest in reform.

7. Note that the figures discussed thus far pertain only to the costs of subsidies to taxpayers. They exclude costs to consumers, which are difficult to calculate. Estimates that exist indicate that excess consumer costs in 1980 came to $8.4 billion and for 1983 $13.2 billion (see Johnson et al. 1985: 23).

8. This is not to say that the agrarian myth bears no relationship to reality. The average farmer's income is fairly close to the median income of most American families, and most farms are not large corporate entities. Farm interests also have some basis for insisting on special treatment—the critical nature of food as a commodity, the instability of farming due to the weather and natural disasters, and the biological character of agriculture that make it highly risky and difficult to plan.

9. On the House see the *New York Times*, October 9, 1985, p. 1; on the Senate see *Congressional Quarterly Weekly Report*, December 21, 1985, p. 2.

REFERENCES

Albrecht, D., and S. H. Murdock. 1988. "The Structural Characteristics of U.S. Agriculture: Historical Patterns and Precursors of Producers' Adaptations to the Crisis." Pp. 29–44 in *The Farm Financial Crisis*, ed. S. Murdock and F. Leistritz. Boulder, Colo.: Westview Press.

Birnbaum, J., and A. Murray. 1987. *Showdown at Gucci Gulch: Lawmakers, Lobbyists, and the Unlikely Triumph of Tax Reform*. New York: Random House.

Bonnen, J., and W. Browne. 1989. "Why Is Agricultural Policy So Difficult to Reform?" In *The Political Economy of U.S. Agriculture*, ed. C. Kramer. Washington, D. C.: Resources for the Future.

Browne, W. 1988. *Private Interests, Public Policy, and American Agriculture*. Lawrence: University Press of Kansas.

CBS News/*New York Times*. 1986. The Farm Crisis. *CBS News Poll*. February.

Congressional Quarterly, 1984. *Farm Policy: The Politics of Soil, Surpluses, and Subsidies*. Washington, D.C. Congressional Quarterly, Inc.

Congressional Quarterly Almanac. 1985. "Agriculture." Washington, D.C.: Congressional Quarterly, Inc.

Conlan, T., M. Wrightson, and D. Beam. 1990. *Taxing Choices: The Politics of Tax Reform*. Washington, D.C.: CQ Press.

Davies, D. 1986. *United States Taxes and Tax Policy*. New York: Cambridge University Press.

Derthick, M., and P. Quirk. 1985. *The Politics of Deregulation*. Washington, D.C.: Brookings Institution.

Freeman, R. 1973. *Tax Loopholes: The Legend and the Reality*. Washington, D.C.: American Enterprise Institute.

Gardner, B. 1981. *The Governing of Agriculture*. Lawrence: Regents Press of Kansas.

Greider, W. 1981. "The Education of David Stockman." *Atlantic Monthly*, December, pp. 27–54.

Johnson, G., K. Hemmi, and P. Lardinois. 1985. *Agricultural Policy and Trade: Adjusting Domestic Programs in an International Framework*. A Task Force Report to the Trilateral Commission. New York: New York University Press.

Kingdon, J. 1984. *Agendas, Alternatives, and Public Policies*. Boston: Little, Brown.

Long, R., ed. 1987. *The Farm Crisis*. The Reference Shelf. 59, 6. New York: H. W. Wilson.

Los Angeles Times. 1988. Farm Aid. Cited in *National Journal*, December 10, p. 3157.

McGinley, L. 1985. "The Treasury's Plan to Overhaul Tax Code Sparks Heated Debate." *Wall Street Journal*, April 3, Sec. 1, p. 1.

McKinzie, L., T. Baker, and W. Tyner. 1987. *A Perspective on U.S. Farm Problems and Agricultural Policy*. Boulder, Colo.: Westview Press.

Murray, A. 1986a. "Individuals' Top Rate Would Plunge to 28 Percent: Tax Break Curbs Offset Benefits to Wealthy." *Wall Street Journal*, August 18, Sec. 1, p. 6.

_____. 1986b. "Industry-by-Industry Review of Tax Bill Shows Loss of Special Deductions Offsets Rate Cut." *Wall Street Journal*, August 19, Sec. 1, p. 6.

Olson, M. 1982. *The Rise and Decline of Nations*. New Haven, Conn.: Yale University Press.

Plissner, M. 1987. "Campaign '88—A Year to Go." New York, CBS News Poll.

Rauch, J. 1985. "Farmers' Discord over Government Role Produces a Farm Bill That Pleases Few." *National Journal*, November 9, p. 2538.

Roberts, S. 1985. "Farm Issue: Headaches by the Hundredweight." *New York Times*, February 12, p. B8.

_____. 1986. "How Tax Bill Breezed Past, Despite Wide Doubts." *New York Times*, September 26, p. 20.

Roper Organization, Inc. 1978. *The American Public and the Income Tax System*, vol. 1: Summary Report, July.

_____. 1979. *Third Annual Tax Study*, vol. 1: Summary Report, July.

Schattschneider, E. 1960. *The Semi-Sovereign People*. New York: Holt, Rinehart and Winston.

Schick, A. 1990. *The Capacity to Budget*. Washington, D.C.: Urban Institute Press.

Shribman, D. 1985. "Growing Majority Believes Businesses Don't Pay Fair Tax Share, Poll Finds." *Wall Street Journal*, November 26, p. 20.

Stewart, C. 1989. "The Politics of Tax Reform." Pp. 143–170 in *Politics and Economics in the Eighties*, ed. A. Alesina and G. Carliner. Chicago: University of Chicago Press.

Thompson, P. 1988. "The Philosophical Rationale for U.S. Agricultural Policy." Pp. 34–45 in *U.S. Agriculture in a Global Setting: An Agenda for the Future*, ed. M. A. Tutwiler. Washington, D.C.: Resources for the Future.

Tweeten, L., and B. Jordon. 1988. "Farm Fundamentalism: Support for Farmers Is Widespread, But It May Fade." *Choices* 3:26–27.

U.S. Congress, Joint Committee on Taxation. 1987. *General Explanation of the Tax Reform Act of 1986*, H.R. 3838, 99th Congress; Public Law 99–514. Washington, D.C.: Government Printing Office, May 4.

U.S. Department of Commerce, Bureau of the Census. Various years. *United States Statistical Abstract*. Washington, D.C.: Government Printing Office.

U.S. Office of Management and Budget. Various years. *Budget of the United States Government*. Washington, D.C.: Government Printing Office.

Vogel, D. 1989. *Fluctuating Fortunes: The Political Power of Business in America*. New York: Basic Books.

Wilson, G. 1977. *Special Interests and Policy-making: Agricultural Policies and Politics in Britain and the United States*. New York: John Wiley.

Witte, J. 1985. *The Politics and Development of the Federal Income Tax*. Madison: University of Wisconsin Press.

7

The Tragedy of the Concrete Commons: Defining Traffic Congestion as a Public Problem

Joseph F. Coughlin

THE COMMONS DILEMMA

Twenty-five years ago Garrett Hardin described a common pasture set aside for local herdsmen on which their cattle grazed. Each herdsman attempts to maximize his use of this common by adding as many cattle as he can. Each cow added provides the individual herdsman with a proportional economic benefit. For a time this regime of private interests and a public resource works, because the number of cattle is below the carrying capacity of the pasture. Over time the number of cattle increases to a level where the common pasture becomes overgrazed. Despite the worsening conditions of depleted vegetation and general crowding, the potential benefit to each individual to optimize his use of the common continues to encourage overuse. Hardin laments: "Therein is the tragedy. Each man is locked into a system that compels him to increase his herd without limit—in a world that is limited. Ruin is the destination toward which all men rush, each pursuing his own best interest in a society that believes in the freedom of the commons" (Hardin 1968: 1244).

The tragedy of the commons presents a dilemma that "results from an incentive structure in which the benefits to an individual who increases his use of the resources exceed the costs to him even though the sum of the benefits of the action to all users is less than the sum of the costs to all users" (Godwin and Shepard 1977: 231). This scenario provides a context for understanding various policy problems that are population- or growth-related and that involve collectively owned goods such as air, water, and parks. Commons, however, are not just natural resources (Ostrom 1990). There are man-made, indeed concrete, commons that serve as subjects for policymaking.

Perhaps the country's single largest commons is the national highway system. It comprises nearly 4 million miles of surface. Over 3 million miles are rural roads and another approximately 760,000 miles are urban pavements. Although it bears 22.3 percent of the nation's total travel, the interstate system makes up only 1.2 percent of the nation's total number of road miles (USDOT, 1992). The estimated cost of building the present system would probably be nearly a half trillion dollars. The Highway Users Federation estimates that the replacement cost for the interstate system alone could be as much as $5 to $10 million per mile.

Traffic congestion caused 1.5 to 2 billion hours in delays for drivers and passengers in 1987. This resulted in lost work time, delays in the delivery of goods, wasted fuel, and increased air pollution. Although forecasters do not agree on the precise level of increase, there is a consensus that future levels of congestion in many of the nation's major urban areas will more than double commuting times by the year 2000.

How to preserve the commons while protecting individual freedom is a recurring dilemma in American public policy. Two value systems, one pastoral, or "green," and the other industrial, or growth-biased, have tended to dominate. Transportation policy is a product of these competing cultural views, each attempting to manage automobility to further its vision of how we ought to live, manage our resources, and use technology. A principal tactic employed by opposing groups is to manipulate the definition of the congestion problem to gain strategic advantage in the continuing policy debate over personal mobility.

THE NATIONAL HIGHWAY SYSTEM
AND THE VISION OF AUTOMOBILITY

Almost every aspect of life is affected by transportation. The economy is vitally linked to the health and efficiency of the transportation system. Every product and manufactured good depends on transportation in some way. Business transportation costs may be as much as 18 percent of the total cost of a product and 8 percent of the gross national product (Delaney 1986). For example, General Motors spends an estimated $5 billion to transport its goods (Stemple 1989). Likewise, American life is a story of "going to"—to work, to school, to shop, to church, or to some other social activity. In short, before you can do anything, you have to go there.

The nation's highway system, the roads, and the automobiles that operate on them have facilitated a unique way of life based upon personal mobility. A social premium has been placed on the ability to go from point A to point B, door to door, at any time, in the comfort, security, and convenience of one's own car. This vision of individual freedom has made possible a lifestyle that is built around the "central values intimately associated with automobility—material prosperity and progress through unlimited production and consumption of consumer goods, and the fusing of rural and urban advantages in a suburban Utopia" (Flink 1975: 183). This lifestyle is punctuated by the burgeoning growth of the suburban single-family home development, the shopping mall, and the industrial park.

To support that lifestyle, the majority of American households owned one car in 1969; by 1990 that had changed to at least two vehicles. More striking is that the number of households with three or more autos quadrupled between 1969 and 1990. Despite a decrease in the average family's size, the availability of cars climbed dramatically. By 1992, there were 1.11 cars per licensed driver in the United States.

More Americans are going to more places more often every day using their automobiles. U.S. Department of Transportation statistics reveal that the number of vehicle miles of travel made by private vehicles grew by 150 percent between 1960 and 1990 and that the number of miles traveled by each individual increased by 65 percent (USDOT 1992a).

Americans choose to move by automobile. Approximately 85 percent of all personal trips in 1990 were by car. Although the average number of vehicle trips between home and work has remained relatively unchanged, less than a 1 percent increase between 1969 and 1990, the greatest increase in auto use has been for running personal errands, up over 100 percent. These trips include going to the laundry, getting shoes repaired, and so on. Apart from the purchase of services, trips in another category, shopping, rose a dramatic 62 percent (USDOT 1992a: 18).

America's love affair with automobility is likely to continue. Population distribution and land use patterns encourage auto use. More Americans now live in the suburbs than in the nation's cities or rural areas (U.S. Department of Commerce 1991). In contrast to urban centers, where public transit is often readily available, the suburbs are designed around the auto. Shopping centers are spread miles apart and homes are often found in cloistered "executive" developments. Moreover, many employers are relocating out of the city to suburban office parks to take advantage of lower tax rates, new facilities, and amenities demanded by many employees, such as ample parking and outdoor recreation facilities.

THE PROBLEM OF TRAFFIC CONGESTION

Like the grass of the classic common, the nation's highways are experiencing demand well beyond capacity, resulting in the phenomenon called traffic congestion. In 1990, 60 percent of all highway travel in peak hours occurred in congested conditions. Urban interstate highways experienced nearly a 30 percent increase in peak-hour congestion between 1975 and 1990, resulting in millions of hours of delay (USDOT 1991).

Congestion is defined by traffic engineers as an arithmetic function of the number of vehicles per hour over a specified mile of highway—volume of traffic/service flow. As this ratio increases, traffic slows and eventually stops. However, although this quantitative definition may be useful for conducting computer analyses of traffic flows, it does not help the policymaker determine the nature of the problem, what is to be done, or what may be at stake. Paraphrasing one transportation planner in the Washington, D.C., area, congestion is "everywhere and is often the result of no visible problems" (Allen 1991: 5A).

Congestion is not a new problem. Since the 1920s congestion on the nation's highways has been both a policy problem and a source of driver aggravation (Flink 1988). Despite delays and exasperation, Americans continue to choose their automobiles over other transportation alternatives. The cost of this choice remains minimal to the individual. A 1991 Federal Highway Administration study reveals that the total average cost of owning and operating an automobile is only 33 cents per mile, while the larger costs of construction, maintenance, and policing of the nation's highways are underwritten by all levels of government (USDOT 1992b).

Though lane space may be in short supply, the inner space of the auto has expanded. While delayed in traffic the driver can be cooled by air conditioning, listen to language instruction tapes, use the car phone, or conduct business via a portable FAX. Thus the automobile continues to be a comfortable and productive transportation choice. Although these amenities may make delay more tolerable, traffic congestion is still seen as hindering personal mobility. Over 60 percent of the drivers surveyed in a *Washington Post* poll said that they would not be willing to car pool or to leave their car for some alternative at least half the time to help relieve congestion (Prabhakar and Blood 1991). Consequently, congestion remains a significant private inconvenience and a major public issue in most metropolitan areas (Downs 1992; Wright 1992).

There are generally two sets of policy strategies for managing traffic congestion—supply management and demand management. Supply management defines traffic congestion as a function of too little highway to meet demand and simply adds to the common. Unlike the classical common, the carrying capacity of the highway can be increased to meet traffic demand. Historically, the policy of choice has been to pour concrete and lay asphalt until traffic demand is met. As a result, expenditures to build, maintain, and service highways and parking to support auto demand are approximately $175 billion annually (MacKenzie, Dower, and Chen 1992).

Although new highways are being built less frequently than in the road construction boom of the 1960s, policymakers continue to plan and implement transportation supply programs that facilitate automobile use. These programs include lane widening, better signal controls, and large investments in new technologies such as Intelligent Vehicle Highway Systems (IVHS), which will optimize the current system to facilitate traffic flow and operational safety.

Demand management, in contrast, seeks to manage the demand for lane space by changing the behavior of the individual. Traffic congestion from this perspective is defined as too many cars demanding access to a limited good—the highway—and as indicative of undisciplined individual behavior threatening the common good. Demand management for the purposes of this discussion is any policy or set of policies that seeks to dissuade or restrict single-occupant vehicle use. These may include car pooling, transit investments, restricted high occupancy vehicle (HOV) lanes, congestion pricing, and the development of transportation alternatives other than the auto (Institute of Transportation Engineers 1989).

The selection of any one or a mix of supply and demand management strategies is determined by how local transportation policymakers choose to define their congestion problem. Consequently, metropolitan regions with similar congestion problems often differ on what policy alternatives to adopt. Planners in the San Francisco Bay Area defined traffic congestion in terms of too many cars, not too little highway. A coalition of environmentalists and mass transit advocates determined that increasing automobile use was choking the highways with traffic and the air with toxic emissions. As a result, that region spent, and continues to spend, large sums of money on transit. It may be the first metropolitan area in the country to widely implement congestion pricing—the levying of higher tolls on drivers who choose to operate their cars during periods of peak demand, such as the morning and evening commute.

In contrast to San Francisco, Houston and surrounding Harris County defined congestion as a problem of too little highway to meet traffic demand. Therefore, Houston decisionmakers, coupled with a coalition of city business leaders and land developers, opted to develop a strategy based principally on supply management: in short, to build more system capacity rather than attempt to change individual behavior. At a cost of $1 billion per year, Houston built more than 1,600 lane miles, two new toll roads, and only 95 miles of designated car pool and bus lanes.

How does the government formulate policy to address a problem that is as ubiquitous as it is difficult to define? Despite attempts at rational analysis to define congestion and determine the range of acceptable solutions, the issue has been described in conflicting dimensions. Each definition has been the product of a different set of participants influencing the decisionmaking process, and each has produced a distinctive set of policy alternatives.

A CULTURAL BASIS OF PROBLEM DEFINITION

The management of individual behavior and its impact on the commonwealth is derived from how people agree to live with each other and on the basis of what values they choose to share common resources. Douglas and Wildavsky argue that it is how people want to live with other people that matters in their selection or dismissal of various policy choices (Douglas and Wildavsky 1982; Polisar and Wildavsky 1989). If transportation is nothing else, it is a physical system that facilitates how we choose to live with each other. Traffic congestion has provided an opportunity to redefine the traditional surface transportation policy from that of a physical-economic infrastructure to facilitate the movement of people and goods to that of a socio-political tool to re-engineer how we live and use our common resources.

Two themes tend to dominate American political conflict in determining policy that affects lifestyle and the use of common resources: individualist and communitarian. The first places a high value on individual freedom and choice, while the second places a greater premium on community and social equity. While the individualist argues that as each does well the community prospers, the communitarian argues that the common good must be protected from the selfishness of individual behavior. Collective policy problems, such as how to use common resources, are approached differently from these two traditions, making each a political philosophy (Taylor 1992).

The individualist tradition has tended to support policies that afford a more material, technology-assisted lifestyle, while, in contrast, the communitarian philosophy has been predisposed to a more pastoral tradition, placing great importance on policies that protect the environment. These two traditions have persisted throughout American political thought. Where individualist thought has traditionally dominated transportation policy, its greatest support has come from real estate interests, business leaders, and elected officials who promote economic development and regional growth, growth that has often been fueled by aggressive roads and public works building programs funded by all levels of government.

The communitarian tradition has been achieving newly found resonance by capitalizing on events and policy that focus public attention on the import of environmental quality and on the impact of misguided individual choice on the social good. This tradition is reflected in the *greening* of America's transportation policy, finding support within the environmental movement and a loose coalition of transit interests, urban planners, and architects.

Bosso argues that the American political system is structured more in favor of individualist values than communitarian or green values. He compares environmental values with *traditional* "system values," arguing that where "ecological thinking stresses the interconnectedness of the parts that make up the whole," and therefore the importance of the common good, individual freedom values emphasize the importance of personal choice (Bosso 1993: 89). Bosso demonstrates that these values transcend each perspective's view of planning and short- versus long-term policymaking.

Green values emphasize planning: If we were better at planning the use of resources we might benefit everyone, not just a select few, in the long term. This holistic approach would fully assess the benefits of our transportation policy choices against the likely costs each alternative may have on the environment and the community. Individual freedom values, in contrast, emphasize the short term and are generally opposed to long-term planning that may supplant daily individual choice. Policy change to individualists is incremental and policy-specific, while greens suggest that planning and policy decisions should be comprehensive and integrative.

The perspectives also differ on the value and role of technology. Environmentalists tend to be suspicious of technology, for the same reason that individual freedom advocates are supportive. To those supporting individual choice, technology is the savior or cure-all facilitating growth and mitigating its deleterious effects; to the greens, technology has been used as a band-aid or as a means to continue a way of life that is in the long-term detrimental to the common good.

Both perspectives—the individualist, which will hereafter be referred to as the traditional or growth perspective, and the communitarian, which will be described as green—are shaping transportation policy. Both sets of values view transportation as a linchpin in promoting a particular vision of modern life. Likewise, both the traditional and green perspectives see traffic congestion as a symptom of a larger problem and as an opportunity to redefine transportation policy, thereby determining how America uses its common resources and how its citizens live with each other.

Although the green perspective has met with mixed political success at the local level, it has recently made considerable progress at the federal level, where a substantial amount of transportation funding is controlled. A series of legislative victories affecting transportation has broadened the definition of mobility to include green values that have not been traditionally included in the transportation policy community.

Supported largely by environmentalists and a coalition of planners, transit interests, historical preservationists, and a vocal bicycle and pedestrian lobby, the environment and transportation were linked as never before in the passage of the 1990 Clean Air Act Amendments (CAAA) and the 1991 Intermodal Surface Transportation Efficiency Act (ISTEA). ISTEA, the five-year surface transportation authorization bill, dictates that local decisions to build future roads to alleviate congestion be assessed in terms of their impact on clean air. Although the linkage between auto use and air quality has been debated for twenty years, the CAAA and ISTEA now require that transportation policymakers bear the responsibility with smokestack industries for emissions in regions with severe air pollution problems. The legislative mandate compels regional authorities to implement demand management policies to regulate individual driver behavior to ensure that their metropolitan regions attain clean air standards set forth in the CAAA (Bryner 1993). Similarly, the passage of the Energy Act of 1992 formally incorporates the value of energy efficiency into the transportation planning process.

In the social context, the Americans with Disabilities Act (ADA), which guarantees access to public transportation facilities to the physically disabled, effectively introduced social equity as a value to be included in defining transportation policy. The ADA coalition continues to argue for a more humanized transportation system that guarantees mobility and access to social centers, health care, and jobs for the disabled, the poor, and the elderly.

Reflecting upon these pieces of legislation, and on the impact of ISTEA in particular, one state transportation planner declared the legislative environment to be "an opportunity to renegotiate a new contract . . . on mobility and quality of life; and, to try to sort out the conflicting values confronting society" (Transportation Research Board 1993).

REDEFINING TRANSPORTATION:
COMPETING VALUES AND CONFLICTING
DIMENSIONS OF THE CONGESTION PROBLEM

The green and the traditional perspectives choose to define the causes of congestion differently. Each emphasizes different issues associated with the problem. The values of environmental quality, energy efficiency, social equity, safety, economic health, system efficiency, and mobility are all points of emphasis in the congestion debate. No one perspective, green or growth, disagrees absolutely with the role of any one of these values in defining the problem. However, it is how each prioritizes these values that determines the polemics of defining the congestion problem and, in turn, the list of legitimate policy alternatives. Figure 7.1 depicts the relative priority afforded to each value by both perspectives.

The green perspective sees demands for highway expansion to relieve congestion as inextricably linked to growth and its related costs of diminished environmental quality, urban sprawl, and an insatiable demand for finite energy resources. The underlying assumption linking transportation and the environment is that if highways were built to spur development, development can be stopped by not building them, and growth can be limited by controlling their use. Congestion to many environmentalists is simply a

GREEN PERSPECTIVE

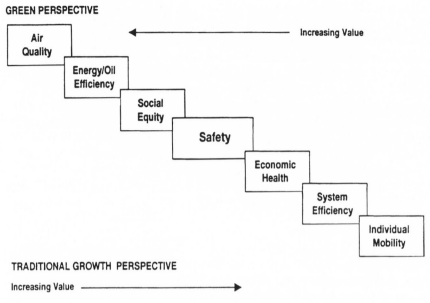

Figure 7.1. Transportation Policy Perspectives and Values

symptom that the country has reached the limits of growth. Consequently, it is those perceived costs of growth that are emphasized in defining the problem.

The major cost most frequently emphasized is diminished environmental quality. One environmentalist described many freeways as "so congested that they look like eerily animated parking lots—animated not because they are moving, but because of the photochemical activity dancing in the air" (Lyman 1990: 36). Air pollution resulting from auto use and exacerbated by congestion is the most frequently cited environmental cost of auto use. It is regularly argued that the organic and inorganic emissions from automobiles contribute to ozone depletion, regional smog problems, and the greenhouse effect. When more people choose to drive, highways become more congested, resulting in more idling cars producing a greater volume of pollutants.

Closely linked to the green emphasis on diminishing air quality is energy consumption. Congestion is cast as an additional byproduct of continued and growing auto use that is fostering the nation's dependence on foreign petroleum. Environmental groups contend that, in the long run, our nation's current approach to automobile use is unsustainable due to the finite availability of petroleum and to the unpredictability of foreign sources.

The third dimension of congestion that environmentalists focus upon is land use and its relationship to social equity. Congestion is now a suburban phenomenon. Between 1960 and 1990 congestion increased 58 percent in the suburbs. Urban centers grew by 30 million people between 1950 and 1990, while the suburbs grew by 80 million. This increased traffic reflects a boom both in suburban housing and in the number of employers moving from the city to the suburbs (Stewart 1990). Because the suburbs are generally not serviced by public transportation, some argue that the migration of jobs from the city to the outlying edge cities has blocked opportunities for many, particularly the urban poor, for employment. Moreover, the auto, and the roads built to serve it, have facilitated middle-class flight from the typically inner-city problems of substandard education and crime. The problem of congestion provides an opportunity to cast poor land use planning and the automobile as accomplices to an "erosion in the quality of urban life and modern stratification of urban society in terms of race, income, and wealth—a level of urban stratification the world has never known before" (Johnson 1992: 14).

Interestingly, the issue of safety can be described as a common-ground value shared by the two perspectives. Despite an average of forty-five thousand deaths and nearly one million highway-related injuries a year, highway safety receives only intermittent emphasis. Although the high import placed upon air quality is usually linked to public health and the priority placed upon individual mobility is said to preserve a way of life, neither perspective has chosen to place continuous emphasis on highway safety.

In defining the problem of traffic congestion the traditional growth perspective emphasizes the values of economic vitality, system efficiency, and personal mobility. The traditional transportation perspective tends to promote the economic growth paradigm: economic vitality is critical to improving the quality of life for all and is the engine for technological innovations that will solve growth-related problems. Anything that impedes economic growth, therefore, is a threat to our quality of life and to any hopes there might be for improvement.

Those advocating a traditional approach to congestion argue that the economic cost of traffic delay is more important than the inconvenience it produces. Paradoxically, this perspective also admits that as a region becomes more affluent, use of automobiles increases; therefore congestion may, in a sense, be a positive indicator of a vibrant economy. Despite this, the traditional perspective argues that billions of productive work hours are lost each year and that delays in the delivery of goods and services diminish the competitiveness of American business.

The emphasis on the costs of congestion to economic vitality has frequently provided a common ground between business leaders and elected officials. Business is dependent upon the productivity of its workers and upon the transportation services this requires; consequently, industry will locate where it believes it can operate the most efficiently. Elected officials, on the other hand, see business as key to providing more jobs and regional prosperity to their constituency. Therefore, they tend to form coalitions on policies that further highway expansion to alleviate traffic congestion.

Where business emphasizes economic efficiency, traditional-minded highway engineers in many state transportation departments place a high value on the efficient and productive use of the highways built by them over the past fifty or more years. The goal of transportation policy from this perspective is to move traffic generated by economic activity. As one spokesman from the highway engineering community put it, "our job as transportation professionals is to plan for and serve these desired economic interests as best we can" (Lamm 1989: 20). If there is a congestion problem, highway engineers look at what can be done to correct the system's inefficiency or mismanagement, whether through construction, improved traffic signals, or signs. Transportation planning tends to have a bias in favor of servicing individual highway demand rather than modifying individual driver behavior.

Hinged upon the value of individual freedom, the third value is the one on which the traditional perspective places the greatest emphasis. This is the *right* to mobility, redefined over the past fifty years as automobility. Automobility enables individuals to choose where they want to live, work, and play. According to Beyers, two cars and a garage are the hallowed staples of suburban life, enabling individuals to travel wherever they please in the convenience, comfort, and privacy that for now only a car can provide. One man in the Washington, D.C., area described his family's dependence on automobiles: "Once I would have thought four cars is a luxury . . . but this is just bread and butter transportation for us" (Beyers 1993: A1).

FOUNDATIONS OF THE MOBILITY PROBLEM: WHO AND WHAT IS TO BLAME?

Rochefort and Cobb argue that who and what is portrayed as the cause of a policy problem is crucial to determining how that issue is to be resolved. Predictably, the two perspectives diverge on the level of analysis they commonly use to define the problem of congestion and offer different alternatives to allocate blame for the problem.

The green perspective focuses upon the individual level of analysis, arguing that it is the individual's choice to continue his or her unlimited use of the common that threatens the health of the environment and society. The individual culprit may be the individual driver, the planner, or the land developer. Although the car is said to pollute or blemish the landscape, it has become emblematic of individual choice. One author reflects upon drivers and their contribution to congestion and air pollution: "cars are the most democratic of pollution sources, pollution from cars comes down to millions of personal choices" (Wald 1990: 1E). Although the individual is seen as making environmentally costly choices every day, it is often asserted that this is due to misguided self-interest. Explaining the dramatic rise in auto use, the driver has been compared to a Dr. Jekyll and Mr. Hyde, where "the Hydes of the world, not to mention the Smiths and the Joneses, are victims of circumstances seemingly beyond their control or anyone else's" (Wald 1990: 1E). Shifting the blame to individual highway planners, a representative of the Sierra Club in the mid 1970s articulated his opinion that "time has shown their vision was inadequate. They put us into a horrible kind of box, committing us to a transportation system that was fundamentally evil" (Flink 1975: 75).

Anthony Downs attributes congestion, environmental degradation, and other maladies of growth ironically to the success of the "ideal vision" of development that included the auto, the single family home, and suburban living. Downs argues that there is a need to replace this dominant paradigm fostered by developers, political institutions, and real estate investors over the past few decades with "a new vision of development" (Downs 1989: 1–3).

Whether rational decisions or misguided self-interest is culpable for the congestion problem, the traditional policy of financing highway development has been called the largest public subsidy of private transportation in history. Although many have benefited, greens argue that the urban poor and transportation alternatives to the automobile have paid the price. Continued highway development would only encourage the middle-class to flee the cities, taking with them jobs and leaving behind a racial divide and a social inequity that can only result in continued urban decay. Moreover, the continued subsidy of auto use takes money away from the promotion of cleaner, more energy-efficient transportation alternatives, such as mass transit, bicycling, and walking. The congestion problem illustrates that the traditional policy of encouraging auto use is misdirected; public money should be redistributed to those groups and alternatives that have been neglected in favor of the auto.

In contrast, the traditional perspective focuses upon the physical capacity or management of the transportation system as the primary cause of congestion. From the vantage point of those supporting construction to promote economic growth, for example, congestion is the result of insufficient capacity, which can best be remedied either by widening the existing road or by building a new highway to service the excess traffic demand. Building additional highway capacity was the predominant policy strategy until the 1980s, when the budgetary context of road building changed. From the 1920s to the 1980s there was ample government funding available to expand existing pavements and to build new highways; however, over the past ten years the federal deficit, coupled with fiscal crises in many states, has made new construction a less viable alternative. Consequently, there is now greater stress on new technologies and improved management techniques to optimize the existing road capacity.

The traditional approach tends to use technology to mitigate the costs of automobility. Congestion management, from this perspective, is looking not to change individual driving behavior but to use electronics to improve the "flow" of traffic. Even the language of the technology—Intelligent Vehicle Highway Systems (IVHS), so-called smart cars and smart highways—argues that if we can only make the existing roadway smarter we can make it more efficient. Technologies such as radio tags to eliminate backups at toll booths, sensors that enable autos to drive closer together at higher speeds, and radar to avoid possible collisions are all ways to aid the "function of the driver's brain" to make the road safer and more productive (Eisenstein 1993: G6).

Similarly, if roads were managed more efficiently, congestion could be reduced. Incident delays, defined as congestion caused by accidents or other events on the highway, are a leading cause of tie-ups. Rubbernecking, or in technical parlance, gawker delay, when drivers slow to view an accident scene or a construction sight, is a major management challenge. It has led many highway departments to place screens around work areas or to limit the use of emergency lights by police and repair crews.

NATURE OF THE PROBLEM: STANDARDS, STATISTICS, AND STUDIES

Information is often the primary currency of political power in a policy debate. Often the more technical and complex the data, the more credible it seems. Opposing interests actively develop and present competing, and often conflicting, standards, statistics, and studies to argue the correctness or efficacy of their positions. With this documentation they attempt to communicate the severity, incidence, costs to personal interests, and even the novelty of the policy problem.

The greens use the problem of congestion as an opportunity to focus on the air pollution costs of automobility and its relationship to public health. Motor vehicles contribute between 20 and 30 percent of all carbon dioxide emissions, which are considered to be a principal contributor to the greenhouse effect. Cars are also a primary contributor to ground-level ozone pollution—a major component of urban smog.

The 1990 CAAA establish attainment standards for urban regions for several pollutants, such as 0.13 parts per million (ppm) for ozone. Another standard exists for carbon dioxide, another for carbon monoxide, and yet another for sulfur-based emissions. Metropolitan areas must attain these standards by limiting automobile use or by enacting legislation that requires "green cars" that are battery-powered or that use alternative fuels such as methanol.

But what pollutants should be measured and how? Which are safe in what volume? The answers to such questions must be determined in a policy environment that is highly technical and political. For example, the technical criteria and the methodology for measuring and monitoring pollutants emitted by automobiles are unclear. Should a single type of air sampling device be used to measure air quality uniformly across the United States? And what model or models should be used to analyze the data once collected?

Though often presented as scientific findings, standards are debatable. A National Academy of Sciences study, for example, suggests that the government, for nearly twenty-five years, may have cost the public billions of dollars by regulating a set of organic pollutants that are emitted by automobiles but are also found in nature. What may be necessary to reduce urban air pollution, researchers now argue, is the regulation of nitrogen oxides (NOX), which are believed to be the leading ingredient in the catalytic process that leads to smog (National Research Council 1991). A recent Harvard School of Public Health study underscores the indeterminate nature of measuring and establishing air pollution standards. The study states that the standards currently established for acceptable levels of air particulate matter released by industry and automobiles may not be safe; in fact, "serious health effects have been observed at exposure levels far below this standard" (Harvard School of Public Health 1993: 2; see also Dockery et al. 1993).

Even though standards are ambiguous, they can become powerful tools in political debate. Standards provide a basis to communicate both the relative severity and the relative incidence of a problem. In *The Green Commuter*, for example, Joel Makower cites Environmental Protection Agency data that identify about 100 metropolitan areas that did not meet ozone attainment standards in 1991, an increase of approximately 40 regions from 1987 (Makower 1992).

Once a standard establishes a baseline, statistics proliferate about whether progress is being made to resolve the problem or whether ground is being lost. Moreover, the perceived widespread incidence of a problem can be easily linked to impacts on the public. One study conducted for the American Lung Association stated "nearly 40 states contain at least one non-attainment level, many states contain several. Almost 100 million Americans still live in areas which exceed healthy air levels" (Walsh 1988: 1). The same study suggests that despite improvements in auto pollution standards, increased auto use has mitigated their effectiveness. Noting that transportation sources were responsible for 73 percent of the lead, 70 percent of the carbon monoxide, 34 percent of the hydrocarbons, 45 percent of the nitrogen oxides, and 18 percent of the air particulates released, the study notes that "a gradual build-up of carbon dioxide is occurring, raising the specter of global warming unless the rate can be slowed" (Walsh 1988: 23). Although the threat of these pollutants may be global, the study reveals a personal cost closer to home: health costs related to motor vehicle emissions alone may cost the public between $14 and $93 billion (Walsh 1990: 2).

In contrast to the greens, proponents of the traditional growth perspective focus principally on the economic costs of delay resulting from congestion. Like the greens, however, the advocates of the traditional transportation perspective use standards and measures to communicate the wide import of the problem. Following the traditional perspective view that accommodating demand is a fundamental role for the transportation system, traffic engineers use a standard that includes "service levels" to indicate the flow of cars per hour and the number of cars per mile. As the number of cars increases, the average speed decreases, making the optimal flow level of A decrease to B, and so on, until a service level of F, stop-and-go traffic, is reached. Using this standard measure as a means to acquire additional state and federal funds, many regions define their situation as either serious or severe (U.S. General Accounting Office 1992).

Organizations such as the Road Information Program, a nonprofit research group financed by construction and other highway interests, have declared that congestion clogs 40 percent of all urban highways and "in 11 states congestion is plugging more than half of all highways" (Sharn and Kady 1992: 7a). Likewise, a traffic engineering publication warned that congestion may be four times worse than present levels early in the twenty-first century (Rowe 1990). Thomas Hanna of the Motor Vehicles Manufacturing Association declared that congestion is "an impending catastrophe" for the country (Torvik 1990: 1).

But what of the costs to the public? Estimates of the costs of congestion abound and vary widely. The Motor Vehicle Manufacturers Association estimates 2 billion hours are lost due to congestion. The Federal Highway Administration has estimated that gawker delay resulting from accidents and even billboard signs may cost the country 1.3 billion hours in delay and as much as $10 billion in lost productivity (Tierney 1993). Another study, conducted by the Texas Transportation Institute, estimates congestion-related delay in Los Angeles alone may cost drivers $8 billion; the same study suggests that New Yorkers may pay as much as $1 billion for congestion in their city (Cushman 1990).

ENGINEERING A SUSTAINABLE
TRANSPORTATION POLICY

The traditional approach to transportation policy was to service traffic demand and to ensure that the technology used to build roads, bridges, or arte-

GREEN PERSPECTIVE

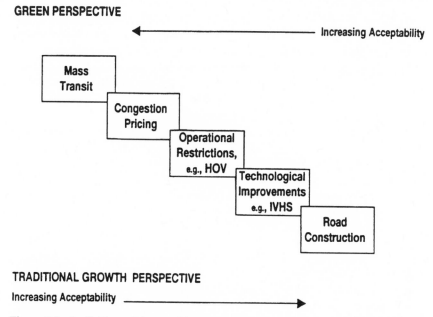

TRADITIONAL GROWTH PERSPECTIVE

Figure 7.2. Available and Acceptable Alternatives toward a Sustainable Transportation Policy

rials had the physical capacity for the job at hand. Generally, the selection of a policy alternative to alleviate congestion or any transportation problem was based on its ability to contribute to economic development, and construction methods were determined largely by technical criteria. Today, policy planning and the selection of policy solutions is based less on their ready availability and cost-effectiveness than on their political sustainability. Congestion relief, and to a greater extent, transportation policy, is now determined by evolving political criteria engineered out of the continuing conflict between the greens and traditional regional growth advocates. Each perspective offers a long-term vision and a range of solutions to the nation's congestion problems.

In Chapter 1 Rochefort and Cobb offered a three-part criterion for determining whether one alternative or another is likely to become government policy. The first part is availability—does a viable alternative exist? Second, is it acceptable? That is, what is the moral efficaciousness of the candidate alternative? And third, is the alternative affordable? Do the necessary resources exist to implement the policy choice? Figure 7.2 depicts the range, availability, and general acceptability of policy solutions to the congestion problem as defined by both perspectives.

Clearly, vocal segments of the green perspective see the automobile as an unsustainable alternative. According to the World Watch Institute, "the automobile-based modern era . . . with its damaging air pollution and traffic congestion does not represent the pinnacle in human social evolution . . . ultimately, a more efficient society is likely to be less congested and polluted" (Brown, Flavin, and Postel 1991: 41). Sustainable transportation policy choices, therefore, are those that promise social equity, energy efficiency, and environmental harmony. To make those choices politically viable, however, the public's perception of what it wants will have to be changed. "Perceived needs [such as automobility] are socially and culturally determined, and sustainable development requires the promotion of values that encourage consumption standards that are within the bounds of the ecologically possible and to which all can reasonably aspire" (World Commission on Environment and Development 1987: 44).

The long-term green vision, then, is to change the tide of suburban development that is both pushed by the auto and in turn pulls for continued highway development. A "back to the center" movement, which favors the redevelopment of town centers, the replacement of the single family home as an ideal, and a restructuring of the institutions that have supported the traditional vision, is gaining popularity among adherents to this perspective.

The greens offer an immediate alternative—public transit. It is already in existence in most urbanized areas, and in most cases it is an environmental improvement over auto use; it pollutes less and is more energy efficient. Responding to the fact that transit ridership has decreased in recent years in favor of the car, transit advocates argue that the costs of automobility must be increased to level the playing field between public transportation and the private car. Higher tolls, gasoline taxes, and congestion pricing could be used as a means to levy the true cost of automobility on drivers. The revenues could then be diverted to transit to improve and expand its service, thereby making it cost competitive as a transportation alternative.

Transit is inherently egalitarian. A transportation system based largely on transit could help assure that economic development, housing, and job opportunities are planned rationally and made accessible to all, not just to those who have the resources to live in the suburbs and operate an automobile. As one transportation planner put it, "planners deal in aggregates—they're not much interested in individuals" (Allen 1991: 5A). But even those who support mass transit admit that developing public transportation at the expense of the personal mobility provided by the auto may not be an acceptable alternative. According to Michael R. Deland, Chairman of the Council on Environmental Quality, personal mobility "is consistent with our most cherished national values of independence. I don't think we're going to change that in the near future" (Wald 1990: 1e).

And certainly those who support the traditional transportation perspective agree that the kind of change the greens advocate may be neither politically possible nor necessary, arguing that technological innovation will continue to solve our transportation and related environmental problems. The traditional growth perspective's long-term vision for transportation policy is incremental, acknowledging that there is limited funding to build new roads and that new technologies will be used to serve the demands placed upon the transportation system by a changing economy and an increasingly mobile public. Growth advocates reason that solutions to many of the problems posed by the greens are readily available. Engines powered by electric batteries and alternative fuels, which are both energy efficient and clean, are being developed and used nationwide. Smart electronics, such as antilock brakes or computer-aided navigation systems, embodied in a family of technologies collectively referred to as IVHS, promises to lessen congestion and to improve safety.

Many greens, however, argue that technological fixes are neither acceptable nor affordable. The use of technology, it is argued, may solve immediate problems only to cause greater problems later. Nostrums such as IVHS will only continue to support a lifestyle that is damaging to the long-term social good. According to Deborah Gordon, Transportation Director for the Union of Concerned Scientists, "investing large sums of money in high-tech solutions is likely to wed Americans even more tightly to cars while claiming significant resources to the detriment of alternative transportation modes . . . strategies such as ride-sharing and high occupancy vehicle facilities, pedestrian walkways, bicycle facilities, parking policies, and land use planning are a better investment of limited transportation dollars" (Gordon 1992: 24–25).

PROBLEM DEFINITION AND THE COMMONS DILEMMA

Although institutional factors and the characteristics of an issue are certainly strong influences, the political process and policy products of problem definition are greatly determined by the mix of participants and the values they introduce into the policy debate. Although the import of values in a policy debate may seem readily apparent, what appears to be a rational, and often technical, debate between differing perspectives often hides political agendas. The conscious selection of language, such as smart highways, and the development of technical measures, such as attainment standards, contribute to the social construction of a seemingly rational policy process.

Exploring the dimensions of problem definition provides an opportunity to examine the dynamics of issues that involve collective action and common resources. It also points out the potential difficulty in formulating policy within an issue area where the scope of participation is expanding and where the values are in flux. Different cultural conceptions of how a problem is formulated provide alternative world views for participants in the policy process. Such perspectives are often not amenable to compromise, which can lead to prolonged, contentious, and confusing debate over the nature of a problem and the legitimate range of acceptable solutions. Such divisiveness can paralyze decisionmakers and can lead to policy gridlock.

What is the near-term outlook for regional transportation policy? Although many would like policies that would legislate or price the driving public out of their automobiles, the political sustainability of such a policy is doubtful. It is far more difficult to take something away from people than it is to offer a better alternative. Likewise, a transportation policy that depends on unlimited road construction is equally unsustainable. Therein is the paradox: as important as clean air and personal health are to all, reliable and convenient personal mobility is seen as equally important.

Nearly 200 million automobiles will be produced in the United States alone over the next ten years. Auto use, and the desire for a personal car, is rising dramatically in the United States, in the developing world, and even in industrialized countries with well-developed transit systems. The automobile is not going to travel its last mile for some time. Technology will make the car greener to satisfy the environmental criteria now evolving. Until transit, either rail or bus services, can be made as convenient, safe, and reliable as the auto, there is little hope that it can be regarded as a comparable transportation alternative.

What is likely to evolve is a mixed transportation system, one that is not as dependent on the automobile and that does not subscribe to the traditional model of transit service. Because suburban growth is likely to continue and edge cities are likely to expand, population densities in the suburbs will continue to increase. Population density is key to transit ridership. Rather than viewing public transit as a purely urban system servicing only a city's central business district and limited radial commutes suburb to city to suburb, regional transit operators should be planning now to develop circumferential bus, rail, and shuttle services connecting edge cities and outlying suburbia. The focus of such a balanced transportation policy should be to take people where they are going, not where we think they ought to be.

REFERENCES

Allen, H. 1991. "Driving Us Crazy: Anatomy of Traffic Jam." *Washington Post*, October 22, p. A5.

Beyers, D. 1993. "Not the Family Car, but the Family Fleet." *Washington Post*, April 4, p. A1.

Brown L. R., C. Flavin, and S. Postel. 1991. *Saving the Planet*. Washington, D.C.: Worldwatch Institute.

Bosso, C. J. 1993. "Environmental Values and Democratic Institutions." Pp. 72–93 in *Environmental Risk, Environmental Values, and Political Choices: Beyond Efficiency Trade-offs in Public Policy Analysis*, ed. J. M. Gillroy. Boulder, Colo.: Westview Press.

Bryner, G. C. 1993. *Blue Skies, Green Politics: The Clean Air Act of 1990*. Washington, D.C.: Congressional Quarterly Press.

Cushman, J. H., Jr. 1990. "Smart Cars and Highways to Help Unsnarl Gridlock." *New York Times*, April 12, p. A16.

Delaney, R. V. 1986. "Freight Transport Deregulation." Paper presented at the Council of Logistics Management, Anaheim, Calif., October.

Dockery, D. W., C. A. Pope III, X. Xu, J. D. Spengler, J. H. Ware, M. E. Fay, B. G. Ferris, Jr., and F. E. Speizer. 1993. "An Association between Air Pollution and Mortality in Six U.S. Cities." *New England Journal of Medicine* 329, 24 (December 9): 1754–1808.

Douglas, M., and A. Wildavsky. 1982. *Risk and Culture*. Berkeley and Los Angeles: University of California Press.

Downs, A. 1989. "The Need for a New Vision for the Development of Large U.S. Metropolitan Areas." Salomon Brothers Bond Market Research, August.

————. 1992. *Stuck in Traffic: Coping with Peak-Hour Traffic Congestion*. Washington, D.C., and Cambridge, Mass.: Brookings Institution and Lincoln Institute of Land Policy.

Eisenstein, P. A. 1993. "Smart Cars, Smart Highways Make Roads More 'Productive.' " *Washington Times*, April 2, p. G6.

Federal Highway Administration. 1992. *Our Nation's Highways*. Washington, D.C.

Flink, J. J. 1975. *The Car Culture*. Cambridge, Mass.: MIT Press.

————. 1988. *The Automobile Age*. Cambridge, Mass.: MIT Press.

Godwin, K. R., and W. B. Shepard. 1977. "Population Issues and Commons Dilemmas." *Policy Studies Journal* 6, 2 (Winter): 231–238.

Gordon, D. 1992. "Intelligent Vehicle Highway Systems: An Environmental Perspective." Paper presented at IVHS Policy: A Workshop on Institutional and Environmental Issues, Monterey, Calif., sponsored by the Institute of Public Policy, George Mason University, April.

Hardin, G. 1968. "Tragedy of the Commons." *Science*, December, 1243–1248.

Harvard School of Public Health. 1993. Press release of an unpublished study by C. Alden Pope. Boston, Mass.: Harvard University, May 16.

Institute of Transportation Engineers. 1989. *A Toolbox for Alleviating Traffic Congestion*. Washington, D.C.: Institute of Transportation Engineers.

Johnson, E. 1992. "Project Report: The Future of the Automobile in the Urban Environment." *Bulletin of the American Academy of Arts and Sciences* 45, 7 (April): 7–22.

Lamm, L. P. 1989. Remarks at the 59th Annual Meeting of the Institute of Transportation Engineers. *Institute of Transportation Engineers Journal*, December, 17–20.

Lyman, F. 1990. "Rethinking Our Transportation Future." *E: The Environmental Magazine* 1, 5. September/October: 34–41.

MacKenzie, J. J., R. C. Dower, and D. D. T. Chen. 1992. *The Going Rate: What It Really Costs to Drive*. Washington, D.C.: World Resources Institute.

Makower, J. 1992. *The Green Commuter*. Bethesda, Md.: National Press Books.

National Research Council. 1991. *Rethinking the Ozone Problem in Urban and Regional Air Pollution*. Washington, D.C.: National Academy Press.

Ostrom, E. 1990. *Governing the Commons: The Evolution of Institutions for Collective Action*. New York: Cambridge University Press.

Pacey, A. 1983. *The Culture of Technology*. Cambridge, Mass.: MIT Press.

Polisar, D., and A. Wildavsky. 1989. "From Individual to System Blame: A Cultural Analysis of Historical Change in the Law of Torts." *Journal of Policy History* 1, 2: 27–42.

Prabhakar, A. S., and B. E. Blood. 1991. *A Survey of Recent Public Opinion Polls on Transportation.* Cambridge, Mass.: U.S. Department of Transportation, Volpe National Transportation Systems Center, December 2.

Rowe, E. S. 1990. "Transportation in the 1990's: A Historical Juncture." *Institute of Transportation Engineers Journal.* December, pp. 13–16.

Sharn, L., and M. Kady. 1992. "Congestion Clogs 40 Percent of Urban Highways." *USA Today*, July 14, p. 10A.

Stemple, R. C. 1989. "Suggested Topics in Formulating a National Transportation Policy." *Moving America: A Look Ahead to the 21st Century.* Washington, D.C.: U.S. Department of Transportation, July 24, pp. 12–21.

Stewart, R. W. 1990. "GAO Report Says Federal Government Lacks Plan to Battle Traffic Congestion." *Los Angeles Times*, January 7, p. A4.

Taylor, B. P. 1992. *Our Limits Transgressed: Environmental Political Thought in America.* Lawrence: University Press of Kansas.

Tierney, J. 1993. "Rubbernecking: Analyzing a Commuter Psychosis." *New York Times*, March 12, p. B4.

Torvik, S. 1990. "The Gridlock Crisis." *Seattle Post-Intelligencer*, January 21, p. B1.

Transportation Research Board. 1993. Comments recorded at the session on "Crafting Regional Vision: Coordinating Transportation and the New Interests." Annual Meeting of the Transportation Research Board, Washington, D.C., January 11.

U.S. Department of Commerce. 1991. *1991 Statistical Abstract of the United States*, Washington, D.C.: Government Printing Office.

U.S. Department of Transportation (USDOT). 1991. "Transportation Issues 1991 and Beyond: A Background Paper." Washington, D.C., November.

———. 1992a. *1990 Nationwide Personal Transportation Survey: Summary of Travel Trends.* Washington, D.C.: Federal Highway Administration.

———. 1992b. *Cost of Owning and Operating Personal Passenger Vehicles, 1991.* Washington, D.C.: Federal Highway Administration.

U.S. General Accounting Office. 1992. *Traffic Congestion: Activities to Reduce Travel Demand and Air Pollution Are Not Widely Implemented.* Washington, D.C.: U. S. General Accounting Office, GAO/PEMD-93-2, November.

Wald, M. L. 1990. "How Dreams of Clean Air Get Stuck in Traffic." *New York Times*, March 11, p. E1.

Walsh, M. P. 1988. *Pollution on Wheels.* Washington D.C.: American Lung Association, January 11.

———. 1990. *Pollution on Wheels II: The Car of the Future.* Washington D.C.: American Lung Association, January 19.

World Commission on Environment and Development. 1987. *Our Common Future.* New York: Oxford University Press.

Wright, C. L. 1992. *Fast Wheels Slow Traffic: Urban Transport Choices.* Philadelphia: Temple University Press.

8

Instrumental versus Expressive Definitions of AIDS Policymaking

David A. Rochefort and Roger W. Cobb

The AIDS disease was first identified in the United States in 1981. By the end of December 1992, the U.S. Centers for Disease Control had recorded more than 250,000 cases (CDC 1993). In 1991, AIDS overtook homicide and liver disease to become the nation's ninth leading cause of death (CDC 1992). More than 150,000 lives have now been claimed by the epidemic. It is impossible to determine precisely the number of Americans infected with the HIV virus, many of whom have yet to seek medical attention. The number is generally believed, however, to be several times the number of diagnosed AIDS cases—in the neighborhood of 1.5 million—leading to projections of increasing AIDS deaths well into the twenty-first century (e.g., Sexton and Feinstein 1991).

Amid all the controversy surrounding this devastating social problem, there is broad consensus on at least one point: the response of government at all levels to the strategic, organizational, and ethical challenges that AIDS has thrust before it has been disappointing. Very often, this public policy failure has been attributed to a conflict between "science" and "politics."

> Even the most far-reaching discoveries of medical science are useless unless coupled with enlightened public policy. It is unfortunate that despite 10 years and more than 100,000 American deaths from AIDS, our national leaders seem to have learned little. (Essex 1991: 23)

> For the first time in the history of human plagues, science has given policy makers an opportunity to respond without panic and without resort to extreme measures. Not that policy makers are taking advantage of this opportunity for rational action—only that they could if available knowledge were deployed wisely. (Osborn 1988: 444)

Even in this country, where outstanding public health surveillance and communications systems exist, it is taking a very long time for people in leadership positions, particularly political and spiritual leaders, to grasp the enormous future dimensions of the AIDS problem, and to take public positions that promote humane and rational policies. (Krim 1987: xvi)

Although the idea of a politics/science dichotomy is appealing to many, drawing strength as it does from facile stereotypes of the vicious ineptness of politicians and the virtuous proficiency of scientists, it miscasts the central dynamic of AIDS policy development. In truth, there is no necessary split between the political and scientific worlds, as numerous large-scale joint endeavors, from space exploration to nuclear power, demonstrate. Rather, the relationship is a nuanced one, in which gains in knowledge may or may not be expected to facilitate policy choice depending on ideology and interest differences for the issue at hand (Graham, Green, and Roberts 1988). The special difficulties encountered in AIDS policymaking—over and above financial, bureaucratic, and implementation obstacles (see, e.g., Panem 1988; Perrow and Guillen 1990)—reflect a volatile struggle over the proper role of government, means/ends relationships in AIDS policy formulation, and utilitarian and moral values. At once philosophical, psychological, and sociological in nature, this clash can be understood in terms of the distinction between "instrumental" and "expressive" definitions of public policy that will be examined in this chapter. Though many past science-related causes have benefited from an irresistible coalignment of instrumental and expressive standpoints, AIDS concerns repeatedly set the two at odds, resulting in fierce debates that make for good political theater but fitful decisionmaking.

The cleavages that enliven American political life are many, among them party, ideology, region, class, race, and religion. The instrumental/expressive duality is not reducible to any of these divisions, however. And it is precisely where other well-worn categories of political explanation fall short—as in the "odd political coupling" of North Carolina Republican Senator Jesse Helms and northern black community leaders in their opposition to the distribution of sterile needles (Kirp and Bayer 1993) or in the clash between Massachusetts' Democratic Governor Michael Dukakis and Boston's Democratic Mayor Raymond Flynn over this same issue (Rochefort and Pezza 1991)—that our alternative framework demonstrates its value.

DEFINITIONAL QUANDARIES OF AIDS

AIDS is a relatively new political issue. There are still many factual uncertainties about the disease, it is strongly associated with lifestyles that are

criminal or considered deviant, and its contagiousness and fatal consequences stimulate widespread public fear. These qualities are a wellspring
from which flow a variety of competing interpretations of the problem and
its meaning for U.S. society.

Ambiguities begin with AIDS, the clinical entity (Office of Technology
Assessment 1992). The CDC developed their first case definition of AIDS in
1982 in order to carry out standardized surveillance of the disease, including
the epidemic's demographic distribution and spread. Local health care providers and facilities are required to report new AIDS cases under the CDC
definition to their state and territorial health departments. These departments, in turn, must relay the information to the CDC. As more data about
the cause of AIDS and its clinical manifestations became available, the CDC
adjusted their definition, first in 1985 and again in 1987. According to this
latter version, a person was diagnosed with AIDS who had one of twenty-
three specified conditions, such as pneumocystis carinii pneumonia, toxo-
plasmosis of the brain, and Kaposi's sarcoma, and who met other condition-
specific criteria, such as a positive HIV test.

Subsequently, this 1987 definition came under fire for reasons related to
politics and policymaking as much as to medicine (Office of Technology Assessment 1992: 2; Osborn 1991). Thousands of HIV-infected people were becoming very ill without developing any of the twenty-three AIDS-defining
conditions. For AIDS advocates, to exclude these persons from the count of
AIDS patients was to understate the true scope of the problem, thus undercutting AIDS as a national issue. Because its list of conditions was oriented
to the kinds of symptoms typically appearing in gay males, the definition
also was criticized for bias against HIV-infected women and intravenous
drug users. A further concern about discrimination arose because these
same two groups tended to be disproportionately black and Hispanic.

The CDC's relatively restrictive definition was also controversial because
it governed the distribution of resources under numerous public and private
programs (OTA 1992: 3) For example, the diagnosis of AIDS according to
CDC criteria helped determine eligibility for Social Security Disability Insurance, Supplemental Security Income, and the Medicaid program. Private
health insurers commonly adopted this same rule for approving reimburse-
ment for AIDS-related services. Distribution of federal funds to states and
cities under the Ryan White Comprehensive AIDS Resources Emergency
Act of 1990 also hinges on a geographic district's AIDS target population,
again using the CDC definition. Thus, the CDC's detractors accused them
of stanching the flow of funds and services needed by thousands of desper-
ately ill patients.

Responding to such attacks, the CDC proposed a fourth revision of their
AIDS definition in the fall of 1991. It would have added to those persons
meeting existing criteria all HIV-positive individuals with $CD4^+$ cell counts

below 200 per cubic millimeter of blood. The CD4$^+$ lymphocyte is an immune system cell whose count ranges from 800 to 1,200 in the blood of healthy persons.

The CDC intended to implement the new definition at the start of 1992 but ran into stiff opposition from women's groups and other advocates who insisted on a more inclusive list of AIDS-defining conditions. Under the pressure of a nationwide campaign, including public demonstrations, congressional testimony, and other tactics, the CDC capitulated (Navarro 1992c). The new federal AIDS definition that went into effect on January 1, 1993, added three more illnesses common among HIV-infected women and drug users (pulmonary tuberculosis, invasive cancer of the cervix, and repeated bacterial pneumonia) as well as the CD4$^+$ cell test.

Perforce, troubling new estimates soon were compiled of the magnitude of the AIDS epidemic. The CDC had projected a 75 percent increase in cases for 1993, owing to the broadened definition. In fact, during the first quarter of the year the increase exceeded 200 percent, with 60 percent of all reported cases qualifying under the new definitional criteria (L. Altman 1993a). And still to be seen is the impact of the 1992 definition in altering distributional patterns, since states are likely to differ in their ability to identify AIDS cases under the revised methodology and because previously underreported groups are not spread uniformly across the nation.

Measurements of a public problem's scope define one aspect of its perceived seriousness. Another aspect is the immediacy of the threat posed by the problem. The perceived contagiousness of AIDS heightens the fear felt by persons not now affected that they are at risk of joining the problem population. But the determinacy of that chance of infection is hardly clear-cut, and varying epidemiological estimates have alternately fanned and dampened public fears. Although subsequently criticized, publications, such as the work of Masters, Johnson, and Kolodny entitled *Crisis: Heterosexual Behavior in the Age of AIDS* (1988; see also Oleske et al. 1983), initially have captured great attention by releasing findings of the rapid spread of AIDS among the heterosexual population and by warnings of transmission by casual contact. Reflecting on his own analysis, team leader Masters commented to a reporter: "It scares the hell out of me" (Alpern 1988: 44).

Over time, however, dire assessments of this kind have not held sway with most researchers. To the contrary, latest reports, such as the one issued in February 1992 by the National Research Council of the National Academy of Sciences, emphasize the illness's confinement among "socially marginalized groups" such as homosexuals, drug users, the poor, and the undereducated. According to one astute commentator, while mainstream society might well be reassured by such news, solidarity behind AIDS as a political issue is likely to wane: "The attitude has become, 'When I thought I was going to get infected I was interested in AIDS, but now that I look around and see that my white, middle-class friends are not infected, I'm not interested' " (Kolata 1993a).

As Rochefort and Cobb indicated in chapter one, causation is a central element of problem definition. To name a problem's cause is to dispel its disconcerting mystery and to turn in the direction of certain kinds of remedies and away from others. For this fundamental dimension of the AIDS issue, one notes additional, if muted, debate. The dominant paradigm of the disease, accepted and disseminated by the U.S. Public Health Service among other important scientific authorities, attributes AIDS to infection with the human immunodeficiency virus transmitted via blood or semen. But there are other less well-known views that, in some cases, contradict the virus-AIDS hypothesis (Root-Bernstein 1993). For example, Professor Peter Duesberg, a retrovirus and cancer expert at the University of California, Berkeley, has proposed a theory that HIV is a mere bystander or marker of AIDS, but not its cause (Duesberg 1992). The key factor in western societies, according to Duesberg and his followers, is prolonged use of recreational drugs, which weakens immune system functioning and causes additional clinical abnormalities. It is no coincidence, by this view, that the groups at highest risk for AIDS, intravenous drug users and male homosexuals who sometimes use aphrodisiacs, muscle relaxants, and psychoactive drugs, are also known substance abusers. Meanwhile, Duesberg asks, how do we make sense of the patients with AIDS and AIDS-like diseases who never test positively for HIV infection (see, for example, Navarro 1992b)?

This is not the place, and we are not the ones, to attempt an assessment of the scientific merits of this debate. Nor is this assessment necessary to appreciate the far-reaching policy implications of the alternate AIDS-causation theory, were it ever to dislodge the reigning HIV view. If AIDS does not result from infection transmitted by sexual activity, then prevention programs centering on safe sex are off base. Distribution of sterile needles, another mainstay of current prevention strategy, would actually be harmful by facilitating drug use, AIDS' supposed cause under this theory. Duesberg has gone so far as to call AZT, the primary drug now given to HIV-infected persons, "AIDS by prescription," since it kills infected *and* uninfected immune system cells. And the drug-use theory of AIDS condemns as foolhardy current HIV research support of more than $4 billion a year. There is no sign that these funding priorities are about to change, but the conventional wisdom that HIV alone causes AIDS increasingly is being questioned by scientists frustrated with the unresolved mysteries of the disease (Kolata 1993b; L. Altman 1993b). Meanwhile, Duesberg feels he has paid a steep penalty for his unconventional AIDS theory—the sudden unexplained loss of NIH funding for his cancer research (Heimoff and Sommer 1991).

Value concerns drive the process of public policymaking in all fields. Claims that AIDS is communicated primarily by sharing dirty needles and

by unprotected homosexual intercourse enhance the disease's moral dimension, injecting notions of culpability, deservingness, blame, and punish-
ment. Indeed, some argue that "the AIDS epidemic has become 'moralized'
far more than 'medicalized'" (Perrow and Guillen 1990: 7). Opinion polls,
the popular media, and discriminatory incidents reported by the press all
confirm the existence of deep hostility toward persons with AIDS.

The process of moralization is not unprecedented in the history of medicine, but the lengths to which it has been carried with AIDS may be. According to Sontag (1989), a partial analogy may be found in societal disapproval
of cancer patients whose illnesses seemingly result from weak-willed personal habits like smoking and drinking; but the behaviors productive of
AIDS are judged by many to be indulgent and delinquent, not just weak.
Syphilis, she reminds us, was also a heavily stigmatized, widely feared infec-
tious disease spread by sexual activity; but AIDS prompts negative reactions
toward "unnatural" sexual behavior, not just promiscuity. Perceptions such
as these help to cast the typical AIDS sufferer in the societal role of "The
Other," to use Dennis Altman's (1986) phrase, in contrast to a smaller number of "innocent victims" who are neither homosexual nor drug users. Shilts
(1991; see also Shilts 1987) calls it the distinction between "Good AIDS"
and "Bad AIDS" and credits popular and leadership prejudice against the
latter for halting government action in areas from research funding to prevention.

The connection is difficult to prove conclusively. Opponents of AIDS policy initiatives cite numerous factors to account for their opposition. Without
question, however, U.S. social welfare history demonstrates that groups
viewed in negative terms are most likely to receive limited, stigmatizing, and
even coercive public policy responses (Rochefort 1986). Given intolerant attitudes, the great wonder perhaps is that AIDS has not turned into more of a
backlash political issue (Zaller 1992: 330).

The qualities of scope, severity, causation, and personal blame underscore
that much public discourse on AIDS is really a debate over how the problem
should be gauged, characterized, and interpreted. The feasibility of ever
finding an effective vaccine or cure and the affordability of funding the
massive research effort to that end are essential definitional struggles on the
solution side of the AIDS policy equation (L. Altman 1993b; Pear 1993).

INSTRUMENTAL AND EXPRESSIVE ORIENTATIONS:
PAST RESEARCH

The distinction between instrumental and expressive perspectives has been in
place for at least four decades across various disciplinary boundaries in the
social sciences. Several related dichotomies are encompassed, including ra-

tionality vs. affect, ends vs. means, and economic interests vs. status interests. Our purpose in sampling this literature is not to delve into fine points of scholarly debate, but rather to show the theoretical import of the instrumental/expressive framework for diverse streams of inquiry and to introduce concepts that inform the policy case studies following.

Sociological and Psychological Foundations

It was sociological theorists who first attempted to incorporate all social behavior into a synthetic systems approach. For Parsons (1951; see also Parsons and Shils 1951), a most important polarity was that between instrumental and expressive action. According to Parsons, instrumental behavior was aimed toward achievement of a particular goal. Expressive action was focused on emotional gratification. Different social orders give primacy to one or the other basis of social organization, but stability depends in all cases on a degree of integration between the two.

Social psychologists have also distinguished between instrumental and expressive orientations to describe two different types of adaptation by individuals to their environment. The instrumental person is one who is goal-oriented and self-directed, "with independence, assertiveness, and decisiveness" (Spence, Deaux, and Helmreich 1988: 154). The expressive individual is more emotionally than practically oriented and more prone to interpersonal sensitivity.

Among cognitive psychologists, a distinction is noted between thinking about ends and about means. These are portrayed as fundamentally different dimensions of decisionmaking, involving different modes of information-processing and utility calculations that encompass both practical and value-based aims, such as aesthetics (Anderson 1975: 303–314). By implication, conflict between the two foci may arise, with one person differing from another in how the tension is resolved.

Opinion Formation and Politics

A number of analysts working on opinion formation have made use of the instrumental/expressive distinction or kindred concepts. Smith (1973), for example, proposed that all attitudes may perform three functions for the individual. The first is an object appraisal function, in which information is used to decide what view of a subject is consistent with personal interests. As Smith (1973: 79) writes, this exercise is the hallmark of "the rational man." The other two functions relate to social adjustment, a process in which attitudes are adopted to support relationships with others or to externalize deep-seated personality needs. In related work, Katz (1968) specified four attitudinal functions: instrumental, value-expressive, ego-defensive, and knowledge organization.

Nimmo (1975) has argued that popular understanding of the political world revolves around "images." In contrast to instrumental, or profit, ends are concerns such as legitimacy and deference. As to the latter, he wrote: "our views of customs, traditions, conventions, ceremonies, rituals, institutions, and habits . . . [give] meaning to our political lives beyond simply pursuit of material gain. Although a sense of legitimacy and status is less tangible than the material profits associated with using images as tools for profit, that sense is no less subjectively rewarding" (1975: 17).

Analyzing the relationship between attitudes and behavior in a number of issue areas, Sears and Citrin also came up with a relevant dichotomy. Their instrumental factor is called "self-interest." A self-interest model advances that "voters are essentially egocentric, that a person's politics depends upon his personal circumstances and how the proffered choices impinge upon them" (Sears and Citrin 1982: 13). In an alternative model stressing symbolic protest, people respond based on early socialization involving "conditioning of specific affects to specific stimuli; for example, of strong negative affects toward 'welfare' or 'blacks.' In adulthood, related stimuli evoke the same emotional response" (Sears and Citrin 1982: 15). After studying the tax revolt in California during the late 1970s, these authors concluded that "symbolic attitudes invariably play an important role" in the political process (Sears and Citrin 1982: 232).

The most recent public opinion literature with a psychological bent continues to be preoccupied with the broad question of what roles reason and affect play in position-taking on political issues (see, for example, Sniderman, Brody, and Tetlock 1991).

Language in Politics

By what means are instrumental and expressive concerns communicated in the political arena? In his classic work, Sapir (1934) pointed out that the public use of language is crucial in rendering political issues meaningful for individuals and groups. In this regard, he spoke of a symbol's "actual significance . . . being out of all proportion to the apparent triviality of meaning suggested by its mere form" (Sapir 1934: 493). Paralleling the instrumental/expressive pairing, Sapir postulated two types of symbols, referential and condensational. The former, such as a statistic, has a clear tangible or factual basis. The latter, such as a patriotic icon or slogan, is an affective creation capable of representing a wide variety of meanings to different individuals. Sapir believed that condensational symbols were particularly powerful because they allowed "for the ready release of emotional tension in conscious or unconscious form" (1934: 493).

Edelman (1985) carried this approach further, stating that fact-based language holds major importance for only a relatively few people and for well-organized interest groups. For the majority, politics is "a parade of abstractions" (Edelman 1985: 10). In Edelman's view, use of condensation symbols in "hortatory rhetoric" takes on immense significance because it can either mobilize or pacify the mass public by "a threat or reassurance" (Edelman 1985: 7).

Status Politics

The role of social status concerns in political conflict as an alternative or adjunct to economic-based motivations is now well recognized. Lipset (1955) and Hofstadter (1965) both called attention to status factors in their studies of right-wing politics. Gusfield (1963) took a related approach in explaining the temperance movement in early twentieth-century America. Zurcher and his colleagues found certain parallels between this temperance movement and present-day antipornography crusades, concluding that the latter was "not primarily utilitarian, but symbolic" (1971: 231) and driven by participants' desire to protect what they saw as a lifestyle under threat. Thus, status politics can develop out of a group's concern about loss of prestige in society or the elevation of values and mores that are deemed objectionable.

Research on Attitudes toward AIDS

Existing work on instrumental and expressive themes of the AIDS issue has only begun to tap into this rich body of sociological, psychological, and political science investigation. The most systematic research to date has focused on the factors underlying surveyed attitudes on AIDS.

In a series of studies, Pryor et al. (1989) sought to test the instrumental and symbolic (or "value-expressive") bases of attitudes toward persons with AIDS. In this research, the former was operationalized as beliefs about the probability of oneself or one's child contracting AIDS. The latter was operationalized as general attitudes toward homosexuality. Both factors proved to have an independent effect on rejection of nonhomosexual AIDS sufferers. Jelen and Wilcox (1992) confirmed the dual importance of instrumental and symbolic attitudes in dispositions toward the AIDS issue. In their analysis, the relative impact of these predictors depended on the specific type of policy intervention.

Finally, another survey research project by Pollock, Lilie, and Vittes (1993) adds an interesting wrinkle on the interaction between political activity levels and instrumental/symbolic attitudes. They found that for the most politically involved citizens, symbolic attitudes pro and con gay rights tended to shape the subsequent development of instrumental beliefs about risk; in other words, political involvement helped to polarize views about the contagiousness of AIDS. They summarize: "Thus symbolic values, once invoked, become durable and versatile touchstones of belief. What is more, debates over what to do about AIDS sufferers are likely to be most rancorous and divisive among the attentive and involved—the stratum of citizens in the best position to mediate the controversy for others" (Pollock, Lilie, and Vitles 1993: 132).

It is that rancorous, divisive world of real politics that we enter now for a different kind of analysis of the interplay between instrumental and expressive definitions in AIDS policy controversies, including the sources, forms, and consequences of these definitions.

NEEDLE EXCHANGE

The connection between intravenous drug use and AIDS is accepted as one of the strongest relationships in epidemiological research on the disease. Sharing of unsterilized needles acts as a highly effective means of communicating the HIV virus. In addition, drug users may spread the virus to non-drug users through sexual contact and during pregnancy and delivery. It is estimated that half or more of intravenous drug users are HIV-infected (*New York Times* 1987). Nearly 60 percent of all pediatric AIDS cases are related to IV drug use (*State ADM Reports* 1992).

The first program to permit drug addicts to exchange their dirty needles for clean ones was undertaken in Amsterdam, the Netherlands (Buning et al. 1986). In 1985, the first full year of the program, 100,000 needles and syringes were turned in. Similar programs soon were established in the United Kingdom, Sweden, Australia, and Canada. In 1986, the World Health Organization held a conference on HIV infection and concluded that "initiatives of this kind could have an important role to play in stopping the spread of HIV" (W. Anderson 1991: 1508).

By the late 1980s, needle exchange programs were on the agenda in the United States as well. For example, a 1985 study by the New Jersey Department of Health found that "making sterile hypodermic equipment available to IV drug users will reduce needle sharing and hence viral transmission by this mode" (Bayer 1989: 221). The National Academy of Sciences also urged needle exchange experiments. In 1991, the National Commission on AIDS, created to advise the president and Congress, added its voice to the chorus, recommending that legal barriers for the purchase of needles and syringes be eliminated.

The U.S. Congress, however, has prohibited states' use of federal funds for distribution of sterile needles. As of the end of 1992, there were thirty-two needle exchange programs in the U.S., none statewide and most without explicit legal sanction (U.S. GAO 1993). Time and again, proposal of these initiatives has sparked explosive community battles preventing or sharply limiting their implementation. A recent report on the states' AIDS prevention efforts for drug users stated that "programs in which people who inject drugs exchange used needles for sterile ones are the most controversial and least legislated of all of the responses to ID [injection drug] use and HIV transmission" (*State ADM Reports* 1992: 2).

Basic to the case for needle distribution is the instrumental definition of this policy approach as one that can achieve its objective and do so efficiently. That overriding objective is fighting the spread of AIDS. And the high prevalence of HIV infection among intravenous drug users (and their sexual partners) makes this population a logical target for intervention. Drug users have a subculture of their own, distrustful of outsiders, which authorities find difficult to penetrate. Proponents of needle exchange cite evidence from studies showing that by employing this technique, other societies have had a marked impact on HIV infection rates without increasing the use of drugs. One forecasting model developed at Yale University indicated the likely effect of a needle exchange program in New Haven to be a 33 percent reduction in new HIV infections over the period of a year (U.S. GAO 1993). Meanwhile, needle exchange programs are inexpensive to operate, costing less in many cases than the care of a single AIDS patient. The pro argument does not fail to recognize needle exchange as an extreme measure; justifying such extremism, however, is the great danger of AIDS. According to the instrumental perspective, needle exchange is defined as a pragmatic response to a worsening social problem.

On the anti–needle exchange side are some who dispute the facts and analysis of the instrumental case in favor. Much more significant, however, is an expressive definition of the policy proposal that approaches it on very different grounds. Use of drugs is a violation of law; so, too, is possession of drug paraphernalia or needles without a medical prescription in several states. Opponents have complained that needle exchange programs undermine respect for the law by involving government in the commission of an illegal act. The programs seem to many to condone, if not outright endorse, drug use, a personally destructive and morally reprehensible form of behavior. In a *New York Times/CBS* poll in 1988, a majority of those who saw addiction as an illness supported needle exchange, while only one-quarter of those who saw addiction as a crime did (Rochefort and Pezza 1991). Opponents also question the deservingness of AIDS victims who are drug users. Significantly, in that same national poll, only 25 percent indicated they had any sympathy for "people who get AIDS from sharing needles while using illegal drugs." Thus, for those defining needle exchange expressively, not even meeting the challenge of AIDS is an end to justify the means of an improper government action to assist an unpopular group engaged in immoral behavior.

The struggle between these divergent sets of views has been played out in dramatic fashion in local political arenas, from Boston (Rochefort and Pezza 1991) to Tacoma (*New York Times* 1989). Consider events in one major American city.

Public health commissioner Dr. David Sencer first proposed the distribution of sterile needles in New York City in late 1985 with Mayor Edward Koch's tacit support (Bayer 1989: 221). A vehement negative reaction was not long in coming. Drug enforcement and police officials lashed out against the plan. One mayoral candidate called it "one of the most harebrained ideas I've heard from city government" (W. Anderson 1991: 1507). The *New York Times* (1985) gave cautious support but asked the troubling question, "How can cities ravaged by heroin condone its use?" Mayor Koch eventually withdrew his backing and said the idea was one "whose time has not come and, based upon the response, will never come" (W. Anderson 1991: 1507). The program was scrubbed. Furor subsided.

Yet the number of AIDS cases among drug users in the city continued its startling growth, and each year hundreds of HIV infected infants were being born to mothers who were IV drug users. In 1987, New York City's new health commissioner, Dr. Stephen Joseph, revived the idea of needle exchange, this time in the form of an experimental study for which he sought state sanction (Joseph 1992: chapter 8). Again, strong criticism arose from many quarters, including state officials, who said the city's research methodology did not measure up to stringent scientific standards.

This deadlock was finally broken in 1988 when a community action group, the Association for Drug Abuse Prevention and Treatment (ADAPT), threatened its own illegal needle distribution in the city. Finding its hand forced, the state approved a limited, revised needle exchange as a clinical trial by the city. Participants were to carry I.D. cards, and the program would run with treatment and control groups. Albeit a modest effort in scale, this would be the first time in the U.S. that drug paraphernalia was given to addicts by the government.

The plan never did attain widespread support. Its friends came primarily from the medical community, AIDS activists, and others who said they wanted decisive action against a mounting public health crisis. Some addicts told reporters they appreciated the offer of help in avoiding AIDS (W. Anderson 1991: 1510).

Arrayed against the plan, by contrast, was an impressive phalanx of powerful interests who freely used moralistic, emotional, and "hortatory" language in their attacks. New York City's special narcotics prosecutor stated, "What a terrible signal this sends in the war on drugs"(Joseph 1992: 202). The city council called on Mayor Koch to halt the program, and the chairman of the council's Black and Hispanic caucus complained, "the city is sending the wrong message when it distributes free needles to drug addicts while we are trying to convince our children to say no to drugs" (W. Anderson 1991: 1512). Other black leaders were even more outspoken, such as another member of the caucus who characterized the needle exchange as "planned assassination in the Black community. It's a damnable, intolerable, unforgivable project" (Joseph 1992: 205). Earlier, New York City's John Cardinal O'Connor had accused the city of "dragging down the standards of all society" (W. Anderson 1991: 1509).

Against this onslaught, health commissioner Joseph defended the initiative with a reasoned, dignified, and, by comparison, feeble response. He recited a litany of HIV and AIDS statistics. He reminded opponents that this was a trial program, intended to carry out objective research to yield needed information in the fight against AIDS: "People are taking positions based on opinions and assumptions without any data, and that's what we want to get" (W. Anderson 1991: 1512). When the *New York Daily News* published a stinging editorial against the initiative, Joseph wrote in reply that "the *News*'s recent attempt to fan the flames of irrationality and whoop up neighborhood hysteria, all in the name of strangling the Health Department's needle-exchange study in the cradle, is inexcusable. . . . As the person charged with protecting the health of this city's people, I must take every reasonable measure available to me to arrest the rampaging AIDS virus. I believe this study reasonable, based on dispassionate review of the evidence before me" (Joseph 1992: 211).

Still, to mollify the critics administrators scaled back the program repeatedly. When it began in November 1988, there was only one distribution center in lower Manhattan. Just two addicts enrolled on the first day; after two months, only fifty-six users had signed up and seventy-six needles were exchanged (W. Anderson 1991: 1512, 1514). The program ended in February 1990, killed by newly elected Mayor David Dinkins in fulfillment of a campaign promise. Paradoxically, however, Dinkins would reverse his position two years later and announce a new program, reportedly after seeing study findings on the effectiveness of needle exchange programs elsewhere in curbing new HIV infections (Navarro 1992a).

Warwick Anderson writes:

Although evidence from abroad suggested by early 1989 that the distribution of clean needles and syringes could reduce the sharing of drug paraphernalia without increasing addiction, this evidence clearly, in the end, was outweighed by the magnitude of the policy's symbolic affront to social order. Thus the control over the definition of the relevant issues had been wrested from the health professionals and, in the end, the explicit moral and political aspects of the problem proved paramount in defining society's response. (Anderson 1991: 1515)

This explanation captures the experience of New York City and many other municipalities that have taken up a needle exchange proposal in recent years, only to be thrown into tumult by contending instrumental and expressive definitions of the nature and worth of the policy before them. Whichever side has won—more often, the opponents of needle exchange—the battle defies conventional political analysis while dramatizing the agonizing public choices that AIDS imposes.

Condom Distribution in Public Schools

The current debate about condoms and their place in AIDS prevention programs is but the latest chapter in a long history of controversy in the United States over the social meaning of condoms (Gamson 1990). At the root of the conflict lie the two uses of condoms: as prophylactics against sexually transmitted disease and as contraceptive devices. Different parties with different interests, from condom manufacturers to medical professionals to religious leaders, have emphasized one aspect or the other in acrimonious battles to determine the definition, acceptability, and availability of this product.

During the 1980s and 1990s, a third definition of the condom has also come to be promoted, exacerbating the dispute (Gamson 1990: 277–278). For many gay activists, condoms are an essential part of sex education programs granting legitimacy to their sexual practices. This definition advances a provocative "resexualized" use of condoms, in contrast to a strict public health rationale. Symbolic of the culture clash between mainstream and gay groups, one AIDS activist in the early 1990s began selling "Old Glory" condoms whose logo was an unfurled red-white-and-blue American flag in the shape of a condom (Tousignant 1992).

It is against this backdrop that the debate over distribution of condoms in public schools has taken place. Across the nation, dozens of school districts have reviewed proposals, and by late 1992, school-based condom distribution was under way in several large urban areas, including New York City, Chicago, Los Angeles, Philadelphia, and Dallas (Baurac, 1992). In one state, Massachusetts, the Board of Education passed a policy calling on all local school systems to consider allowing condom distribution; only a small handful of districts, however, have chosen to act positively (Mednick 1991). Nowhere in the country has the issue failed to generate strong reaction.

The struggle over condom distribution in the schools is dominated by the two perspectives we have called instrumental and expressive, the first oriented to rational problem-solving and the second to defense of moral values.

PRO:

The arguments of the proponents are short-term, pragmatic, and health oriented: young people are sexually active; it is unlikely that they will abstain regardless of how often they are exhorted; and they are in danger of contracting a fatal disease. The logical consequence of this position is the provision of age-appropriate sex education that includes information about same-gender sex, modes of HIV transmission and methods of prevention, as well as the provision of condoms without either mandatory counseling or parental consent.

CON:

The opponents of safer sex education and the provision of condoms stress the long term, the role of the parent and church versus the school and the state, and issues of morality. In their view, the control of the sexuality of young people properly resides with parents and the religious institutions to which parents and children belong, which emphasize chastity before marriage and fidelity afterward. The provision of safer sex education and condoms threaten [sic] these goals and appear to condone sexual experimentation. For some religious groups, such as the Roman Catholic church, condoms are a completely forbidden form of birth control. (National Research Council 1993: 292)

Again, developments in New York City, the location of one of the earliest and most ambitious condom distribution plans, provide a vivid illustration of the political interplay of these ideas. Briefly in 1986, condoms had been given to students through school-based health clinics. But that activity was soon ended by the city's Board of Education. The first signal that a new condom distribution plan was under preparation came in late September 1990, when Schools Chancellor Joseph A. Fernandez released the announcement (Barbanel 1990). Once the actual plan was presented in early December, it included all 120 high schools in the city, and it made no provision for mandatory counseling or for parental consent (Berger 1990b).

From the first indication that a plan was forthcoming until the Board of Education's final vote on it, the architects of the condom distribution program drew heavily on statistics to make their case. Fact sheets were distributed; slide presentations were made. According to the data introduced, 80 percent of New York City's 261,000 high school teenagers were sexually active (Berger 1990a and 1990b). Further, 20 percent of all AIDS victims in the country between the ages of 13 and 21 lived in New York City, even though only 3 percent of the entire U.S. population in this age group dwelled there. The incidence of AIDS among the city's teenagers was reported to have climbed 51 percent between 1988 and 1989. Considering the long interval between HIV infection and the development of AIDS, officials projected a continuing upward spiral in such figures.

That the condom proposal faced a tough political road was never in doubt. The Catholic Archdiocese of New York was unwavering in its denunciation of the proposal. At one point, there was even talk of an organized boycott of the public schools by Catholic parents, should the plan win adoption (Verhovek 1991). School principals themselves registered mixed feelings about making condoms available, as they weighed concerns for the health of their students against personal moral and religious beliefs (Berger 1990c). On the Board of Education, a clear majority in favor of the general concept of condom distribution was converted into a close split "for" and "against" by the city's specific plan because of its uncompromising approach.

Large public turnouts and vigorous debate characterized the several open sessions that the Board of Education held to discuss condom distribution. One of the final meetings in February 1991 went from 10 a.m. until late evening, with 277 speakers coming forward (National Research Council 1993: 294). The instrumental arguments of supporters and the expressive protestations of opponents were central to these public exchanges, which captivated attention for six months in the political life of one of this nation's greatest cities.

Chancellor Fernandez portrayed his plan as a logical and commensurate response to the AIDS problem and maintained that "we cannot afford to ignore this crisis" (Berger 1990b). He also described New York City as "sitting on a ticking time bomb" with respect to AIDS (Berger 1990d). For Fernandez and many other supporters, the program was a clear case of ends over means, as illustrated in one principal's comment that "if it saves one life, it would be worth it" (Berger 1990c). Whether or not adults approved of adolescent sexual activity was beside the point for condom distribution advocates. Typical of the fatalism on this question, a *New York Times* (1990) editorial columnist wrote: "It's painful for many adults to acknowledge that teen-agers are sexually active. But to deny it, and fail to help protect teen-agers from the consequences of early, unsafe sex, is folly." Fernandez, similarly, was against permitting a parental "opt out" or requiring the counseling of students, because these elements promised to undermine the effectiveness of his strategy by reducing participation. The issue was not principle, but practicality.

For opponents of the condom plan, like the vice-president of the Board of Education, "it sends a message that we expect that young people will engage in sexual activity" (Berger 1990a: B6). And many parents agreed with Catholic Bishop Thomas Dealy of the Diocese of Brooklyn that this proposal was "an affront to parents" that intruded on the family's domain of moral instruction (Berger 1990a: B6). "Will the next step be the distribution of hypodermic needles [in school]?" an outraged Board of Education member asked (Berger 1990a: B6; 1990b). At one meeting of the board, the vice-president claimed that students receiving sex education in the public schools were being taught how to perform anal intercourse (Berger 1990e).

On the eve of the final Board of Education vote, the *New York Times* (1991: A22) portrayed it as a choice between "whether to be swayed by those who mind our children's health or those who would mind their morals." Over the months as the trenches filled, a clear line was demarcated: city education officials, health professionals, AIDS advocates, homosexual groups, and some parents stood in favor; Roman Catholic clergy and lay leaders, Orthodox Jews, and other parents stood against. When the board at last made its decision, the former side prevailed, but only narrowly, in a 4-3 vote (Berger 1991a). (Nearly three years later, a state appellate court would overturn the policy on the grounds that parental consent was necessary. At the time of this writing the city was redrafting the plan [Barbanel 1993]).

New York City's battle over condom distribution in the schools supplies a telling case study of the role of instrumental and expressive definitions in policy debate. But there is nothing unique about the nature of events in this locale, aside perhaps from the extensive documentation undertaken by the New York media.

Falmouth, Massachusetts, a seaside community on Cape Cod with a population of less than 30,000, could not be more different from New York City in most respects, but it hosted a very similar controversy over condom availability in the town's public schools. The Falmouth school committee took up the issue not long after New York City did, in September of 1991 following the state Board of Education's August recommendation that all local school systems consider condom distribution (P. Anderson 1991). What followed was a series of public meetings attended by hundreds and featuring dozens of concerned residents as speakers.

John Collins, a former mayor of Boston, was a leading opponent. He articulated the familiar "it sends the wrong message" objection: "To distribute contraceptives in a public school conveys a message of explicit approval and tolerance for teen-age promiscuity" (Currier 1991: A12). Falmouth is not the archdiocese of New York, but five local Catholic churches did launch "a moral crusade" against the proposal, including a letter-writing campaign and sermons from the pulpit (Borg 1991). Most speakers at the public meetings weighed in against the plan, and an anticondom petition with more than three thousand signatures was presented by a committee of concerned citizens. Yet the school committee voted in October to approve the plan, one member explaining, "We decided that if we could save one kid's life, then we had the responsibility to try to do so" (McLaughlin 1991: 33)

Broadway plays generally open first on the road and then head for New York City. This political drama previewed in the big city *then* went out of town, and the dialogue in Falmouth surely seemed to have been scripted by a New York City playwright.

In July 1993, the condom issue played on the national stage when surgeon general nominee Dr. Joycelyn Elders came under fire for her support of condom distribution to teenagers while she was health director of Arkansas (Friedman 1993).

INSTRUMENTAL AND EXPRESSIVE ORIENTATIONS: CONCLUSIONS AND COMPLICATIONS

A contrast and comparison of the needle exchange and condom distribution issues permits several concluding observations about instrumental and expressive policy definitions and their intricacies in practice.

1. *The adoption of instrumental and expressive policy definitions can exhibit strong independence across political issues.*

Needle exchange and school-based condom distribution both represent strategies to prevent the spread of AIDS by reducing the dangerousness of high-risk personal behaviors. Even across a pair of issues seemingly so parallel in content, we find striking inconsistencies in the adoption of instrumental and expressive interpretations. In New York City, Mayor Dinkins was anti–needle exchange (until recently) but pro–condom distribution. In Boston, another site of controversy on these same issues, Mayor Flynn was pro–needle exchange but anti–condom distribution (Aucoin 1991). Each of these figures made use of instrumental rhetoric to support his position on one issue and expressive rhetoric to support his position on the other.

As these cases suggest, instrumental and expressive orientations may be less constraining in opinion formation than more standard political ideologies like liberalism and conservatism, which tend to bind positions across a variety of issues. No person is without instrumental and expressive elements in his or her thought process. Organizations, too—especially political organizations, including interest groups (Salisbury 1969; Ornstein and Elder 1978) and political parties (Pomper 1992)—serve both pragmatic and moralistic aims, although the balance may vary. What triggers the choice between these two orientations for a given issue is often obscure, however. To the extent that this is so, the instrumental/expressive distinction will serve as a better tool for political description than for prediction.

2. *Instrumental and expressive policy definitions can be counterposed or combined.*

Needle exchange and condom distribution demonstrate the fireworks that occur when instrumental and expressive views collide politically. But such conflict is not at all necessary; the relationship between the two orientations is variable and potentially quite complex.

Instrumental and expressive definitions may well coincide, the former reflecting logical assessment of a policy and the latter reflecting its emotional appeal. Numerous public activities—from welfare reform (Behn 1991) to the Polaris missile program (Perrow and Guillen 1990)—have the capacity to satisfy on both levels simultaneously. But even in situations where one orientation is primarily determinative, the other orientation can operate in a subordinate capacity to bolster the policy choice favored.

Thus, those who object to the impropriety of premarital sex sometimes offer instrumental counterarguments (such as, "condoms are unreliable") as a way of attacking the condom distribution program. And instrumentalists are invoking moral values, not cost-benefit analysis, when they plead the sanctity of saving "even one life." Finally, there is the New York City Board of Education member who cast the deciding vote in favor of the chancellor's pragmatic condom distribution plan. The daughter of a rural Ohio preacher, this woman made her choice after a painful soul-searching that culminated with fasting and prayer (Berger 1991b).

3. *Instrumental and expressive policy definitions can become entangled with, and influenced by, preexisting social and ideological cleavages.*

A reporter for the *New York Times* noted a recurring pattern of support and opposition in New York City's condom fight (Berger 1990f). Residents of communities where AIDS and teenage pregnancy were most rampant—chiefly minority and poverty areas—were the most likely to support the plan as a justified policy intervention. Residents in more affluent neighborhoods without high levels of these problems tended to object that the availability of condoms would encourage promiscuity. Similarly, on the Board of Education the four votes in favor of the plan came from two black and two Hispanic members; the three votes against were all cast by white members.

Whatever other motivations were at work, it seems plain that New York City residents caught up in the condom debate were influenced to some degree by race and class concerns. And little wonder. If an instrumental position on anti-AIDS policies like this one conveys the willingness to fight the threat of AIDS, then perceptions of the severity of that threat should be expected to shape issue positions.

In another twist on the racial theme, black leaders in New York City and elsewhere have risen up in force against the needle exchange proposal. Recognizing that their black communities are overrepresented among high drug use areas, they feel the program evidences lack of true concern for dealing with the long-neglected social and economic problems faced by residents of these neighborhoods.

4. *No point of view is intrinsically favored in the political struggle between instrumental and expressive policy definitions.*

Every day each one of us ponders decisions of greater or lesser magnitude that engage reason and emotion, require assessment of ends versus means, and pit one valued principle against another. The outcomes vary, depending on innumerable idiosyncrasies of the decision being considered as well as our own state of mind.

The political system, by extension, is no different. It is impossible to generalize about which set of views will prevail when policy proposals defined in opposing instrumental and expressive terms come under review. As with all political questions, it will hinge, in part, on the mobilization of forces behind the two sides of the debate, including the response of political leaders, interest groups, and public opinion. Yet in some instances, the stronger coalition will still fail if decisionmakers elect to exercise personal preference—as apparently occurred in the town of Falmouth, where the school committee resisted great organized popular pressure against that district's condom distribution plan. Moreover, decisions made at one juncture may later be overturned as new information comes to light, or attitudes alter, or the decision-making context is changed. One thing alone is certain: only those policies that are widely perceived as doing both "what's right" and "what will work" will cross untroubled political waters.

REFERENCES

Alpern, D. M. 1988. "It Scares the Hell Out of Me." *Newsweek*, March 14, p. 44.

Altman, L. K. 1993a. "Widened Definition of AIDS Leads to More Reports of It." *New York Times*, April 30, p. A18.

_____. 1993b. "At AIDS Talks, Science Confronts Daunting Maze." *New York Times*, June 6, sec. 1, p. 20.

Anderson, B. F. 1975. *Cognitive Psychology*. New York: Academic Press.

Anderson, P. 1991. "Board Debates Condoms in Schools." *Cape Cod Times*, September 11, p. A8.

Anderson, W. 1991. "The New York Needle Trial: The Politics of Public Health in the Age of Aids." *American Journal of Public Health* 81: 1506–1517.

Aucoin, D. 1991. "A Longtime Ally Lambastes Flynn on Condom Plan." *Boston Globe*, November 12, p. A1.

Barbanel, J. 1990. "Chancellor Has Plan to Distribute Condoms to Students in New York." *New York Times*, September 26, p. A1.

_____. 1993. "Condom Handouts Voided in Schools." *New York Times*, December 31, p. A1.

Baurac, D. R. 1992. "Teen Sex: Condom Distribution Still a Volatile Policy Issue." *Chicago Tribune*, September 20, sec. 6, p. 1.

Bayer, R. 1989. *Private Acts, Social Consequences: AIDS and the Politics of Public Health*. New York: Free Press.

Behn, R. D. 1991. *Leadership Counts: Lessons for Public Managers from the Massachusetts Welfare, Training, and Employment Program*. Cambridge, Mass.: Harvard University Press.

Berger, J. 1990a. "5 of Board's 7 for Condoms in the Schools." *New York Times*, September 27, p. B1.

———. 1990b. "New York School Chief to Offer Plan for Distributing Condoms." *New York Times*, December 4, p. A1.

———. 1990c. "Opposition to Condom Plan by Some Principals." *New York Times*, December 5, p. B3.

———. 1990d. "Condom Plan for Schools Draws Criticism." *New York Times*, December 6, p. B1.

———. 1990e. "New York City Board Members Clash on Condom Proposal." *New York Times*, December 20, p. B4.

———. 1990f. "Condoms in Schools: Divergent Views in New York Debate Are Rooted in Class, Race and Religion." *New York Times*, December 22, p. 30.

———. 1991a. "School Board Approves Plan for Condoms." *New York Times*, February 28, p. A1.

———. 1991b. "A Prayer and a Fast: What Turned Condom Vote." *New York Times*, March 1, p. B1.

Borg, L. 1991. "Falmouth of Two Minds about School Condom Distribution." *Providence Journal-Bulletin*, December 29, p. B1.

Buning, E. C., R. A. Coutinho, G. H. van Brussel, G. W. van Santen, and A. W. van Zadelhoff. 1986. Letter. *Lancet* 1: 1435.

Centers for Disease Control and Prevention, U.S. Department of Health and Human Services. 1993. *HIV/AIDS Surveillance Report*, February, p. 6, Table 1.

———. 1992. *HIV/AIDS Prevention Newsletter*, December, p. 2.

Currier, T. 1991. "Falmouth Finalizes Condom Plan." *Cape Cod Times*, November 20, p. A1.

Duesberg, P. H. 1992. "The Role of Drugs in the Origin of AIDS." *Biomedicine and Pharmacotherapy* 46: 3–15.

Edelman, M. 1985. *The Symbolic Uses of Politics*. Urbana: University of Illinois Press.

Essex, M. 1991. "Needed: Sound Health Policy, Not Hysteria, on AIDS." *Boston Globe*, June 8, p. 23.

Friedman, T. L. 1993. "Clinton Delays Senate Hearings on Health Post." *New York Times*, July 16, p. A1.

Gamson, J. 1990. "Rubber Wars: Struggles over the Condom in the United States." *Journal of the History of Sexuality* 1: 262–282.

Graham, J. D., L. C. Green, and M. J. Roberts. 1988. *In Search of Safety: Chemicals and Cancer Risk*. Cambridge, Mass.: Harvard University Press.

Gusfield, J. 1963. *Symbolic Crusade: Status Politics and the American Temperance Movement*. Urbana: University of Illinois Press.

Heimoff, S. and J. Sommer. 1991. "Is the HIV AIDS Theory All Wrong?" *CALReport*, University of California–Berkeley, November, pp. 6, 18.

Hofstadter, R. 1965. "The Pseudo-Conservative Revolt—1954." Pp. 41–65. in *The Paranoid Style in American Politics and Other Essays*, ed. R. Hofstadter. Chicago: University of Chicago Press.

Jelen, T. G., and C. Wilcox. 1992. "Symbolic and Instrumental Values as Predictors of AIDS Policy Attitudes." *Social Science Quarterly* 73: 737–749.

Joseph, S. C. 1992. *Dragon within the Gates*. New York: Carroll & Graf.

Katz, D. 1968. "Consistent for What? The Functional Approach." Pp. 179–191 in *Theories of Cognitive Consistency: A Sourcebook*, eds. R. P. Abelson et al. Chicago: Rand McNally.

Kirp, D. L., and R. Bayer. 1993. "Needles and Race." *Atlantic*, July, pp. 38–39, 42.

Kolata, G. 1993a. "AIDS Groups Dismayed by Report They See as Discounting Concerns." *New York Times*, February 7, p. 30.

―――. 1993b. "Debunking Doubts That H.I.V. Causes AIDS. *New York Times*, March 11, p. B13.

Krim, M. 1987. "Introduction." Pp. xv–xxxiv in *AIDS: Public Policy Dimensions*, ed. J. Griggs. New York: United Hospital Fund of New York.

Lipset, S. M. 1955. "The Radical Right: A Problem for American Democracy." *British Journal of Sociology* 6: 176–209.

Masters, W. H., V. E. Johnson, and R. C. Kolodny. 1988. *Crisis: Heterosexual Behavior in the Age of AIDS*. New York: Grove Press.

McLaughlin, J. 1991. "Falmouth OK's School Distribution of Condoms." *Boston Globe*, October 24, p. 33.

Mednick, A. 1991. "Schools Say No to Condom Distribution." *Boston Globe*, November 24, South Weekly sec., p. 1.

National Research Council, Committee on AIDS Research and the Behavioral, Social, and Statistical Sciences. 1993. *The Social Impact of AIDS in the United States*. Washington, D.C.: National Academy Press.

Navarro, M. 1992a. "New York City Resurrects Plan on Needle Swap." *New York Times*, May 14, p. A1.

―――. 1992b. "68 U.S. Patients in Limbo: Caught in Medical Enigma." *New York Times*, October 21, p. B7.

―――. 1992c. "More Cases, Costs and Fears under Wider AIDS Umbrella." *New York Times*, October 29, p. A1.

New York Times. 1985. "Choosing Between Two Killers." Editorial. September 15, p. E20.

New York Times. 1987. "AIDS, Sex and Needles." Editorial. March 29, p. IV: 24.

New York Times. 1989. "Tacoma Backs Needle Swap." February 11, p. A32.

New York Times. 1990. "The Facts of Life about Teen-Age Sex." Editorial. September 27, p. A22.

New York Times. 1991. "Vote Yes for Condoms." Editorial. February 26, p. A22.

Nimmo, D. 1975. *Popular Images of Politics*. Englewood Cliffs, N.J.: Prentice-Hall.

Office of Technology Assessment, Congress of the United States. 1992. *The CDC's Case Definition of AIDS: Implications of Proposed Revisions*. HIV-Related Issues Background Paper 8. Washington, D.C.: U.S. Government Printing Office, August.

Oleske, J., A. Minnefor, R. Cooper, Jr., K. Thomas, A. dela Cruz, H. Ahdieh, I. Guerrero, V. V. Joshi, and F. Desposito. 1983. "Immune Deficiency Syndrome in Children." *Journal of the American Medical Association* 249: 2345–2349.

Ornstein, N. J. and S. Elder. 1978. *Interest Groups, Lobbying and Policymaking*. Washington, D.C.: Congressional Quarterly Press.

Osborn, J. 1988. "AIDS: Politics and Science." *The New England Journal of Medicine* 318: 444–447.

―――. 1991. "The Changing Definition of AIDS: What's in a Name?" *Journal of American Health Policy* 1: 19–22.

Panem, S. 1988. *The AIDS Bureaucracy*. Cambridge, Mass.: Harvard University Press.

Parsons, T. 1951. *The Social System*. New York: Free Press.

Parsons, T. and E. Shils, ed. 1951. *Toward a Theory of Social Action*. Cambridge, Mass.: Harvard University Press.

Pear, R. 1993. "As AIDS Money Is Parceled Out, Political Questions." *New York Times*, February 27, p. E3.

Perrow, C., and M. F. Guillen. 1990. *The AIDS Disaster*. New Haven, Conn.: Yale University Press.

Pollock, P. H., S. A. Lilie, and M. E. Vittes. 1993. "On the Nature and Dynamics of Social Construction: The Case of AIDS." *Social Science Quarterly* 74: 123–135.

Pomper, G. M. 1992. *Passions and Interests: Political Party Concepts of American Democracy*. Lawrence: University Press of Kansas.

Pryor, J. B., G. D. Reeder, and R. Vinacco, Jr. 1989. "The Instrumental and Symbolic Functions of Attitudes toward Persons with AIDS." *Journal of Applied Social Psychology* 19: 377–404.

Rochefort, D. A. 1986. *American Social Welfare Policy: Dynamics of Formulation and Change*. Boulder, Colo.: Westview Press.

Rochefort, D. A., and P. E. Pezza. 1991. "Public Opinion and Health Policy." Pp. 247–269 in *Health Politics and Policy*, ed. T. J. Litman and L. S. Robins. New York: Delmar.

Root-Bernstein, R. S. 1993. *Rethinking AIDS: The Tragic Cost of Premature Consensus*. New York: Free Press.

Salisbury, R. H. 1969. "An Exchange Theory of Interest Groups." *Midwest Journal of Political Science* 13: 1–32.

Sapir, E. 1934. "Symbolism." Pp. 492–495 in *Encyclopedia of the Social Sciences*, vol. 14, ed. E. R. A. Seligman. New York: Macmillan.

Sears, D., and J. Citrin. 1982. *Tax Revolt: Something for Nothing in California*. Cambridge, Mass.: Harvard University Press.

Sexton, T. R., and J. Feinstein. 1991. "Long-Term Projections of the AIDS Epidemic." *Interfaces* 21: 64–79.

Shilts, R. 1987. *And the Band Played On*. New York: St. Martin's Press.

———. 1991. "Good AIDS, Bad AIDS." *New York Times*, December 10, p. A31.

Smith, M. B. 1973. "Political Attitudes." Pp. 57–82 in *Handbook of Political Psychology*, ed. J. Knutson. San Francisco: Jossey-Bass.

Sniderman, P. M., R. Brody, and P. E. Tetlock. 1991. *Reasoning and Choice: Explorations in Political Psychology*. Cambridge: Cambridge University Press.

Sontag, S. 1989. *AIDS and Its Metaphors*. New York: Farrar, Straus, and Giroux.

Spence, J. T., K. Deaux, and R. L. Hemreich. 1988. "Sex Roles in Contemporary American Society." Pp. 149–178 in *Handbook of Social Psychology*, 3rd ed., vol. 2, ed. G. Lindzey and E. Aronson. New York: Random House.

State ADM Reports. 1992. *Straight to the Point: State Legislatures Revisit the Needle Exchange and Prescription-for-Needles Controversy*. Washington, D.C.: Intergovernmental Health Policy Project, George Washington University, May, pp. 1, 2, 6–9.

Tousignant, M. 1992. "Drawing the Line on Patriotic Activity." *Washington Post*, May 21, p. A1.

U.S. General Accounting Office. 1993. *Needle Exchange Programs: Research Suggests Promise as an AIDS Prevention Strategy*. Washington, D.C., March.

Verhovek, S. H. 1991. "Regents Leave Decision on Condoms to Districts." *New York Times*, February 22, p. B2.

Zaller, J. R. 1992. *The Nature and Origins of Mass Opinion*. Cambridge: Cambridge University Press.

Zurcher, L., R. G. Kirkpatrick, R. G. Cushing, and C. K. Bowman. 1971. "The Anti-Pornography Campaign: A Symbolic Crusade." *Social Problems* 19: 217–238.

9

The Contextual Bases
of Problem Definition

Christopher J. Bosso

The cases in this volume are evidence of a flourishing subfield within policy studies. The question, of course, is why. One obvious answer is that, as always, students of public policy are following the flag. That is, the study of problem definition has blossomed because the *politics* of problem definition has become so critical to success or failure in policy formation. To appreciate this all one needs to do is consult just a few of the many case studies published during the last decade: Light (1985) on social security; Rochefort (1986) on social welfare policy; Birnbaum and Murray (1987) on tax reform; Bosso (1987) on pesticides; Light (1992) on creating the Department of Veterans Affairs; Cohen (1992) on clean air. Some of this heightened focus on the nature of problems may be the result of a keener scholarly attention to the subject, since we can revisit old cases and "discover" that problem definition was more important than acknowledged by most scholars (though certainly not politicians) at the time. Even so, one still gets the impression that the struggle over problem definition is more nakedly critical than ever in our politics.

But, why? Perhaps problem definition is so important because our politics has become more fluid over the past couple of decades as more traditional bases for generating policy support in the American context—for example, political party and regional loyalties—no longer exhibit their old potency. Perhaps it is because the post–Cold War world has produced a state of ideological anarchy, one that has scrambled the very definitions of "liberal" and "conservative," much less "socialist" or "radical." As a result, perhaps we are in an indeterminate period where definitions of *all* public problems are up for grabs, a free-for-all of meaning that eventually will settle into new cleavages. Perhaps it is because macro-level social and economic trends—the globalization of everything, it seems—have destroyed once stable policy and political alignments, or because the penetration of virtually instantaneous electronic mass media into every facet of policy formation makes rhetoric and symbolism all the more critical to framing policy debates and policy directions. Or, perhaps all of the above taken together are relevant, and it may take a new generation of scholars just to sort it all out.

A sharpened focus on problem definition also may have roots within social science itself, as part of a broader rebellion against the seductive but simplistic determinism embodied in the more economics-based theories of policymaking that have dominated academic and political discourse over the past three decades. These angles of vision, which at their core posit that human behavior extends primarily from economic incentives, in many ways provided powerful scholarly support for the intellectual dominance of conservative—or, at least, libertarian—ideas and policies (see Almond 1990; Dionne 1991; Lowi 1992). In this vein, it isn't too much of a stretch to suggest that a focus on problem definition is part of a broader effort within the social sciences to revisit concepts and factors (e.g., culture, societal values, formal institutions) that may have been undervalued in, for example, the literature on rational choice.

But such a broad assessment about why the study of problem definition has blossomed is for another time and place. My purpose here is to think about the cases presented in this volume from a more contextual perspective. I start with a presumption that the conflict model linked to political scientists such as E. E. Schattschneider (1960) and the social construction of reality model linked to such scholars as Murray Edelman (1988) both contribute in distinct ways, and at different levels of analysis, to our understanding of how societies define problems—and why it *matters* how societies define problems. Indeed, the struggle to define public problems takes place within regime-level contexts, some which are relatively immutable, others more susceptible to change over time. This said, I start by thinking about the boundaries imposed by societal value systems—commonly known as "culture"—on any struggle over problem definition. Despite any effort to be more "scientific" in how we study politics, the *practice* of politics still is a social phenomenon. What else can it be? Thus, any social construction of reality must be affected by culture, shared values, and other "irrational" or nonmaterial factors, though how still is not well understood.

CULTURE AND THE ILLUSION OF ALTERNATIVES

"Consensus" Values and the Socially "Advantaged"

If problem definition hinges on the social construction of reality, then culture, commonly held values, ideology, political socialization, and ideas all matter. In this vein, we might recall the definition of "target populations" offered by Schneider and Ingram: "*stereotypes* about particular groups of people that have been created by politics, culture, socialization, history, the media, literature, religion, and the like" (1993: 335; emphasis supplied). Images of target populations themselves are socially constructed. One of the factors in this dynamic must be the prevailing culture or, to put it another way, its dominant value paradigm.

The cases in this volume in different ways contribute strongly to this insight. What is more, the cases reinforce the impression that for any problem *at the regime or macro-level of discussion and analysis there are remarkably few alternatives actually under debate.* In the United States a powerful and enduring political culture (as distinct from an arguably much more variegated popular culture) helps to whittle down the range of "legitimate" alternatives to a pitiful few long before any quasi-pluralist "conflict" over problem definition ever ensues. What Goodwyn (1978) calls the "received" culture has a powerful effect on how a people perceive the meanings of public problems and, by extension, those populations affected by such policies. In the American context this culture is built around core beliefs in individual liberty—defined as freedom *from* government constraints—private property, the Protestant work ethic, social mobility based on merit, civic duty, faith in progress, and, most telling, the absence of social class.

These "myths," buttressed by an ardent faith in the "invisible hand" of the market, make politics subordinate to the private sector and reinforce beliefs that there is little need for more than some minimal "Lockean government" (Zisk 1992: 214). So powerful are these values, many of which are buttressed legally by the Constitution, that they create the conditions for, in the words of Charles Lindblom, a "privileged position of business" in any political debate. In any economic system based on private enterprise, Lindblom argues, "a large category of major decisions is turned over to businessmen, both small and larger. *They are taken off the agenda of government.* Businessmen thus become a kind of public official and exercise what, on a broad view of their role, are public functions" (1977: 172; emphasis supplied). Whether one agrees entirely with Lindblom's conclusion— Vogel (1989) for one suggests conditions under which the position of business isn't always so privileged—there is little doubt that the sanctity of private property and the deification of the "free" market are cornerstones of the American value system.

To what practical effect on problem definition? Nowhere in the cases discussed by Portz is the possibility of public ownership of the threatened plants ever discussed seriously, even, apparently, among the workers for whom such a "statist" response (a term itself alien to the American political lexicon) might be a rational and community-oriented alternative to devastating job losses. Certainly the situation at Rath eventually deteriorated to the point where an employee stock-ownership plan seemed the only option, and certainly some activists in the Mon Valley pushed for eminent domain, but in both cases these tactics were seen as acts of desperation. It is useful in this context to note that employee stock ownership programs themselves usually are subject to the whims of private capital and investors—or, more telling, the lack thereof—and the failures are more notable than the odd success. Indeed, American policymakers during the Cold War era typically promoted "industrial policy" of any kind only when it came to promoting national security needs. Even the interstate highway system and post-Sputnik spending on higher education, to name but two policy areas, had to be cloaked publicly in the mantle of "national defense" to be rationalized as "exceptions" to the rule of minimal government.

The national ideology of free-market capitalism is so potent that anyone who suggests real alternatives is labeled quickly a radical or dreamer, an image that ultimately exiles advocates to the margins of mainstream discourse. So powerful is the ideology of the free and demonstrably *impersonal* market that even those most harmed—the workers playing their assigned roles as unfortunate victims—usually can only shake their heads and shrug their shoulders. What, after all, is to be done if "the market" takes away your job? Not much, it seems. And, as if to rub salt in the wound, this construct places any blame on "unproductive" workers and their "bloated" unions because *their* obviously inefficient plants had to be closed. The market regime itself simply is what it is—impersonal, imponderable, and immutable. Even the purpose of employment policy in the United States, as Mucciaroni points out elsewhere, is largely "to offset and ameliorate some of the undesirable impacts of private market activity" (1990: 7). It is not to intervene in that market, whose increasing internationalization undoubtedly will put even more workers and communities at an even greater disadvantage vis-à-vis the mobility of capital and labor. Why? Mucciaroni concludes:

> Employment policy developed largely within the limits established by the values and general beliefs widely accepted in American society. These are grounded in the history and culture of the nation and are transmitted through agents of socialization. Struggles over employment policy are fundamentally about where to draw the line demarcating the appropriate role of government in the economy and its obligations toward individual citizens. The American structure of values and beliefs reveals a tension between democracy and equality, on the one hand, and capitalism and individualism on the other. This tension manifests itself clearly on economic issues. (1990: 266–267)

The tensions to which Mucciaroni alludes are at the core of the debate over the North American Free Trade Agreement, in which foes of the agreement, particularly workers and unions worried about the flight of manufacturing jobs to Mexico, are pitted against advocates of "free" trade. The opponents speak about shielding communities and families against "unfair" competition from low-wage foreign workers, for which they are labeled protectionist. The proponents, on the other hand, enjoy a rhetorical and symbolic edge as they talk of open markets, increased exports, and better deals for consumers.

The potency of private property and free market values also can be seen in the case of the American airline industry which, as Baumgartner and Jones show, is to be regulated only to the degree that competition is kept honest and consumers are protected from fraud or dangerous practices. Of course the industry itself is never to be nationalized, an option certainly exercised for openly nonmarket reasons in more than a few other nations. In fact, the American airline industry was *deregulated* to allow the market to operate more efficiently. But deregulation could go only so far, since totally unchecked competition might lead to oligopoly. Thus, both nationalization and total deregulation are seen as paths to monopoly control, one by government, the other by big business, so the range of acceptable policy debate lies somewhere in between. In this sense the notion of positive and negative construction (or "image") suggested by Baumgartner and Jones is useful: the "airline industry" is in an advantaged position save for when government is brought in to referee the rules of competition or to ensure that customers are not getting gouged. Otherwise, let the market reign.

This ideology of minimal government intervention infuses even the case of sexual harassment. As Paul notes, employers of fewer than fifteen workers were exempted from 1964 Civil Rights Act prohibitions against discrimination in hiring, promotion, and firing. What constitutes a small business seems to fluctuate, but this highly elastic exemption is common in American regulatory policy and consistent with long-standing cultural views about small business as the backbone of the economy. It also in no small way coheres with strong populist values about small business operators as akin to the mythic George Bailey, the local business owner standing firm against the power of the big and impersonal corporation. Not surprisingly, how to treat "small business" is a major sticking point in debates over NAFTA and national health care.

These exceptions to the total triumph of free market orthodoxy in the United States point out the impact of other potent cultural values. On agricultural subsidies, as Mucciaroni shows, an agrarian mythology rooted in democratic ideals clouds any clearheaded popular assessment of objective reality. Or, to be less pedantic about it, a parade of Hollywood film stars testifying before congressional committees evokes images of the typical family farm that square little with the realities of contemporary agribusiness. Farmers are an exceptionally "advantaged" target population: politically powerful, enjoying the same kind of positive social construction as the elderly or veterans and thus deserving of *direct* government support (Schneider and Ingram 1993). Such images of farming may connect urban Americans to an arguably more virtuous agrarian past, the *symbolic* loss of which would disturb more than a few citizens, even if their consumption patterns have little to do with family farming. Browne et al. suggest that these myths "are contested symbols, vague images of how agriculture ought to be, or once was. Their lack of specificity means that competing political interests can easily appropriate them" (1992: 13). To what effect? Browne et al. conclude:

> Our unexamined traditional agrarian beliefs play havoc with the agricultural policy process. Because Americans rightly want to preserve the values expressed in agrarian imagery, they resist attacks on agrarian myths. Indeed, calling them myths, we acknowledge the enduring truth of the values that these beliefs transmit, but not every statement or application of agrarian values is sacred. Our desire to protect those mythic, self-reliant stewards of democracy that are part of our constitutional foundation has led Americans to enact and to persist in policies that have contradictory and destructive consequences. (1992: 141)

That agriculture is one of the most heavily socialized sectors in the American economy seems to make no difference. And Americans are no different from their Japanese or French cousins, for whom a romantic and mythic agrarian past also precludes any real debate about agricultural policy.

The current debate over national health care is another good example of the power of cultural values. On the one hand, the nation is discussing the idea in remarkably open ways, possibly because the demise of the Cold War dichotomy between "communism" and "American values" has made it finally safe to talk about national health care without raising automatically the grim specter of Stalinist five-year plans. On the other hand, whatever policy option emerges probably is going to bear a strong incremental similarity to the dominant traits of the pre-existing private health care system. Private health insurers, the medical community, and their political allies certainly are not going to support any plan that undermines their privileged status in the health care system, and their public rhetoric will strike hard at any option that chafes against dominant societal values such as choosing one's own doctor. For their part, supporters of a Canadian-style single payer system face a deep-seated cultural bias against such a statist approach to social policy, a bias which defenders of the private system certainly will do everything to reinforce. In many respects those promoting the single payer option at present may be doomed from the outset to sit on the margins of pragmatic policy debate. Their views, like those about legalizing drugs (see Sharp), may provide a useful intellectual counterpoint to dominant values but are unlikely to be accepted broadly at the moment. The prevailing values a generation from now, after the nation has had experience with some kind of national health care system, may offer a far different set of opportunities.

Negatively Constructed Target Populations

Two cases—drug use and tax reform—also exhibit little real debate over core values, but do buttress arguments made by Schneider and Ingram about negatively constructed target populations. The distinction made by Rochefort and Cobb between instrumental and expressive arguments also is useful here. Expressive arguments typically reflect broader and deeper cultural and ideological values and therefore can be potent in assigning negatively viewed target populations to their socially constructed ghettos. Cracking down on "welfare queens" or getting "tough on crime" shows how regime values percolate through policy choices, even when instrumental arguments might show that the social or fiscal costs of such policies will outweigh their real benefits.

Sharp, for example, notes the continuity throughout the century of the *problem* of drugs in America—the weakness of human nature. Whether drug users are criminals ("dangerous classes") or just plain weak (the "medically needy"), they remain essentially deviants to most Americans, even if not to the so-called cultural elite who dominate popular culture. Which of the two images of drug use prevails at any one time may depend on the capacity of strategic elites to paint target populations in desired ways, but the *opportunities to do so* are bounded by culture and, as is discussed below, by structural factors outside their control. But the point here is that the range of acceptable debate over the problem of drug use still is relatively narrow; either construction fits in nicely with the culture's basic view about the capacity to reform deviant behavior via jail or medicine, if not religion or psychotherapy. Other cultures don't seem quite so missionary in their reformist impulses, but in the United States any libertarian argument for legalizing drug sale and use is easily marginalized.

On tax policy, as contrasted with agriculture, Mucciaroni shows how dominant cultural myths about "fairness" and about the "middle class" can be potent in overcoming the entrenched clout of organized producer interests. As he notes, "whether producer groups will be defeated or not depends upon whether they are perceived as victims of economic misfortune beyond their control, or, instead, as greedy claimants feeding at the public trough" (p. 120). If farmers-as-victims were shielded by powerful agrarian myths, "entrenched special interests" using the tax code for their own benefit certainly were not. They were instead the powerful but despised "contenders" whose benefits must be hidden so as not to arouse public anger (Schneider and Ingram 1993). Farmers win when "fairness" *to them* (not necessarily to the consumer) is an issue, but "special interests" could not prevail once the fairness of the tax code itself became the issue. Besides, as Mucciaroni concludes, businesses hardly can hide behind the mythology of "free enterprise," with its supposition of minimal government intervention and still defend tax breaks.

In both cases one also can see how negatively viewed target populations probably are hurt by high public issue salience. Positively regarded target populations, however, seem more immune to or are generally *helped* by high issue saliency. The same point has been made elsewhere about the Ethiopian famine of the mid 1980s: starving children whose condition is no fault of their own certainly generate more widespread attention and greater sympathy than do people whose travails are the more obvious result of a civil war or of their own government's failed ideology (Bosso 1989). By "obvious" I mean to imply that, even in the case of widely acknowledged famines, how blame is assigned will influence whether anybody will come to the rescue. Little Western assistance came to Ethiopia so long as the famine was seen as the fault of the country's Soviet-supported rulers, a view pushed mightily by a United States government firmly entrenched in the Cold War. Only when that definition of the problem was overwhelmed by raw televised images of starving children did aid pour in.

Policy Intellectuals and Paradigmatic Evolution

Benjamin and Duvall (1991) argue that social scientists have underappreciated the cultural foundations of economic and political institutions. More important, they argue that "culture change is itself not exogenous, but rather is the *product of evolving human practices*, which, themselves, are a direct outgrowth of the cognitive orientations extant in society" (1991: 22; emphasis supplied). In this vein, the points made by Baumgartner and Jones about spillover effects, the impacts of debates within professional communities, and the accretion of seemingly small changes leading to macro-level shifts in problem definition are relevant. Cultural contexts, and their impacts on the parameters of policy debate, can be transformed. How such regime-level contextual change happens is the key question.

The case of traffic congestion examined by Coughlin perhaps is the best example of how evolving human practices may slowly be leading to the kinds of cultural change that will alter significantly the social construction of a public problem. The other cases discussed so far have displayed little macro-level conflict over problem definition, while the cases of sexual harassment and AIDS-related issues exhibit full-blown cultural conflict. However, with traffic congestion we see the emergence of a still nascent macro-level debate between the norms of a traditionally individualist culture and a newer set of as yet subordinate "green" values. The reigning paradigm remains potent—particularly in states and localities wherever defenders of orthodoxy wield structurally enhanced leverage (see below)—but the "green" paradigm is making headway, particularly as such "objective" conditions as traffic congestion, wasteful energy use, and limited public resources become more widely acknowledged. More than two decades of environmental debate, activism, and education thus have had their cumulative impacts. Though the automobile still is so woven into the culture that to criticize it is to pose ideological threats to a whole set of values, expectations, and "rights," an evolution in problem definition is under way.

It is during this nascent competition over core values that the social construction of an entire problem is most up for grabs. The role of policy professionals and other intellectuals may be especially telling in these periods, since debates over nonsalient problems take place far more in the seminar rooms of universities and the halls of policy-related institutions than out in the open. Other work by Baumgartner and Jones (1993) on the societal images of problems like tobacco, pesticides, and nuclear power suggests that the roles played by policy experts may be central during the early, faintest stirrings of controversy, before the grand societal coalitions of support or opposition can be marshaled. The hard intellectual discourse on airline deregulation, patterns of development and commuting, sexual harassment, changes in the tax code, and so forth was under way long before some recognized "triggering event" sparked broad issue saliency and subsequent mass discussion. Indeed, in several cases discussed here the intellectual impacts on problem definition stand out: feminist legal scholars like Catherine McKinnon on definitions of sexual harassment; Robert McIntyre on the fairness of the tax code; medical experts on AIDS; environmental and energy advocates on the social construction of transportation; economists on airline deregulation. If some problems are now so constricted by consensus that little macro-level debate occurs, and others have become so explosive that instrumental arguments are lost amidst the smoke and heat, then there also are problems where a "grand conversation" is under way, contributing slowly, often imperceptibly to major shifts in how society thinks. For the scholar this might be the most interesting "phase" in the dynamic we call problem definition, since it addresses the question of paradigmatic *change*, of how reigning ideas or value paradigms eventually are replaced (see Kuhn 1962).

Cultural Conflict and Paradigm Change

If in any polity there is relatively little sharp and highly salient regime-level debate over the definition of most problems—unless that polity is undergoing profound regime-level traumas—the exceptions are telling. In this volume these exceptions essentially are *cultural* debates over the meaning of gender, sexuality, and religious values, which, with race, have been America's sharpest societal cleavages since the 1950s (see Mayer 1992). True macro-level debate is under way in the realm of sexual harassment, inarguably as part of a truly epochal transformation in attitudes about the role of women in the home and workforce and in the overall relations between the sexes. Ideological (and often partisan) camps are formed, battle lines drawn, and the fight is on, with starkly distinct images of the "real world" pitted against one another. The same is true to some degree with efforts to fight AIDS through needle exchanges and condom distribution in the public schools. Such battles, as Rochefort and Cobb show, largely pit health care professionals and other experts against defenders of long-held cultural values. In such a battle it is no surprise that those fighting against needle exchanges or condom distribution in the schools rely predominantly on expressive arguments. To "condone" drug use through needle exchanges certainly flies in the face of what Sharp shows are mainstream society's palpable fears about the impacts of drugs. Instrumental language about the "efficiency" or "effectiveness" of needle exchange programs is blunted by even more potent arguments that such practices undermine respect for law or that they merely comprise another component of a greater white establishment conspiracy against minorities—a view with surprising (to whites) resiliency within much of the black community. With condoms in the schools, instrumental arguments come up against strong religious values about sexual behavior and, in particular, fears about ceding parental control over children to "experts" with alternative values and agendas. In such conflicts "reasoned" arguments run smack up against strong social and cultural values, and rare is the elected official who will side with the experts against angry parents and voters.

This said, the threat of AIDS also has powerfully challenged long-held religious and social values about sex, homosexuality, sex education, and the public role in preventing the spread of sexually transmitted diseases. AIDS at first was perceived solely as a homosexual disease but later as one that claimed "innocent" victims (children, lovers, health care workers). Note that a major federal AIDS grant program—the Ryan White Comprehensive AIDS Resources Emergency Act—was named after a youth who contracted the disease in a blood transfusion for hemophilia and whose plight (being ostracized in one town) became the kind of "human interest" story so prevalent in mass culture. It isn't an exaggeration to suggest that only after AIDS claimed enough original victims, thus generating plenty of grieving and heterosexual relatives, and spread on to "innocents" like Ryan White did the disease break out of its socially constructed ghetto. Indeed, it is not too much to argue that AIDS has helped to humanize homosexuality in the United States, though at a huge human cost.

The Social Construction of Culture

Benjamin and Duvall argue that models of decisionmaking where human motivations are based primarily on economic incentives tend to avoid or discount "the social construction of the *elements* of rational choice—interests, preferences, knowledge of various alternative courses of action, awareness of and expectations about the consequences of different courses of action, etc.—*none* of which are either inherent in the individual agent nor simply exogenously given. Instead, they are deeply social, resting on and made possible by some socially shared knowledge and understandings" (1991: 4–5). Social scientists, they argue, must take seriously "the practices, emotional responses, obligations, and volitional choices of human agency, on the one hand, *and* the historically continuous and changing structures of society that constitute the social context of human agency, on the other hand" (1991: 6). Culture itself is such a social context for human thought and behavior; as such, it also is changeable. It provides contexts for conflict but is itself changed *by* conflict. With AIDS and sexual harassment we see a society redefining its values and perspectives, a painful and not always edifying dynamic where traditional cultural constructs are being altered or even replaced. This is what full-blown macro-level value change looks like: messy, fractious, and seemingly without letup until a new "consensus" reigns.

HOW DOES STRUCTURE MATTER?

The Mobilization of Bias

So culture matters, but not in a reductionist, monocausal way. Any explanation of the impacts of values, Skocpol adds, must show how "experiences with governmental institutions and political processes profoundly affect the way people understand and evaluate alternative policy possibilities within a given cultural frame" (1992: 22). In this vein, Truman long ago noted, "the formal institutions of government in the United States do not prescribe all the meanderings of the stream of politics. They do mark some of the limits, however, and designate certain points through which it must flow whatever uncharted courses it may follow between these limits" (Truman 1964: 322). The process of problem definition is part of that political "stream." As such, it not only is affected by culture, societal values, and prevailing norms, but also by the formal structure of governing institutions and procedures within which politics takes place.

"There are an incredible number of devices for checking the development of conflict within the system," argued Schattschneider about the general impacts of structure. "All forms of political organization have a bias in favor of the exploitation of some kinds of conflict and the suppression of others because *organization is the mobilization of bias*. Some issues are organized into politics and others are organized out" (1960: 71). A generation of scholarship on interest group power and public policy has affirmed Schattschneider's premise that government is more than some "neutral referee" over group conflict. Yet there is remarkably little straightforward discussion about how features like federalism, separation of institutional power, or distinct means of selection have had *independent* impacts on problem definition. What is more, there is precious little comparative analysis of the differential impact of structure on problem definition across political systems. Policymakers certainly have appreciated the importance of formal structure, yet, Schattschneider continues, "one difficulty scholars have experienced in interpreting American politics has always been that the grand strategy of politics has concerned itself first of all with the structure of institutions. The function of institutions is to channel conflict; institutions do not treat all forms of conflict impartially" (1960: 72).

As in our discussion about culture, the roles played in defining problems by strategic elites, organized interests, political parties, and other actors without doubt are critical, but they make sense *only* within the boundaries imposed by the formal structure of governance. By virtue of constitutionally mandated function, fundamental design, and legal jurisdiction, formal institutions *must* influence the way problems get defined. Policy entrepreneurs may compete to define issues, but their freedom must be constrained at least in part by the system's topography. Also like culture, structures are not necessarily immutable, but some facets are hardier than others.

The Question of Constitutionality

In the United States debates over public problems invariably are framed not in terms of whether proposals are "good" or "right" but whether they are "constitutional." This legal construct has no small bearing on what kinds of problems are or are not considered within the legitimate purview of government. The British scholar H. G. Nicholas argues that the capacity to fall back on constitutionality as a last defense has profound effects:

> Thus the history of American politics is also, at almost every point, a constitutional history and, as often as not, the constitutional conflicts are not the real ones, but the smoke-screen behind which the real differences are being thrashed out. . . . This often introduces an element of unreality, not to say casuistry and play-acting, into the arguments of American politics. The great slavery debate was seldom joined about the merits of slavery as such, much less about the relations of black and white, but rather about whether or not Congress had the right to legislate slavery into or out of the territories. The great and continuing

struggle between *laissez-faire* and public control was—and is still—fought in the largely outworn language of states' rights and what the Founding Fathers meant by terms like "general welfare." (1980: 24)

The specter of constitutionality is everywhere in this volume. On plant closings, the Constitution gives private property legal superiority over the needs of the state or some broader community. Says Lindblom, "constitutional rules—especially the law of private property—specify that, though governments can forbid certain kinds of activity, they cannot command business to perform. They must induce rather than command" (1977: 173). Even when challenges emerge, as in Pittsburgh, they must be carried out according to constitutional rules that buttress already strong societal values about private property. Eminent domain proceedings, for example, must go through the courts, which will demand "fair" compensation in line with constitutional guarantees against the taking of private property. As long as U.S. Steel owns the plant site it has the legal upper hand.

Because every problem at some time is defined as a constitutional question it also is, in effect, taken temporarily out of more openly political realms. First Amendment guarantees of freedom of religion must influence how localities, much less the federal government, even discuss volatile issues like sex education or how to prevent the spread of sexually transmitted diseases. Behind any such discussion lies the probability that the loser will go to court to fight the battle on purely constitutional grounds. The judiciary, for its part, always is sensitive to how secular law affects religious institutions such as schools or hospitals. Prohibitions against unreasonable search and seizure are part of the drug issue and an inflammatory focal point for proponents of harsher actions against drug possession. The courts have had to decide whether the Constitution covers possible sexual harassment in the private workplace, and even whether it provides judicial standing to cases alleging harassment. The courts also no doubt will have to decide whether and how the Americans with Disabilities Act will guarantee equal access to public transportation, a right of access issue that, as Coughlin points out, introduces the element of social equity into what was once a narrowly drawn issue about traffic congestion.

A great deal of this element of constitutionality, of course, is not set in stone, if American social and legal history is any guide. Slavery is long gone, more blatant forms of discrimination based on a whole host of characteristics or practices are proscribed, and rights that not long ago were the stuff of legal advocates or philosophers are now established as law. As with culture, much of this change has come about because of conflicts over the very meaning of a law or policy, of what is or is not constitutional. It is a moving standard to some degree, but one whose current boundaries always impose themselves on the definition of any problem.

The Potency of Localism

Beyond laying out what is or is not within the realm of government authority, the Constitution imposes structural contexts within which governance and political conflict take place. The most apparent if frequently overlooked of these contexts, particularly compared to many other political systems, must be federalism. The American style of noncentralized governance, with its multiple venues of authority and responsibility, buttressed by strong cultural predispositions toward local control, dramatically complicates and diffuses policymaking. It also powerfully affects problem definition beyond the dimension of constitutionality already alluded to above. The most obvious example in this volume is in the area of plant closings, which, Portz notes, are perceived largely as *local* issues. The relatively minimal role of the national government in economic development matters enables corporations to shop around freely, to play plants and localities off against one another. The states, meanwhile, vie strenuously for new employers, a form of interstate cannibalism over which the national government plays little or no role. Such conditions generally enhance private business power and, more critically, a business definition of the problem as one of competitive disadvantage with respect to other plants, other states, or other nations. The 1992 case in which General Motors mulled over closing an assembly plant in Michigan or its rival in Texas is but a more openly debated version of this zero-sum condition. Such local issues can have major national repercussions, as witness the anxieties about job loss that were a palpable part of the 1992 presidential election, but rarely are they framed as national issues at the level of the plant itself.

Coughlin underscores the impacts of federalism in debates over national transportation policy, such as it is. As Nicholas reminds us, the Constitution "gives the federal government very little power to oblige the states to take positive action when they have a mind not to" (1980: 21). States frequently must be lured into compliance with federal laws by outright grants or, more telling, threats to cut off funding. Even today states and localities retain tremendous primary authority over much of the transportation system, so it is no surprise that the problem of traffic congestion can be defined in such different ways in San Francisco and Houston. Each locality is responding to local cultural, economic, and political variables, not the least of them being the always pervasive threat that businesses will leave for more lucrative pastures. Coughlin's case also shows the side effects of such local and state competition over business location, as new employers not only move to places offering better deals but also bring their congestion with them. Debates over transportation at this level inevitably get framed in terms of economic development, leaving proponents of alternative green values to seek more sympathetic policy venues in the federal government, where local developers arguably have less clout.

The effects of federalism also can be seen in the cases discussed by Rochefort and Cobb, since health and education issues in the United States tend to devolve to the states, municipalities, and local school boards. No education ministry simply mandates national standards for sex education or condom distribution in school clinics—there wasn't even such an education ministry in the United States until the late 1970s, for that matter—and certainly the states and localities would not stand easily for federal preemption in these policy realms. The result is a patchwork quilt of debates and policies, with local conditions playing central roles. Within the broadest of boundaries imposed by the Constitution or the federal government, the variations in state and local drug laws, standards on sexual harassment, laws of business incorporation, tax codes, health systems, and so on provide testimony not only to the sheer complexity of law in the American context, but also to the very policy contexts within which national debates proceed.

That same localism is refracted structurally through state and national legislatures, whose systems of representation are based on geography, and accentuated in legislative committee systems where constituency interests prevail. These conditions readily grant a great deal of preferential access to narrowly defined economic and political interest. So it is no surprise that constituency-based producer interests wield great clout in Congress, with agriculture particularly influential in a Senate where rural overrepresentation is virtually guaranteed by the Constitution. Most problems inevitably get framed in local and state terms, with members normally concerned less about "rational" policy than with their own district or state interests. National "transportation policy" thus becomes little more than an amalgam of discrete highway or mass-transit projects, while "agriculture policy" actually is a jumble of separate commodity programs. This localism pervades legislative policy debate save when it is dominated by a far more powerful construct, like fairness in the case of tax reform.

On the other hand, federalism can provide relatively low-cost ways to raise alternative ideas and try out new approaches. The states, reflecting local conditions and subcultures, in many ways are the laboratories of American politics, contexts within which those marginalized nationally may have greater access and clout. It may be no surprise that localities have been far more open than the national government to experiment with needle exchanges, new avenues for economic development, alternative drug abuse treatments, or new standards for gender equity. Yet we really know relatively little about variations in problem definition across the American states, in particular the kinds of cultural and structural factors that promote experimentation.

Institutionally Induced Conflict

The Constitution's separation of institutional power, buttressed by an array of formal checks and balances, also means that these institutions—particularly Congress and the presidency—often actively vie for primacy over problem definition in ways rarer in other national systems of governance. For example, as Harrison and Hoberg find in comparing regulatory styles in the United States and Canada, "conflict between legislative and executive branches in the U.S. often publicizes the regulatory agenda. In contrast, Canadian regulatory agencies and ministers exercise greater discretion with respect to publicizing their agenda" (1991: 6). Separate means of selection, separate terms of office, and even distinct constituencies guarantee tensions among the branches. These structural realities alone (much less when exacerbated by partisan divisions) guarantee some degree of conflict over problem definition, particularly when institutional prerogatives are at stake.

Sharp for one shows how competition between Congress and the executive over the problem of drug abuse was fed in no small way by the kind of divisions in partisan control over the separate branches that the American system so easily produces. It is also easy to see how tensions between the branches over the Clarence Thomas appointment, exacerbated by partisan frictions, fed the flames that engulfed the Anita Hill episode. Yet partisan divisions are not necessary to ensure conflict, since the centrifugal forces embedded in the system of representation make it just as likely that the branches will chafe against one another even when dominated by the same party. The Surgeon General may define AIDS as a health matter and promote condoms as a reasonable option to prevent the spread of the disease, but such instrumental arguments may find little support among House members or senators defending their own ideological and policymaking turf. Presidents may insist on policy leadership across a whole range of domestic and foreign problems, but members of Congress of both parties insist on their prerogatives, particularly when it comes to impacts on their districts or states. The Senate, as Clarence Thomas discovered, also insists on a more than perfunctory constitutional duty to "advise and consent" on presidential appointments. Conflicts are guaranteed, but take place within prescribed institutional arenas according to specific rules and procedures.

The American system also provides a unique *periodicity* to its issue dynamics via its constitutional provisions for separate means of selection, staggered terms of office, and rigid electoral timetables. As Sharp shows, the major pieces of drug-related legislation in the 1980s *all* passed in even-numbered election years, a regularized cycle of partisan and, by extension, institutional conflict that provides useful opportunities for reawakening particularly passionate conflicts. On the other hand, the rigidity of the U.S. electoral system also means that legislators and, particularly, executives have much less control over the context for problem definition than those where governments can call elections or where the selection of one set of officials can determine that of the other. Had George Bush been a prime minister with the capacity to call elections after a major triumph (such as the 1991 Persian Gulf War), he might have shared British Prime Minister John Major's postwar electoral success. But Bush had to wait until late 1992, by which time the luster of the war victory was replaced by unease over the nation's economic future. The definition of what that election was all about was taken at least partially out of Bush's hands by the very tyranny of the election calendar, an independent structural factor if there ever was one.

A POLITY-CENTERED APPROACH
TO PROBLEM DEFINITION

So where does all of this discussion about the impacts of culture and structure leave the policy elites, interest groups, and other political actors that we presume are central players in any conflict over problem definition? Baumgartner (1989) elsewhere argues that all political elites pursue variations on Schattschneider's strategies of expanding ("socializing") or narrowing ("privatizing") conflicts. As he shows in comparing U.S. and French nuclear power policymaking, precisely *how* respective elites pursue those strategies depends on the system itself:

> The complicated institutional structures of the United States and the autonomy of a number of governmental authorities allowed opponents many opportunities to shift the venue of the debate to one where they could be successful. In France, on the other hand, a determined set of governmental agencies use a streamlined set of institutions and procedures in order to keep consideration of nuclear power restricted to a small set of experts with a shared interest in the growth of the program. (1989: 196)

If problem definition is contextual, then policy elites, interest groups, and even the mass media are not free to act in any way they want. If, as Robert Alford argues, "the course of conflicts may be partially understood by reference to the ability of groups to establish their definition of the situation as the appropriate one," the freedom of groups to maneuver is remarkably constrained by public values and by the topography of the system of governance (1969: 31). Policy elites, interest groups, media organizations, and other elites certainly play key roles in defining problems and setting agendas. There also is more than a little fighting among elites and groups over whose alternative construction of reality will stick. But none of this takes place in a vacuum.

What can we conclude, then? These cases taken together suggest first that conflict over problem definition is not guaranteed, that there are a great many times when prevailing values or the rules of the game simply screen out most (and sometimes all) alternative definitions of a problem. Interest groups or policy elites in the short term seemed to have little chance to alter dominant social constructions of such problems as plant closings, drug use, agricultural subsidies, or, to some degree, government intervention in the airline industry. In each case the "received culture" seems to have had a greater role in defining the range of legitimate alternatives than any policy elite or interest group. In fact, one also can see in these cases how hard it is to change strongly held public values. Mass media in such cases are unlikely to challenge the received culture, but will instead publicize deviations from (e.g., tax breaks for "special interests") or threats to (e.g., the "farm crisis") orthodoxy. During cases of full-blown cultural conflict, by contrast, at some point the broad public itself becomes the central and not necessarily predictable player, its influence felt through electoral returns or other mechanisms that tell policy elites just how far they can go. For example, the Hill/Thomas hearings and the Tailhook affair may have been triggering events with major impacts on the problem of sexual harassment, but one doubts whether either event would have triggered *anything* had a macro-level debate over gender roles and relations not been already under way for more than two decades.

These cases suggest that neither culture nor structure is necessarily immutable. From my perspective, the most intriguing cases are those where nascent conflicts over problem definition seem under way, where a longstanding value no longer retains its cohesion but where a full-blown replacement has yet to achieve widespread legitimacy. The two cases where we can identify this dynamic most are airline *de*regulation and traffic congestion. In the one we see the eventual impacts of a decade of policy advocacy for loosening up the greatest of governmental constraints on industry competition; in the second we witness the emergence of a particularly potent challenge to long-held development and property values. The roles played by policy elites and advocacy groups, either in defense of the old order or as the vanguard for change, seem more central in these cases than elsewhere, probably because it is in such early debates that elites can have disproportionate impacts over the intellectual and symbolic boundaries of problems. It also is during such early conflicts that whether governing structure or institutional rules act as bulwarks against or avenues for change themselves becomes an issue. At this point in the process the independent effects of such factors as federalism or congressional committee systems seem most manifest. In this regard it is small wonder that so many public debates about institutional reform really have substantive policy impacts in mind.

All of this comprises what might be called, to borrow from Theda Skocpol (1992), a polity-centered approach to problem definition and policy change. None of the models of problem definition discussed in chapter 1 suffices by itself, but they work well together. Societal characteristics and cultural values converge with existing structural and political conditions to create the contexts within which political actors jockey to promote competing problem definitions and formulate public policy. These conflicts, in turn, influence dominant values and policy processes. Or, as Skocpol puts it, "as politics creates policies, policies also remake politics" (1992: 58). Any social construction of reality takes place in cultural contexts, any conflict among groups or elites is refracted through structures and processes. It is an image of constant if not seamless change that challenges scholars to rethink more static models of policymaking and to revisit more carefully such factors as culture, socioeconomic conditions, institutions, and history.

A polity-centered approach to problem definition also raises the question about whether the dominant literature on problem definition, particularly those approaches coming more out of the conflict model, is overly nation-specific. That is, are there "styles" of problem definition that pertain to other political systems? What commonalities and what differences can be found? In some ways we need to ask more questions about the "dog that did not bark" posed by Sherlock Holmes in the "Mystery of Silver Blaze." Why do other nations have industrial policies where plant closings are defined in very different frames of reference from those seen in the United States? How is the problem of drugs defined in Western European nations and why? To what extent do we see American exceptionalism on some problems but perceptual conformity on others? To what degree is problem definition a function of the intrinsic technical or economic nature of a condition itself versus the result of polity-centered factors like culture or structures of governance? A fruitful avenue of inquiry in this regard lies in expanding upon the notion of national styles of policymaking explored by such works as Lundqvist (1980) and Kelman (1981) on the United States and Sweden; Nelkin and Pollack (1982) on France and West Germany; Harrison and Hoberg (1991) on the United States and Canada; and Vogel (1986) on the United States and Great Britain. Yael Yishai (1993), for example, suggests that differences in abortion policy in four nations (the United States, Israel, Sweden, and Ireland) reflect widely shared "public ideas" about abortion in each nation, perceptual and value constructs that establish the boundaries for legitimate debate within each polity. To look harder at how distinct polities define problems to begin with may give us renewed appreciation for the relative *distinctiveness* of national policy styles amidst problem-induced similarities.

Comparative studies of problem definition can go a long way toward separating out what is shared and what remains unique.

Finally, one must ask whether the impression of a messier and far less linear policymaking process that we get from looking at problem definition squares with reality or merely is the result of looking at policymaking through new lenses. Can we even know the difference? Perhaps, as Mucciaroni concludes about employment policy in the United States, "if the explanation seems inelegant and complex, it is because the subject matter itself—the evolution of a major public policy over the course of some forty years—is inelegant, complex, and changeable" (1990: 258). Despite efforts to construct grand theories of rational decisionmaking, students of public policy deep down have suspected this all along. Understanding better how polities define problems and act on those perceptions may free us to to admit openly that policymaking is just that sloppy and complicated, even while giving us the conceptual tools for making better and more meaningful sense about the whys and hows of change. That may not be a bad way to spend our time.

REFERENCES

Alford, R. 1969. *Bureaucracy and Participation*. Chicago: Rand McNally.

Almond, G. A. 1990. *A Discipline Divided: Schools and Sects in Political Science*. Newbury Park, Calif: Sage Publications.

Baumgartner, F. R. 1989. *Conflict and Rhetoric in French Policymaking*. Pittsburgh: University of Pittsburgh Press.

Baumgartner, F. R., and B. D. Jones. 1993. *Agendas and Instability in American Politics*. Chicago: University of Chicago Press.

Benjamin, R., and R. Duvall. 1991. "Structure and Practice in Comparative Research: Taking Cultural Context Seriously." Paper delivered at the annual meeting of the American Political Science Association, Washington, D.C., August 29–September 1.

Birnbaum, J. H., and A. S. Murray. 1987. *Showdown at Gucci Gulch: Lawmakers, Lobbyists, and the Unlikely Triumph of Tax Reform*. New York: Random House.

Bosso, C. J. 1987. *Pesticides and Politics: The Life Cycle of a Public Issue*. Pittsburgh: University of Pittsburgh Press.

———. 1989. "Setting the Public Agenda: Mass Media and the Ethiopian Famine." Pp. 153–174 in *Manipulating Public Opinion: Essays on Public Opinion as a Dependent Variable*, ed. M. Margolis and G. Mauser. Monterey, Calif: Brooks-Cole.

Browne, W. P., J. R. Skees, L. E. Swanson, P. B. Thompson, and L. J. Unnevehr. 1992. *Sacred Cows and Hot Potatoes: Agrarian Myths in Agricultural Policy*. Boulder, Colo: Westview Press.

Cohen, R. E. 1992. *Washington at Work: Back Rooms and Clean Air*. New York: Macmillan.

Dionne, E. J. 1991. *Why Americans Hate Politics*. New York: Simon and Schuster.

Edelman, M. 1988. *Constructing the Political Spectacle*. Chicago: University of Chicago Press.

Goodwyn, L. 1978. *The Populist Movement: A Short History of the Agrarian Revolt in America*. Oxford: Oxford University Press.

Harrison, K. and G. Hoberg. 1991. "Setting the Environmental Agenda in Canada and the United States: The Cases of Dioxin and Radon." *Canadian Journal of Political Science* 24, 1: 3–27.

Howlett, M. 1991. "Policy Instruments, Policy Styles, and Policy Implementation: National Approaches to Theories of Instrument Choice. *Policy Studies Journal* 19 (Spring): 1–21.

Kelman, S. 1981. *Regulating America, Regulating Sweden: A Comparative Study of Occupational Safety and Health Policy*. Cambridge, Mass.: MIT Press.

Kuhn, T. 1962. *The Structure of Scientific Revolutions*. Chicago: University of Chicago Press.

Light, P. C. 1985. *Artful Work: The Politics of Social Security Reform*. New York: Random House.

———. 1992. *Forging Legislation*. New York: W.W. Norton.

Lindblom, C. E. 1977. *Politics and Markets: The World's Political-Economic Systems*. New York: Basic Books.

Lippmann, W. 1922. *Public Opinion*. New York: Free Press (1965 ed.).

Lowi, T. J. 1992. "The State of Political Science: How We Became What We Study." *American Political Science Review* 86 (March): 1–7.

Lundqvist, L. J. 1980. *The Hare and the Tortoise: Clean Air Policies in the United States and Sweden*. Ann Arbor: University of Michigan Press.

Mayer, W. G. 1992. *The Changing American Mind: How and Why American Public Opinion Changed between 1960 and 1988*. Ann Arbor: University of Michigan Press.

Mucciaroni, Gary. 1990. *The Political Failure of Employment Policy, 1945–1982*. Pittsburgh: University of Pittsburgh Press.

———. 1991. "A Critique of the Garbage Can Model of Policy-Making." *Polity* 24, 3 (Spring): 459–482.

Nelkin, D. and M. Pollack. 1982. *The Atom Besieged: Antinuclear Movements in France and Germany*. Cambridge, Mass.: MIT Press.

Nicholas, H. G. 1980. *The Nature of American Politics*. Oxford: Oxford University Press.

Rochefort, D. A. 1986. *American Social Welfare Policy: Dynamics of Formulation and Change*. Boulder, Colo.: Westview Press.

Schattschneider, E. E. 1960. *The Semi-Sovereign People: A Realist's View of Democracy in America*. Hinsdale, Ill.: Dryden Press.

Schneider, A., and Ingram, H. 1993. "The Social Construction of Target Populations: Implications for Politics and Policy." *American Political Science Review* 87, 2 (June): 334–347.

Skocpol, T. 1992. *Protecting Soldiers and Mothers: The Political Origins of Social Policy in the United States*. Cambridge, Mass.: Harvard University Press.

Truman, D. B. 1964. *The Governmental Process: Political Interests and Public Opinion*. New York: Knopf.

Vogel, D. 1986. *National Styles of Regulation: Environmental Policy in Great Britain and the United States*. Ithaca, N.Y.: Cornell University Press.

———. 1989. *Fluctuating Fortunes: The Political Power of Business in America*. New York: Basic Books.

Weaver, R. K., and B. A. Rockman. 1993. *Do Institutions Matter? Government Ca-*

pabilities in the United States and Abroad. Washington, D.C.: Brookings Institution.

Yishai, Y. 1993. "Public Ideas and Public Policy: Abortion Politics in Four Democracies." *Comparative Politics* 25, 2: 207–228.

Zisk, B. H. 1992. *The Politics of Transformation: Legal Activism in the Peace and Environmental Movements.* Westport, Conn.: Praeger.

The Contributors

FRANK R. BAUMGARTNER is associate professor of political science at Texas A&M University. He is the author of *Conflict and Rhetoric in French Policymaking* (1989), coauthor (with Bryan D. Jones) of *Agendas and Instability in American Politics* (1993), and author or coauthor of a variety of articles on agenda setting, interest groups, and policymaking in both France and the United States.

CHRISTOPHER J. BOSSO is associate professor of political science at Northeastern University, specializing in American politics and policymaking, interest groups, and environmental politics. He is the author of *Pesticides and Politics: The Life Cycle of a Public Issue* (1987), winner of the 1988 Policy Studies Organization award for the best book in policy studies. In addition to recent writings on environmental activism and values, he is the author of a chapter on policy formation in the *Encyclopedia of Policy Studies*, 2d ed. (1994).

ROGER W. COBB is professor of political science at Brown University. His books (with Charles D. Elder) include *Participation in American Politics: The Dynamics of Agenda Building* (1983) and *The Political Uses of Symbols* (1985). His recent journal articles concern aging policy and homelessness.

JOSEPH F. COUGHLIN is senior policy analyst and director of transportation and logistics services for EG&G Dynatrend at the Volpe National Transportation Systems Center in Cambridge, Massachusetts. He is a member of the National Research Council's Transportation Research Board Advisory Committee on Intergovernmental Relations and Policy Processes and is chair of the Subcommittee on Sustainable Development and Transportation.

BRYAN D. JONES is head of the Department of Political Science and Puryear Professor of Liberal Arts at Texas A&M University. His books include *Service Delivery in the City* (1980), *Governing Buildings and Building Government* (1985), *The Sustaining Hand* (1986) with Lynn W. Bachelor, and *Agendas and Instability in American Politics* (1993) with Frank R. Baumgartner.

GARY MUCCIARONI is associate professor of political science at Temple University. He has held teaching appointments at Brown University, New York University, and the College of William and Mary. His research has been supported by the Brookings Institution, where he was a research fellow and guest scholar, the Russell Sage Foundation, where he was a visiting scholar, and the U.S. Department of Labor. His books include *The Political Failure of Employment Policy, 1945–1982* (1990) and *Issues, Institutions and Public Policies* (forthcoming, 1994).

ELLEN FRANKEL PAUL is deputy director of the Social Philosophy and Policy Center and professor of political science and philosophy at Bowling Green State University. She is the author of numerous scholarly articles and the author or editor of twenty-seven books, including *Moral Revolution and Economic Science* (1979), *Property Rights and Eminent Domain* (1987), and *Equity and Gender: The Comparable Worth Debate* (1989).

JOHN PORTZ is associate professor of political science at Northeastern University. His research interest is state and local public policy, particularly the areas of economic development and education. Recent publications include *The Politics of Plant Closings* (1990) and journal articles on biotechnology, health, and industrial policy. He is currently examining education reform in Boston as part of an eleven-city study of urban education.

DAVID A. ROCHEFORT is associate professor of political science at Northeastern University. He has published in the areas of policy analysis, social welfare, mental health care, and health policy and politics, including three books: *American Social Welfare Policy: Dynamics of Formulation and Change* (1986), (editor) *Handbook on Mental Health Policy in the United States* (1989), and *From Poorhouses to Homelessness: Policy Analysis and Mental Health Care* (1993). Rochefort is a former National Institute of Mental Health postdoctoral fellow at Rutgers University and visiting associate professor of public policy at Brown University.

ELAINE B. SHARP is professor of political science and chair of the Department of Political Science at the University of Kansas. She is the author of *Citizen Demand-Making in the Urban Context* (1986), *Urban Politics and Adminis-*

tration (1990), and *The Dilemma of Drug Policy in the United States* (1994). Other recent publications include articles on economic development policy in the *Western Political Quarterly* and *Economic Development Quarterly*, on agenda setting and drug policy in the *Policy Studies Journal*, and, with Steven Maynard-Moody, on welfare policy in the *American Journal of Political Science*.

Index